RAISE THE FLOOR

Any properly footnoted quotation of up to 500 sequential words
may be used without permission, as long as the total number of words
quoted does not exceed 2,000. For longer quotations or for a greater
number of total words, please write for permission to South End Press,
7 Brookline Street, #1, Cambridge MA 02139-4146.
www.southendpress.org
Design and production by Gates Sisters Studio, Inc.
Printed in the United States • First edition 2001

Library of Congress Cataloging-in-Publication Data
Sklar, Holly, 1955—
Raise the floor : wages and policies that work for all of us /
Holly Sklar, Laryssa Mykyta, Susan Wefald.
p. cm.
Includes bibliographic references.
ISBN: 0-89608-683-6 (alk. paper)
1. Wages—Government policy—United States. 2. Poor—
Government policy—United States. 3. Women—United States—
Economic conditions. I. Mykyta, Laryssa. II. Wefald, Susan. III. Title.
HD4975 .S485 2002
331.2'973—dc21
                                                            2002021838
          05 04 03 02 01   1 2 3 4 5

RAISE THE FLOOR

WAGES AND POLICIES THAT WORK FOR ALL OF US

Holly Sklar
Laryssa Mykyta
Susan Wefald

· · ·

AFTERWORD BY Marie C. Wilson

WITH RESEARCH BY Solutions for Progress, Inc.
AND Social Research Corporation

ms. foundation for women

ACKNOWLEDGEMENTS

■ ■ ■ ■ ■

We would like to thank Robert Brand and Ross Koppel who provided invaluable insight and research as well as Solutions for Progress staff members Rachel Burton, Frederick Ngoga Gateretse, Stephanie Levin, Christine Piven and Deborah Zubow.

Our thanks to the following people who helped shape this book and Raise the Floor project through thought-provoking conversation, review of draft manuscripts or other assistance: Marie Wilson, Sara Gould, Nora Grip, Anna Wadia, Kelly Parisi, Judy Evans and other Ms. Foundation staff, John Demeter, Kathy Engel, Judy Arthur, John Barros, Jared Bernstein, Ellen Bravo, Carolina Briones, Chauna Brocht, Jennifer Brooks, Alice Burton, Chuck Collins, Tim Costello, Amy Dean, Trinh Duong, Ros Everdell, Truth Freemyn, Carol Goertzel, Rosemarie Greico, Tara Gruzen, Chris Hartman, Heidi Hartmann, Lisa Hoyos, Allen Hunter, Anabel Ibanez, Madeline Janis-Aparicio, Scott Klinger, Karen Kraut, Mike Lapham, Betsy Leondar-Wright, Gail Leondar-Wright, Al Lovata, Bonnie Macri, Cindy Marano, Nadia Marin-Molina, Sara Mersha, Amy Millman, Stephanie Monroe, Gail Nicholson, Karen Nussbaum, Chris Owens, Dana Paredes, Kim Pate, Maureen Ridge, Rinku Sen, Amy Stear, Ellen Teninty, Mark Toney, Betty Yu, Rosemarie Vardell, Miriam Walden, Susan Winning, Leah Wise and website designer Garrett Rieman. Thanks also to Daniel Chomsky; Trey Cole of the U.S. Census Bureau; Ken Petrick of the U.S. Commerce Department Bureau of Economic Analysis; and Ken Simonson and Brian Headd of the Small Business Administration Office of Advocacy for providing helpful data.

A very special thanks to Linda Gates and Gates Sisters Studio for beautiful design work—on a very unfriendly work schedule.

Finally, we gratefully acknowledge the Ford Foundation and the Foundation for Child Development whose support made this book possible.

CONTENTS

■ ■ ■ ■ ■

LIST OF TABLES AND FIGURES

■ ■ ■ ■ ■

LIST OF TABLES AND FIGURES

■ ■ ■ ■ ■

Overview

■ ■ ■ ■ ■

They work five days a week, often more.

They work full time in the richest nation on earth, yet they can't make ends meet.

They can't make ends meet because their wages are too low.

They are health care aides who can't afford health insurance.

They work in the food industry, but depend on food banks to help feed their children.

They are child care teachers who don't make enough to save for their own children's education.

They work at vacation resorts, but they have no paid vacation.

They care for the elderly, but they have no pensions.

They work hard.

They work at the backbreaking work of picking lettuce and tomatoes, peaches and strawberries.

They work in the meatpacking plants at jobs so grueling and dangerous they call out for a sequel to *The Jungle*.

They work in fast food places and the finest restaurants where wealthy executives write off lavish meals as business expenses.

They work ringing up purchases at discount stores and luxury boutiques.

They work cleaning the homes and hotel rooms of people who make more in a day than they make in a year.

They work hard and they can't make ends meet in the richest nation on earth.

Most Americans think that's wrong.

Most Americans think work should pay enough to support workers and their families. If you work full time, you should not be poor. It's as simple as that. No one should be working poor.[1]

> **S**hreveport, La.— ...It was early April, and [46-year-old] Ms. Williams was dressed in the dark blue uniform that she wears at her first job, caring for the aged and infirm at a nursing home. Atop that was the gray apron she dons for her second job, cleaning offices at night. The place where she works as a nursing assistant, Harmony House, was paying her $5.55 an hour—barely above the minimum wage—even though she has been there more than 10 years, is a union member and completed college courses to become certified. The cleaning job, which she took up because she couldn't make ends meet, pays right at the federally mandated minimum: $5.15 an hour...
>
> "You think you're moving forward," adds Ms. Williams, "but you're just moving backwards."
>
> **Rick Wartzman**, Wall Street Journal, *July 19, 2001.*

Moving Backward

Despite a decade of record-breaking economic boom, millions of Americans are working poor on punitively low wages. Today's minimum wage is lower than the level of 1950, adjusting for inflation. The share of Americans without health insurance is higher than it was a decade ago. The official poverty rate is higher than it was three decades ago.

One out of six children is growing up poor, according to the official measure—which actually understates poverty, as we'll see in Chapter One. One out of three black and Latino children are poor, by official count, in the richest nation on earth.

There is a strong link between child poverty rates and the percentage of full-time workers paid low wages. The United States has the highest child poverty and highest percentage of low-paid workers among 14 industrialized nations. Moreover, a study by the United Nations Children's Fund looking at the United States, Ireland, Spain, the United Kingdom, Germany and Hungary shows, "American children are less likely to move out of the bottom of the income distribution than children elsewhere, something which challenges common perceptions about mobility and opportunity in the US."[2]

The economic booms of the last three decades left many Americans behind. Average workers make less, adjusting for inflation, than their counterparts did during the long-ago Nixon administration. For families headed by people under age 55, median net worth (assets minus debt)

M r. Valles earns his living serving hamburgers at a McDonald's restaurant in downtown Los Angeles. He's a family man. He and his wife, Lily, have two children...
"I make $5.75 an hour. That's about $240 a week. One hundred ninety dollars after taxes. You can't really live on that. Lily works in a fast-food place, too. She makes the same as me. Two weeks of my pay and two weeks of her pay every month goes for rent. Then you have to pay the fare to go back and forth to work. You gotta pay for your food. You have bills. We're still paying on the sofa..."
I asked if they ever went on vacation. He looked at me as if I'd asked if his children could fly. "No," said Mr. Valles quietly. "There is no money for vacation."

Bob Herbert, New York Times, August 21, 2000.

was lower in 1998 than in 1989, according to the latest figures available from the Federal Reserve Survey of Consumer Finances. (Half the families have net worth below the median, half above it.) The median net worth of families earning less than $50,000 was lower in 1998 than in 1995. Lower real net worth means households had less real wealth to draw on for children's college educations, dealing with unemployment or health crises, or building on for retirement than when the boom began.

The racial wealth gap is wide. White non-Hispanic families had a median net worth of $94,900 in 1998, while nonwhite or Hispanic families had a net worth of $16,400—only a sixth as much as whites. That's counting home equity.[3]

"For the typical household, rising debt, not a rising stock market, was the big story of the 1990s," observed the Economic Policy Institute in the *State of Working America 2000-2001*.[4] Nearly one out of five families has zero or negative net worth.[5]

Consequences

P overty wages and growing inequality have consequences. With an abundance of low-paying jobs, lack of affordable housing and huge cutbacks in the welfare and food stamp rolls, so many people are seeking emergency food and shelter that our homeless shelters and food banks are overwhelmed.

Low-income workers are turning increasingly to food banks, which, like homeless shelters, cannot keep up with the rising demand. In its

We know that deep, persistent poverty is unworthy of our nation's promise... Where there is suffering, there is duty. Americans in need are not strangers, they are citizens; not problems, but priorities, and all of us are diminished when any are hopeless... Many in our country do not know the pain of poverty. But we can listen to those who do. And I pledge our nation to a goal: When we see a wounded traveler on the road to Jericho, we will not pass to the other side.

President George W. Bush, Inaugural Address, *January 2001.*

A true revolution of values will soon cause us to question the fairness and justice of many of our past and present policies. We are called to play the good Samaritan on life's roadside; but... One day the whole Jericho road must be transformed so that men and women will not be beaten and robbed as they make their journey through life. True compassion is more than flinging a coin to a beggar; it understands that an edifice which produces beggars needs restructuring...

There is nothing to prevent us from paying adequate wages to schoolteachers, social workers and other servants of the public... There is nothing but a lack of social vision to prevent us from paying an adequate wage to every American citizen whether he be a hospital worker, laundry worker, maid or day laborer. There is nothing except shortsightedness to prevent us from guaranteeing an annual minimum—and livable—income for every American family.

Martin Luther King Jr., Where Do We Go From Here: Chaos or Community?, *1967.*

2000 survey of 25 cities, the U.S. Conference of Mayors found that requests for emergency food increased an average of 17 percent during the past year; 13 percent of the requests went unmet. Two-thirds of those requesting food assistance were parents and children. One out of three adults requesting food assistance were employed.[6]

We are the richest nation on earth, but many of our children die young because they are poor. If the U.S. government were a parent, it would be guilty of child abuse. Globally, the United States ranks first in wealth and military might, and 32nd in child mortality under 5 years old. The United States is tied with Cyprus and Cuba and behind Canada,

Western Europe, Australia, Israel, Singapore and South Korea.[7]

The United States spends more of its gross domestic product on health care than any other country, but millions of our people don't reap the benefits. We are the richest nation on earth, but we are the only major industrialized nation not to assure health care for all its citizens, whether through a public, private or mixed system. In many other nations, health care is a right. Here it is an increasingly expensive privilege. Here, millions of people don't have health insurance of any kind—public or private.

Many people believe that access to health care is not a major problem for the uninsured. Here's the reality: In the words of the American College of Physicians, "No health insurance? It's enough to make you sick."

The uninsured are at much higher risk for disease, disability and death. Lack of health insurance typically means lack of health care or second-rate treatment. People can't afford to see doctors for preventive screening or illness, fill their prescriptions or get proper care at hospitals (where you may have a "wallet biopsy" checking for health insurance or credit cards before treatment). Uninsured people may be up to three times more likely than privately insured people to experience adverse health outcomes.[8]

Lack of health insurance is generally associated with a 25 percent higher risk of death (adjusting for physical, economic and behavioral factors).[9] Sometimes the risk is much higher. Uninsured women are 49 percent more likely to die than women with insurance during the four to seven years following an initial diagnosis of breast cancer.[10]

Inequality is a matter of life and death—and not just for the poor. In

---

TABLE 0-1

If the 100-member U.S. Senate Were a Microcosm of the Nation

51 SENATORS WOULD BE WOMEN
49 WOULD BE MEN

71 WOULD BE WHITE
12 WOULD BE BLACK
12 WOULD BE LATINO
4 WOULD BE ASIAN OR PACIFIC ISLANDER
1 WOULD BE AMERICAN INDIAN, ESKIMO OR ALEUT

15 WOULD HAVE NO HEALTH INSURANCE
12 WOULD BE BELOW THE OFFICIAL POVERTY LINE
23 WOULD EARN LESS THAN $8 AN HOUR

13 WOULD GET PARTIAL TAX REBATES
26 WOULD GET NO TAX REBATE

1 WOULD HAVE NEARLY AS MUCH WEALTH AS **95** OTHERS COMBINED
THE TYPICAL SENATOR WOULD HAVE HOUSEHOLD INCOME OF ABOUT **$41,000**

No matter how many individual and anecdotal exceptions there may be, the fact remains that the children of the poor simply do not have the same opportunities as the children of the non-poor. Whether measured by...health and survival rates, educational achievement or job prospects, incomes or life expectancies, those who spend their childhood in poverty of income and expectation are at a marked and measurable disadvantage...

The poverty bar may not be written into the laws and institutions of the land; but it is written into both the statistical chances and the everyday realities of millions of children who happen to be born into the poorest strata.

United Nations Children's Fund,
A League Table of Child Poverty in Rich Nations, *June 2000.*

the view of a growing number of health experts, inequality (among countries, states and metropolitan areas) is bad for your health. The United States, the richest country in the world, ranks only 20th when it comes to life expectancy, "lagging behind poorer countries such as Costa Rica, Greece and Spain."[11]

A report in the *American Journal of Public Health* found that higher income inequality is associated with increased mortality at all per capita income levels. "Given the mortality burden associated with income inequality," the report concludes, "business, private, and public sector initiatives to reduce economic inequalities should be a high priority."[12]

Most Americans believe that work should not mean poverty, and poverty should not mean homelessness, malnutrition, lack of health care or shortchanged education. Most Americans support much more comprehensive health care, child care and other needed social programs.

We can create the society we deserve. In the following pages we present:

- national minimum needs budgets, reflecting the minimum income necessary for individuals and families to meet their basic needs;

- a realistic $8 federal minimum wage that would lift millions of workers and their families out of poverty;

- policies to supplement wages in assuring that people can meet their basic needs.

What follows is a summary.[13] If you don't want a preview of findings, we invite you to go right to Chapter One.

EXECUTIVE SUMMARY

National Minimum Needs Budgets

Many Americans living above the official poverty line cannot meet their basic needs. There is a growing gap between what the government says you need to get by and what it actually costs.

People should not have to choose between eating or heating, health care or child care. Our proposed minimum needs budget covers these kind of necessities. It is designed to help us in using the minimum wage and other federal policies such as the Earned Income Tax Credit to set a national floor under wages and living standards.

The minimum needs budget includes the average cost of minimally adequate housing (including utilities), health care, food, child care, transportation, clothing and personal expenses, household expenses, telephone and taxes—factoring in tax credits such as the Earned Income Credit and Child Tax Credit. We present minimum needs budgets for six household compositions: single adult, two adult-no children, single parent-one child, single parent-two children, two adult-one child and two adult-two children. For each of these households, we present budgets with and without some form of employment-provided health coverage. Because most low-income workers do not have employment-based health insurance we present

It is common, among the nonpoor, to think of poverty as a sustainable condition—austere, perhaps, but they get by somehow, don't they? They are "always with us." What is harder for the nonpoor to see is poverty as acute distress. The lunch that consists of Doritos or hot dog rolls, leading to faintness before the end of the shift. The "home" that is also a car or a van. The illness or injury that must be "worked through," with gritted teeth, because there's no sick pay or health insurance and the loss of one day's pay will mean no groceries for the next. These experiences are not part of a sustainable lifestyle, even a lifestyle of chronic deprivation and relentless low-level punishment. They are, by almost any standard of subsistence, emergency situations. And that is how we should see the poverty of so many millions of low-wage workers—as a state of emergency.

Barbara Ehrenreich, Nickel and Dimed, 2001.

minimum needs budgets without employment health benefits in the summary table below.

The minimum needs budgets substantially exceed official federal poverty thresholds. A single person without employment health coverage would need about 190 percent of the federal poverty threshold to meet their minimum needs budgets. Families would need more than double the official poverty level to meet their basic needs. Single-parent families would need double the poverty threshold even if they had employment-based health insurance coverage.

Our budget is based on average national costs, which, by definition, average out higher and lower costs around the country. To provide context, especially for those readers living in atypically high- or low-cost areas, we calculated minimum needs budgets for five sample high-, medium- and low-cost metropolitan areas: New York City; Los Angeles; Des Moines, Iowa; Kansas City, Missouri; and Gadsden, Alabama. While the minimum needs budgets for Kansas City and Des Moines are close to the national budgets, Gadsden's budgets are much lower while New York City's are much higher.

Our focus is on setting a national floor through national policies such as the federal minimum wage and Earned Income Tax Credit. We emphasize the word floor. Today, many states and localities have higher minimum wages and living wage ordinances and higher eligibility thresholds for social services. States should be encouraged to reach higher than the federal standard, but not allowed to engage in a "race to the bottom," by opting out of the federal minimum wage, for example, as President Bush has advocated.

TABLE 0-2

Minimum Needs Budgets Without Employment Health Benefits
1999 dollars

Minimum Needs Budget	Single Adult	Two Adult	Single Parent, One Child	Single Parent, Two Children	Two Adults, One Child	Two Adults, Two Children
Annual Income Needed	16,549	23,522	28,796	32,999	31,255	35,637
Hourly Wage*	7.96	11.30	13.84	15.86	15.03	17.13

Note: The term "without employment health benefits" refers to workers whose employers do not pay any portion of the employee's health insurance costs. The minimum needs budgets "without employment health benefits" reflect the amount these households would pay to purchase health insurance in the private market.

* The hourly wage necessary for one full-time, full-year worker to earn the respective minimum needs budget or the combined wage for two adult workers.

Source: Solutions for Progress.

The Minimum Wage Fell While Productivity, Profits and CEO Pay Climbed

The minimum wage used to bring a family of three with one full-time worker above the official poverty line. Now it doesn't bring a full-time worker with one child above the line. The minimum wage has become a poverty wage instead of an anti-poverty wage.

The minimum wage is well below our minimum needs budget for even a single person—with or without employment health benefits. A full-time, year-round worker earning the current minimum wage of $5.15 per hour makes $10,712 annually (or $21,424 for a full-time two-earner family). Only households with two adults working full time, no children, and employment health benefits can meet their minimum needs budget at this wage. If "minimum wage" doesn't cover necessities, it's no minimum.

The federal minimum wage, enacted in 1938, was meant to put a firm floor under workers and their families, strengthen the economy by increasing consumer purchasing power, create new jobs to meet rising demand, foster economic development in lagging regions of the country—principally the South—and prevent the original "race to the bottom" of employers moving to cheaper labor states in a downward spiral.

Today's minimum wage workers earn a third less in real wages than their counterparts did a third of a century ago. The real value of the minimum wage peaked in 1968 at $7.92 per hour (in 2000 dollars). Now at $5.15, the real value of the minimum wage is 35 percent lower than it was in 1968.

When workers are not paid "a fair day's pay for a fair day's work" they are not just underpaid—they are subsidizing employers, stockholders and consumers. For decades now, workers have been shortchanged in good times and bad. Government let the minimum wage floor drop, dragging down average worker wages as employers followed—and encouraged—the government's stingy lead.

Worker productivity went up, but wages went down. Productivity grew 74.2 percent between 1968 and 2000, but hourly wages for average workers in 2000 were 3 percent lower, adjusting for inflation. Wages for minimum wage workers were 35 percent lower.

What if wages had kept rising with productivity, and were 74.2 percent higher in 2000 than they were in 1968? The average hourly wage would have been $24.56 in 2000, rather than $13.74. That's a difference of nearly $11 an hour—or about $22,000 a year for a full-time, year-round worker.

The minimum wage would have been $13.80 in 2000—not $5.15—if it had kept pace with productivity since 1968. That's a difference of $8.65 an hour, or nearly $18,000 for a full-time year-round worker.

Profits went up, but wages went down. When we look at real domestic corporate profits, we see a dramatic rise in profits compared with workers' earnings. Adjusting for inflation, looking back to 1968—the minimum wage peak—we see that profits rose 64 percent while average earnings dropped 3 percent and the minimum wage fell 35 percent.

The retail trade industry employs more than half the nation's hourly employees paid at or below minimum wage. Retail profits jumped even higher than profits generally. During the 1990s, retail profits skyrocketed 196 percent. Since 1968, retail profits have risen 158 percent.

If the minimum wage had kept pace with domestic profits during 1968-2000, it would be $13.02. If it had kept pace with retail profits, it would be $20.46.

CEO pay went up, but wages went down. The CEO-average worker wage gap has grown ten times wider over the last two decades. In 1980, CEOs made 45 times the pay of average production and non-supervisory workers. In 2000, CEOs made 458 times as much. The gap between CEOs and minimum wage workers has become a grand canyon. In 1980, the average CEO made as much as 97 minimum wage workers. In 2000, they made as much as 1,223 minimum wage workers.

Minimum Wage Critics are Wrong

As if to justify miserly pay, minimum wage opponents often claim that most minimum wage workers are teenagers living with their families. In fact, the typical minimum wage earner is an adult woman, not a teenager. Two out of three minimum wage workers are adults. While women make up just under half the total workforce, two out of three minimum wage workers are women. Only one out of three minimum wage workers is a teenager under age 20—and many of them are already out of school and working for a living. The United States does not provide universal public college education and a significant number of high school graduates cannot afford to go on to college even if they want to. In 1998, more than a third of people who graduated high school within the past year were not enrolled in college.

Many economic and political leaders opposed the minimum wage when it was first enacted, and it is still opposed by many today who predictably try to block raises whenever they are proposed. Opponents argue business can't afford higher minimum wages and that they fuel inflation, increase unemployment, harm low-skill, low-wage workers, and aggravate poverty. Real world recent experience shows the critics are wrong.

We've seen how worker productivity and business profits have greatly—and unjustifiably—outpaced wages. The minimum wage was last raised from $4.25 to $4.75 an hour in October 1996 and to $5.15 in

September 1997. Between 1996 and 2000 the economy boomed, with extraordinarily high growth, low inflation, low unemployment and declining poverty rates. In February 2000, the economy broke the record for the longest expansion in U.S. history. (The expansion began in March 1991.) The unemployment rate reached a low of 3.9 percent in September 2000.

Unemployment has gone down across the board, including for people of color, teenagers and workers in different parts of the country. Unemployment rates also declined for high school graduates with no college and those with less than a high school education. The minimum wage increase reduced poverty, including among teenagers and high school dropouts. Research on past minimum wage increases also shows that minimum wage hikes do not foster higher unemployment.

At this writing, the economy is in a slowdown generated by the Federal Reserve slamming on the brakes too hard with repeated interest rate hikes in 1999-2000. The Fed acted to purposely slow the supposedly overheated economy to maintain low wages—in the name of fighting inflation. Minimum wage critics who said that raising the minimum wage would end the economic boom are now saying the minimum wage can't go up because the boom is over. In reality, the minimum wage was raised during the last recession in 1990-91 with positive effects.

Areas with living wage laws provide more evidence that the minimum wage can be raised significantly. Living wage ordinances typically require that businesses subcontracting with the city, county or university pay their employees a living wage, but some ordinances include city workers and/or businesses receiving economic development subsidies. Despite strong opposition from many of the same people who oppose a higher minimum wage, some 70 living wage laws have been enacted around the country and campaigns are going on in about 80 communities and universities. The wages now required range from $6.50 an hour in Duluth, Minnesota to $11 in Santa Cruz, California with employment health benefits to $12.25 in Santa Monica, California without employment health benefits. Most of the current ordinances mandate wages over $8 an hour. The results from a growing body of research examining living wage ordinances are quite positive.

Good Wages are Good for Business, Large and Small

All around the country, successful business owners have shown that businesses benefit from a higher-paid, highly motivated workforce. Higher wages make it easier for employers to recruit and retain entry-level workers, leading to reduced turnover and absenteeism as well as lower costs associated with training and recruitment. Moreover, businesses report improvements in the quality of products and services.

A higher minimum wage also means that workers will have more purchasing power. Increased demand for goods and services may result in increased employment in a "multiplier effect" generating additional purchasing power. Thus higher payroll costs from a mandated minimum wage increase may be offset by an increase in business revenues.

To take an example of a successful business, In-N-Out Burger was the nation's first drive-through hamburger stand and ranks first among fast food chains in food quality, value and customer service. There are more than 150 In-N-Out Burgers in California, Nevada and Arizona, generating more than $150 million in annual revenues. The owners "have succeeded by rejecting just about everything the rest of the fast food industry has done... The chain pays the highest wages in the fast food industry. The starting wage of a part-time worker at In-N-Out is $8 an hour. Full-time workers get a benefits package that includes medical, dental, vision, and life insurance."[14]

In a study of Baltimore's living wage law "contractors interviewed about the living wage gave generally positive responses. From bus companies to temporary agencies to janitorial services, the prevailing opinion offered was that the living wage 'levels the playing field' and relieves pressure on employers to squeeze labor costs in order to win low-bid contracts."[15]

Opponents of minimum wage increases typically claim that small businesses will be unable to compete and they will have to lay off workers and maybe close their doors. When's the last time you heard a chain store executive worry that their new store would drive the local mom and pop store out of business?

In reality, small businesses can absorb and benefit from a minimum wage increase just as big businesses can. In the words of small business owners Tim Styer, Judy Wicks and Hal Taussig, "All our businesses pay well above the federal minimum wage. We know that today's minimum wage shortchanges workers and undermines the long-term health of businesses, communities and the economy."[16]

Every year the Small Business Administration honors state and national businesspeople. Cindy McEntee, owner of Mo's Enterprises, is the SBA's 2001 Oregon Small Business Person of the Year and first runner-up to the national award. Mo's Enterprises of Newport, Oregon, consists of three restaurants and a chowder factory. "In its 50 years in business, Mo's has always paid more than the required minimum wage and offered major medical health insurance."[17]

Our research shows that small businesses would not be disproportionately affected by a minimum wage increase. We looked at the cost of the wage increase relative to total receipts minus total payroll and benefits and found that it did not vary significantly by firm size. In the few sectors in which there were variations by firm size, small firms were not necessarily the most affected. For example, in the social services sector a wage increase would have a greater impact on the operational costs of firms with more than 500 workers. Sector is far more significant than firm size when it comes to absorbing a minimum wage increase.

Higher wages are good for business in low-income communities. Three years ago *Inc.* magazine and the Initiative for a Competitive Inner City (ICIC) began publishing the annual ICIC-Inc. Magazine Inner City 100, a national listing of 100 successful, fast-growing companies located in low-income urban areas. The 2001 Inner City 100 have increased their number of jobs by 120 percent over the past five years. Their average hourly wage, excluding benefits, is $11.81, more than double the minimum wage. Their benefits for full-time employees are well above average: 98 percent offer health insurance, 81 percent offer a bonus plan, 72 percent offer a 401(k) retirement plan, 41 percent have profit sharing for employees and 13 percent offer employee stock ownership programs. The Inner City 100 have lower than average turnover and most frequently cite customer service as their principal competitive advantage.[18]

Raise the Minimum Wage Floor to $8

Your paycheck should keep you out of poverty, not keep you in it. The federal minimum wage can and should be increased to $8 per hour. Why $8?

- $8 is the amount needed for a single full-time worker to meet their minimum needs budget—without employment health benefits, which most low-income workers don't have;

- $8 matches the 1968 minimum wage peak, adjusting for inflation.

It's time to abolish poverty wages. Certainly, employers can pay a minimum wage equivalent to what their counterparts paid more than three decades ago.

The minimum wage, adjusting for inflation since the 1968 peak year, would be:

- $13.80 if it had kept pace with productivity;

- $13.02 if had kept pace with domestic profits;

- $20.46 if it had kept pace with profits in the retail industry, which employs more than half the nation's hourly employees paid at or below minimum wage.

About a fourth of the workforce would benefit directly from an increase in the minimum wage to $8. This does not include those workers currently making $8 or somewhat above who would benefit from the "ripple effect" from a new minimum wage as wages scales were adjusted to the new floor.

Women are more likely than men to be paid low wages. Women account for 48 percent of the labor force, but 59 percent of workers making less than $8. Women hold a disproportionate share of the jobs in low-wage industries and a disproportionate share of the low-wage jobs in higher paid industries. An increase in the minimum wage to $8 is crucial for women workers and their families.

Low-wage jobs are not distributed evenly throughout the economy. Low-wage workers are disproportionately concentrated in comparatively few industries—primarily agriculture, private household services, retail trade, personal services, social services (including child care, for example) and entertainment/recreation services.

To determine the impact of a wage increase to $8 per hour, we calculated the direct cost of raising the current minimum wage, the indirect effect of increasing the wages of workers paid at or slightly more than our recommended minimum wage, and the additional costs to the employer of employee benefits and taxes within each industry. We compared the total cost of the wage increase to total receipts minus total payroll and benefits and to the cost of goods sold. The cost of goods sold consists of "the direct costs incurred…in producing goods and providing services. Included were costs of materials used in manufacturing; costs of goods purchased for resale; direct labor; and certain overhead expenses, such as rent, utilities, supplies, maintenance and repairs."[19]

The direct cost of an increase in the minimum wage to $8 per hour represents less than 1 percent of receipts minus payroll and benefits and less than 1 percent of the cost of goods sold.

These figures actually overstate the cost. This cost calculation assumes that there are *no exemptions* from minimum wage legislation and that all wage and salary workers are paid at least $8 per hour. More than one-fourth of wage and salary workers—33.9 million workers—were exempt from the minimum wage provisions of the Fair Labor Standards Act in 1999. More than 70 percent of exempt workers were executive, administrative or professional employees, many of whom earn far more than the minimum wage. However, about a third of workers in agriculture, forestry and fisheries and nearly half of private household workers are exempt from minimum wage legislation. Moreover, higher wages can reduce turnover and training costs, enhance productivity and increase worker purchasing power, which in turn can increase sales.

Policies to Make Ends Meet

Throughout our history, generations of Americans have reshaped government policy to better "promote the general welfare." Our legacy from the last century includes the New Deal, with its landmark policies of the minimum wage, 8-hour day, curtailment of child labor and Social Security. What legacy will we build in the 21st century?

The $8 minimum wage is a long overdue companion to the 8-hour day. It will end poverty for millions of workers and their families. With better wages more people will be able to meet their needs without government assistance. But government must do more to assure that everyone can meet their basic needs, whatever their wage.

The United States has universal Social Security for seniors, but not universal child care. We have universal Medicare for seniors, but not for all Americans. Public policy in the United States does much less to reduce poverty, especially for children, than policy in other industrialized countries.

EXPAND THE EARNED INCOME TAX CREDIT

The Earned Income Tax Credit (EIC) was enacted in 1975 to help offset rising payroll taxes and make work pay, and has strong bipartisan support. The EIC is a refundable tax credit—even if tax filers have no income tax liability, they receive a refund check for the amount of the credit.

The EIC should be a supplement to an $8 minimum wage, not a substitute for it. The $8 wage is set to assure that single adults can meet their minimum needs budget. Employers should be required to pay "a fair day's pay for a fair day's work." The EIC should fill the gap between the $8 minimum wage and the minimum needs budgets for all workers and their families.

The EIC should be restructured in order to benefit those workers and families who need it most. We propose a substantially more generous EIC, designed to enable individual workers and working families to meet their minimum needs budgets, assuming that adults work full time, year round.

TOWARD UNIVERSAL HEALTH CARE

For most families, health care is the second highest cost in our minimum needs budgets. Millions of Americans have no health insurance of any kind, putting their health, lives and livelihoods in jeopardy. Nearly one out of six people were uninsured in 1999 (latest data available). One out of three people below the official poverty line and one out of four people in households with incomes less than $25,000 are uninsured. More than one out of six workers are uninsured, including nearly half of all full-time workers below the official poverty line.

Most people and their families rely on work-based health insurance. Six out of ten people are covered by private sector employment-based insurance either through their own employment or a relative. But the share of workers covered by employment health plans drops from 82 percent in the top fifth of wage earners to 69 percent in the middle fifth to less than 30 percent in the lowest fifth. And required employee contributions to health insurance costs tend to be higher in low-wage firms.

The United States spends more of its gross domestic product on health care than any other country, yet unlike many other nations we leave millions of our people with little or no health care protection. Our system is an unhealthy, inadequate, inefficient patchwork of private and public insurance that wastes billions of dollars in the administration of countless private and public eligibility regulations, incompatible time-consuming forms and procedures, and second-guessing of doctors by insurance gatekeepers trained in cost-cutting, not medicine.

The old saying, "An ounce of prevention is worth a pound of cure," couldn't be truer when it comes to health care. Yet our government allows millions of people to fall through the cracks of preventive and acute care when they are young and middle-aged, ensuring they will be unhealthier and more dependent (and costly) when they reach eligibility for Medicare.

Behind all the policy debate, the reality is that people suffer and die for lack of health coverage. We shouldn't lose sight of that. Members of Congress have publicly financed health care—everyone should.

Most Americans believe that everyone should have health insurance coverage whatever their income or job. We propose options to expand health coverage now to all low-income Americans while working towards the universal coverage we need.

Expand Medicaid: Health care coverage should be provided without delay to low-income single adults and families through an expansion of the Medicaid program. Expanding Medicaid builds on the existing Medicaid and SCHIP programs and national and state initiatives to transform children's health programs into family health programs serving low-income parents and children.

Universal Health Insurance: Expanding Medicaid is a practical partial solution, but not a cure to our health care problems. The cure is universal health care, a reality in every major industrialized nation besides the United States.

Many proposals for universal health care build on Medicare—which was enacted after years of determined opposition—and now covers about one out of seven Americans. In recommending "Medicare for All," the Economic Policy Institute notes that the Medicare benefits package would "need to be fully modernized to include prescription drugs, preventive care, improved mental health and substance abuse services, and better cost sharing."[20] One of the major current proposals for universal coverage is the *Proposal of the Physicians' Working Group for Single-Payer National Health Insurance.*

CARE GIVING

While many other countries have reshaped their child care policies to reflect changing realities, our child care policies are stubbornly rooted in the past. In 1960, 38 percent of women were in the paid workforce. Now, 60 percent of women are in the paid workforce. Only 29 percent of married-couple families and 21 percent of all families with children under 18, fit the stereotypical 1950s family of a breadwinner father and a homemaker mother who cares for the children and does not work outside the home.

Looking at child care, parental leave and school policies, you would think working mothers were still a minority. You would also think kids have three parents: two parents with jobs to pay the bills, and another parent to be home in mid-afternoon when school lets out. After-school programs are scarce, as are affordable summer programs. This is harmful to children and to society.

In the long run, we advocate the development of a universal child care and early childhood education system that allows all families to have access to affordable, high quality child care, combined with paid family and medical leave following birth or adoption. We examine existing policies such as tax credits and make recommendations for more immediate improvements.

The 1993 **Family and Medical Leave Act** (FMLA) requires firms with at least 50 employees to allow employees 12 weeks of unpaid, job-protected leave each year for childbirth, adoption or to care for a seriously ill family member. For most Americans, the Act is a pipe dream. Many workers cannot afford to take unpaid leave, and about half the workforce isn't covered because they are employed in small firms. We need to work towards a universal system of paid family leave, which is common in many other countries.

The **Child Tax Credit** is available for taxpayers raising dependent children under 17 years old. It is not directly related to child care expenses. The credit should be raised immediately to $1,000 and made fully refundable to benefit low-income families.

Child care is a huge expense for working families with children. The **Dependent Care Tax Credit** (DCTC), which subsidizes families who need care for a child or dependent adult incapable of caring for themselves in order to work or look for work, is very inadequate. The DCTC should be made refundable so that very low-income families can take advantage of it and the maximum allowable expenditure should be increased significantly. Families earning less than 250 percent of the official poverty line should receive a 100 percent credit (depending on their actual child care expenses and number of children) and not just a small percentage as is the case now.

The **Child Care and Development Fund** (CCDF)—established under the Personal Responsibility and Work Opportunity Reconciliation Act of 1996 (PWRORA)—combined four pre-existing federal child care programs into one funding stream, the Child Care and Development Block Grant (CCDBG). Typically, child care subsidies are available through certificates or vouchers. We spend about $10 billion a year in federal and state funds (not including tax credits) to assist low-income families in paying for child care. This covers only 12 percent of the children eligible. The income eligibility thresholds and appropriations should be raised.

Universal Child Care: Even as we recommend immediate steps be taken to improve existing child care assistance policies, in the longer run we advocate universal affordable child care through a more comprehensive system. For example, Barbara Bergmann recommends replacing the Child Care and Development Fund and the Child and Dependent Care Tax Credit with a comprehensive federal plan for universal, high-quality care. Utilizing a sliding scale, low-income parents would pay little or nothing for child care, while others would pay a fraction of the amount their income exceeds the poverty line. She recommends that the program include after-school care for children up to 12 years old.[21]

Universal pre-kindergarten for 3- and 4-year olds, like universal public school, can provide quality early childhood education while simultaneously helping working parents in need of child care. Numerous studies have demonstrated the positive impact of early intervention programs on later school success. In 1998, only 42 percent of children between the ages of 3 and 5 living in families earning less than $15,000 were enrolled in pre-K, compared with 65 percent of children in families earning more than $50,000. Universal pre-K delivery mechanisms could include public schools, existing preschools and other child care providers that meet quality standards.

There is an increasing need for **child care services for school-age children,** including before- and after-school care as well as summer care, with more adult family members working long hours in the labor market. Research shows that quality school-age care positively impacts children's academic performance, socialization and development. After-school programs also enhance community safety and well-being. No parents should have to leave their preteen children home unsupervised for lack of income.

Raise Child Care Wages: Child care teachers, entrusted with the physical, intellectual and emotional development and well being of our nation's children, are grossly underpaid. Child care workers typically earn about as much as parking lot attendants and much less than animal trainers. Child care centers have difficulty attracting and retaining experienced professionals and are sometimes forced to hire people with virtually no training. Turnover is high. Longtime child care teachers make a tremendous financial sacrifice to stay in the profession. Public subsidies should be linked to higher wages and benefits, and to providing access to training and education for child care workers. To assure fair pay for child care workers, we recommend a wage pass-through of at least one dollar above our recommended $8 federal minimum wage.

"A DECENT HOME"

More than half a century ago, Congress passed the National Housing Act with the goal of assuring a decent home and suitable living environment for every American family. That goal has grown more distant as the number of low-cost rental units greatly exceeds the number of low-income renters, rental and homeownership subsidies are inadequate, and homelessness has risen, especially among working families. We need policies that encourage affordable housing. For example, the National Low Income Housing Coalition (NLIHC) is calling for the establishment of a National Affordable Housing Trust Fund for the production of new housing and preservation or rehabilitation of existing housing that is affordable for low-income people. We should provide greater support for community-based groups that have made important progress in developing affordable housing and revitalizing neighborhoods, using a range of housing funding and models, including subsidized mortgages and downpayment assistance funds, community land trusts, limited-equity cooperatives, mutual housing associations, sweat equity, resident management, nonprofit rentals and so on.

Housing discrimination has remained a problem, as numerous reports by the Department of Housing and Urban Development (HUD), the Federal Reserve Board, regional Federal Reserve Banks, the Urban Institute, ACORN and other governmental and nonprofit organizations and investigative reports have shown. We need much better enforcement of fair housing laws and the Community Reinvestment Act, which requires fair banking practices.

UNIONS AND PAY EQUITY

Union jobs typically provide much better wages and benefits than nonunion ones. The median weekly wage of a full-time worker who belonged to a union in 2000 was $696, compared with $542 for those who did not. That's an annual wage differential of $8,008, not including significantly better health, pension and other benefits paid to union members.

Union jobs have disappeared under waves of downsizing, outsourcing, globalization and union busting. With weaker unions, conservative business and political groups were more successful in their efforts to roll back government social services.

The 1935 National Labor Relations Act gives workers the right to form and join labor unions and to bargain collectively with their employers. Government should significantly strengthen enforcement and implement other measures to support collective bargaining.

"Contingent workers" in nonstandard jobs such as temps, contract workers, leased workers, on-call workers, day laborers and part-time workers typically receive lower pay and benefits than regular full-time workers who do the same job. Contingent workers are excluded from coverage by many employment and labor laws, and lack an effective right to organize a union and bargain collectively. Laws should be reformed to prevent discrimination on the basis of employment status, work schedules or site of work.

Obviously, you can't earn wages if you can't find a job. Government policies should promote **full employment**—the long ignored other mandate of the Federal Reserve Board. Full employment means a job for everyone who needs one, not 6 or 4 percent unemployment.

But to make matters worse for the unemployed, **unemployment insurance** is not ensured. In recent years only about a third of all officially unemployed workers received any unemployment insurance (UI) benefits, and they received less than half of their former weekly wages in benefits. Unemployment benefits should be increased substantially and UI should cover workers seeking part-time work and workers quitting jobs for "good cause" like family care responsibilities and domestic violence. Low-wage and contingent workers should not face discrimination in the form of overly restrictive minimum earnings and work time requirements.

PAY EQUITY

Employment discrimination is a form of theft. Laws prohibiting discrimination on the basis of race, gender, age and disability should be strongly enforced. Further, Congress should pass legislation prohibiting employment discrimination on the basis of sexual orientation as proposed in the Civil Rights Amendments Act of 2001.

Numerous states have enacted pay equity legislation. Pay equity means eliminating gender and race discrimination and setting wages based on legitimate job requirements. Federal legislation such as the

Fair Pay Act, introduced in the House and Senate but not passed, would "expand the Equal Pay Act's protections against wage discrimination to workers in equivalent jobs with similar skills and responsibilities, even if the jobs are not identical."[22]

EDUCATION AND ASSET BUILDING

Free, universal public education is one of the bedrocks of a nation's ability to provide equal opportunity to its citizens and to provide a well-educated workforce to support a strong innovative economy. The federal and state governments should assure equity across race and class lines, and provide public schools with the resources needed to make improvements and sustain effective programs.

The 1944 GI Bill of Rights gave millions of Americans the chance to go to college—many the first in their family. Individuals, families and society all gained. Today, the federal government should greatly expand needs-based grants and refundable tuition tax credits so that college is affordable to everyone. That's good for our democracy and our economy.

Welfare reform should be reformed to encourage education and regular employment with decent wages and benefits and full labor rights. By creating a large category of sub-minimum wage workers and displacing higher-paid workers, workfare undermines unions and puts downward pressure on wages generally.

We have talked about the importance of expanding government support for education and housing, two traditional pillars of asset building. We have talked about the importance of higher wages. Government should also strengthen Individual Retirement Account (IRA) programs, for example, so that they are more helpful to low- and middle-income families and expand support for Individual Development Account (IDA) matching programs targeted to low- and moderate-income households. Participants can withdraw funds from IDAs in order to purchase a home, invest in education or job training, or finance a small business.

Turning Point

We are at a turning point in our nation's history. Will we build on the legacy of the New Deal—or undo it? Will we widen the road to equal opportunity—or narrow it? Will we take the high road to progress?

Public opinion is clear. Poll after poll shows strong support for raising the minimum wage, taking poverty out of full-time work and implementing effective policies to assure adequate housing, child care, nutrition, education, job training and public works, even if this requires higher taxes. Americans want a strong government role in reducing poverty. Americans support the right to universal health care.

Yet our government has gone backward, not forward. The minimum wage is a poverty wage. Millions of Americans are deprived of adequate health care, child care, housing and education. School buildings and bridges are falling apart. Measured as a share of the Gross Domestic Product, federal spending is at the lowest level since 1966 and projected by 2011 to fall to the lowest level since 1951.

We all benefit when government spends our money wisely on preventive policies and a strong safety net. We benefit when everyone is healthier and more educated, reaching their full potential of talents, skills, contributions and creativity.

There are things we can't afford. We cannot afford to give the wealthiest Americans a giant tax break—the real point of the Economic Growth and Tax Relief Reconciliation Act of 2001—while shortchanging the most impoverished Americans.

The Bush plan robs Peter to pay Paul. It pays for the giant tax breaks for the wealthy by undermining Social Security and Medicare, shortchanging children's programs, and cutting the budgets of the Departments of Labor, Justice, Agriculture, Energy and Interior, the Environmental Protection Agency, the Small Business Administration and the Equal Opportunity Commission.

That so-called budget surplus being squandered on the tax cuts is the necessary buildup in the Medicare and Social Security trust funds and the product of years of government shortchanging of budgets for affordable housing, health care, environmental programs, education, public works and so on.

We're getting swindled. When you see you are getting swindled you blow the whistle and stop it. That's what we need to do.

Most of the tax cuts for the top 1 percent take effect after 2001. The ink was barely dry on the tax cut bill before Bush administration officials began warning the "surplus" was shrinking and deeper budget cuts would be needed. Congress must reverse the costly tax cuts for the wealthy scheduled to take effect over the next decade.

We have real surpluses to reduce:

The surplus of Americans whose lives and livelihoods are jeopardized by their lack of health insurance.

The surplus of parents who can't afford to take leave when their children are born or adopted.

The surplus of kids on waiting lists for Head Start.

The surplus of kids going to school in crumbling, overcrowded buildings.

The surplus of women denied unemployment insurance if they leave their job because of domestic violence.

The surplus of homeless families.

The surplus of seniors who can't retire because of inadequate pensions and Social Security.

The surplus of environmental projects we supposedly can't afford.

We have real choices to make. In this book we advocate a higher minimum wage and common sense policies in health care, housing, child care and other crucial areas. What will be our legacy for America?

We're at a turning point. Let's take the high road to progress.

1

■ ■ ■ ■ ■

It Just Doesn't Add Up

Too often, the week stretches longer than her paycheck.
Terry Geier doesn't have a rainy-day fund, at least not
yet, and that term sounds a little breezy for someone
who occasionally can't afford to buy groceries...

Work is not the problem. Geier does plenty of that—five,
sometimes six, days a week. But because she is among
the roughly 9 percent of Ohio workers...whose hourly
earnings are no more than $1 above the minimum
wage, Geier does not make enough to support
herself and her children without help.

Rita Price, Columbus Dispatch, *February 25, 2001.*

Many Americans living above the official poverty line cannot meet their basic needs. There is a growing gap between what the government says you need to get by and what it actually costs.

The government's own studies illuminate the gap. For example, a Census Bureau study found that in 1995 one in five Americans "lived in a household whose members had difficulty satisfying basic needs." These include "households who didn't make mortgage or rent payments, failed to pay utility bills and/or had service shut off, didn't get enough to eat, needed to see a doctor or dentist but didn't, or otherwise could not meet essential expenses."[1]

By the government's own measure, 3 million households—with 5 million adults and 3 million children—experienced hunger at times during 1999 because there was not enough money for food. A total of 31 million people were "food insecure," meaning "they did not have assured access at all times to enough food for an active, healthy life." This doesn't include people who are homeless.[2]

Recent studies by the Economic Policy Institute and the Urban Institute found that many families with incomes up to twice (200 percent) the federal poverty level had difficulty making ends meet.[3] For households below the official poverty line, the difficulties are much worse.

As the table below shows, one out of three Americans lives under 200 percent of the official poverty line. This includes one out of five non-Hispanic whites and one out of two blacks and Latinos. And it includes two out of every five children.

A recent Gallup poll shows significant concern about making ends meet, in proportions similar to the breakdown of Americans living below 200 percent of the official poverty line. Nearly one-third of poll respondents said that they worry about not having enough money to pay their bills. "Women are somewhat more likely than men (35% vs. 27%) to say they are very or moderately worried about paying their monthly bills... A substantial difference in worry about making ends meet is also apparent by race—29% of white Americans are concerned, compared to 46% of blacks and other racial minorities."[4]

Official Poverty Measure

The government says you are not poor if you have incomes above these average thresholds: $8,959 for one person (under 65); $11,869 for a two-person family with one adult and one child under 18 years old; $13,861 for a three-person family with two adults and one child; and $17,463 for a four-person family with two adults and two children (2000 Census Bureau poverty thresholds).[5] By the government's poverty measure, those are income levels sufficient to purchase a minimal standard of living.

Yet, at the same time, some government programs use multiples of the official poverty line to establish eligibility for programs.[6] For example, "Most of the child nutrition programs, including the Special Supplemental Nutrition Program for Women, Infants, and Children (WIC) and the National School Lunch and School Breakfast programs are targeted to those with incomes less than 185 percent of the poverty line. The Food Stamp Program targets households with

TABLE 1-1

Percent of People in Poverty, 1999*

	UNDER 50%	UNDER 100%	UNDER 150%	UNDER 200%
		of official poverty line		
All Persons	4.6	11.8	21.0	30.1
Under 18 years old	6.9	16.9	28.2	38.8
Under 6 years old**	7.6	18.0	29.6	40.9
65 years and over	2.1	9.7	22.9	35.9
White (non-Hispanic)	2.9	7.7	14.8	22.8
Under 18 years old	3.6	9.4	17.6	26.6
Under 6 years old	4.1	10.0	18.6	28.4
65 years and over	1.7	7.6	19.5	32.6
Black	10.1	23.6	36.7	47.8
Under 18 years old	15.3	33.1	48.4	60.8
Under 6 years old	18.3	36.6	50.9	63.3
65 years and over	4.6	22.7	43.7	56.3
Hispanic	8.3	22.8	39.7	53.9
Under 18 years old	11.1	30.3	49.5	64.4
Under 6 years old	11.0	30.6	49.7	65.0
65 years and over	3.3	20.4	41.1	56.1
Male	4.1	10.3	18.8	27.7
White (non-Hispanic)	2.6	6.8	13.1	20.7
Black	8.9	20.2	32.5	43.5
Hispanic	6.9	20.1	37.2	51.7
Female	5.2	13.2	23.0	32.4
White (non-Hispanic)	3.2	8.6	16.5	24.9
Black	11.1	26.6	40.4	51.5
Hispanic	9.6	25.4	42.1	56.1

* These were the latest official poverty rates available at this writing. Poverty thresholds for 1999 included: $8,501 for one person; $11,483 for a 2-person family with one adult and one child under 18; $13,410 for a 3-person family with one child; and $16,895 for a 4-person family with two adults and two children.

** Refers to related children under 6 years old in families.

Source: U.S. Census Bureau, *Poverty in the United States, 1999*, September 2000.

gross incomes below 130 percent of the poverty line."[7] (Households are ineligible for food stamps if their net incomes, after deductions, are higher than the poverty line; limits on countable resources such as the value of cars also apply.) Medicaid allows states flexibility in determining eligibility. According to the Department of Health and Human Services, "The majority of states' Medicaid programs cover children in families between 100 and 150 percent of the FPL [Federal Poverty Level]... Most states provide SCHIP (State Children's Health Insurance Program) coverage for children in families at or above 200 percent of the poverty level."[8] (Coverage for parents in those families is much stingier, as we'll see in Chapter Six.) Unfortunately, there are often big gaps between program eligibility and enrollment because of underfunding and purposely complex and hostile application procedures.

The official federal poverty thresholds were adopted in the 1960s from thresholds developed by Mollie Orshansky of the Social Security Administration. The Orshansky formula was based on U.S. Department of Agriculture (USDA) estimates of the cost of a minimum family diet multiplied by three. An already outdated 1955 USDA Household Consumption Survey provided the basis for the multiplier. The 1955 survey found that families of three or more spent about one-third of their after-tax income on food. The cost of a minimum diet was based on the Economy Food Plan, now called the Thrifty Food Plan, the least costly USDA food plan.[9]

The USDA warned that the plan was meant only for "temporary or emergency use when funds are low." It later "stressed that 'the cost of this plan is not a reasonable measure of basic money needs for a good diet,' and suggested that states designing assistance programs for families consider a food plan that costs 'about 25 percent more than the Economy Plan.'"[10] A USDA survey found that 90 percent of families spending the amount specified by the Thrifty Food Plan did not obtain adequate nutrition.[11]

The Thrifty Food Plan was not only set unreasonably low from the start, but it "still assumes families will bake daily and cook all their food from scratch, never buy fast food or eat out, use dried beans and no canned food, be experts in nutrition, and have a working refrigerator, freezer and stove," among other things.[12]

Mollie Orshansky originally developed two sets of thresholds at the Social Security Administration, one based on the least expensive Economy Food Plan and the other on the next level up, Low-Cost Food Plan. The Office of Economic Opportunity adopted the lower threshold, based on the Economy Food Plan, as a working official definition of poverty in 1965, and it became the official poverty measure in 1969. Orshansky herself preferred the thresholds based on the Low-Cost Food Plan, describing them as "probably more realistic" than poverty measures based on the Economy Food Plan.[13]

When the Social Security Administration sought to adjust the poverty thresholds by adopting food costs based on 1965 revised USDA food plans and increasing the multiplier, to reflect food's

> **T**here are no secret economies that nourish the poor; on the contrary, there are a host of special costs. If you can't put up the two months' rent you need to secure an apartment, you end up paying through the nose for a room by the week. If you have only a room, with a hot plate at best, you can't save by cooking up huge lentil stews that can be frozen for the week ahead... If you have no money for health insurance... you go without routine care or prescription drugs and end up paying the price.
>
> *Barbara Ehrenreich*, Nickel and Dimed.

reduced percentage within family budgets, the Office of Statistics Standards of the Bureau of the Budget overruled the revised thresholds. Orshansky stated that the 1969 decision by the Office of Statistics Standards effectively froze the poverty line "despite changes in buying habits and changes in acceptable living standards."[14]

The inadequacy of the official poverty measure in determining the costs of meeting household needs is widely documented.[15] The poverty thresholds are adjusted for inflation—using the consumer price index for all urban consumers (CPI-U)—but they have not been updated to reflect important underlying economic and social changes.[16]

Today, food costs one-seventh of total average household expenditures, and one-sixth of expenditures for households in the lowest quintile of income—not one-third.[17] (If you divide the U.S. population into five equal parts, a quintile equals one-fifth, or 20 percent, of the population.) Basic needs such as housing and medical care costs have increased more rapidly than food costs. Updating the multiplier to reflect current expenditures would double the official poverty threshold.

Moreover, the official poverty measure ignores changes in family needs such as greater child care expenses and consumption of food outside the home due to women's increased labor force participation and increased family work hours, for example.

Government statisticians know there's a problem with the official measure. As Kathleen Short, then chief of Poverty and Health Statistics at the U.S. Census Bureau, put it, "We haven't changed the way we determine the poverty level since the 1960s. That's a political issue, not because we think it's the best way to measure poverty."[18]

Alternative Poverty Measures and Needs Budgets

I n response to growing concern over the official poverty measure, the Joint Economic Committee of Congress initiated an in-depth review undertaken by the National Research Council of the National Academy of Sciences (NAS). Published in 1995, the NAS study, *Measuring Poverty: A New Approach*, concluded, "The current measure needs to be revised: it no longer provides an accurate picture of the differences in the extent of economic poverty among population groups or geographic areas of the country, nor an accurate picture of trends over time."[19]

The NAS study recommended that the poverty thresholds "represent a budget for food, clothing, shelter (including utilities), and a small additional amount to allow for other needs (e.g., household supplies, personal care, non-work-related transportation)," calculated from actual expenditure data set at a percentage of median annual expenditures for a reference (two adult, two children) family. The budget should be updated yearly and adjusted (using equivalence scales) to reflect the needs of different family types and regional variation in housing costs.

To complete the poverty measure, the NAS study recommended that family resources be defined "as the sum of money income from all sources together with the value of near-money benefits (e.g., food stamps) that are available to buy goods and services in the budget, minus expenses that cannot be used to buy these goods and services. Such expenses include income and payroll taxes, child care and other work-related expenses, child support payments to another household, and out-of-pocket medical care costs, including health insurance premiums." The NAS study also recommended that the poverty measure be regularly reviewed and updated.[20]

Unfortunately, the official poverty measure has not been changed to reflect the NAS recommendations or other critiques. However, the Census Bureau does publish "experimental poverty measures" applying selected elements of NAS methodology, which show higher poverty rates than the official measure. In 1999, for example, the official rate of 11.8 percent rises to rates ranging from 13.8 to 14.4 percent, depending on which experimental measure is used.[21]

The NAS study drew on earlier work by the Bureau of Labor Statistics, Ruggles, Renwick and Bergmann, Schwarz and Volgy, Weinberg and Lamas, and others. For example, Patricia Ruggles used a multiplier approach based on the cost of housing rather than food to measure poverty. Daniel Weinberg and Enrique Lamas used both housing and food costs to calculate a family's expenditure needs.[22]

Numerous researchers in the United States and around the world have formulated detailed budgets to understand minimal household requirements. As a review of family budgets in the Bureau of Labor Statistics *Monthly Labor Review* observes:

> The measurement of family budgets and budget standards dates back to the late 19th century. Such budgets have been used to develop cost-of-living estimates, to assess wage rates, and to examine the standard of living. Early budget standards and family budgets were based on two different methodologies: expert decisions were devised to ascertain how much income a family might require to reach a certain level of living, and estimates were obtained on the actual purchasing behavior of particular families. The first, prescriptive, method was often used to determine the "sufficient" amount needed to provide a "standard of health and decency" or some other measure of the level of living. The second, descriptive, method was often used to describe consumer spending and to determine cost-of-living indexes.[23]

Budgets were also used for such purposes as determining relief payments and government pay scales. At the federal level, family budgets were compiled by the New Deal-era Works Progress Administration and the Bureau of Labor Statistics (BLS).

The BLS began constructing family budgets in 1908. In 1948, the BLS published a "modest but adequate" budget for urban working families, with separate pricing for 34 cities. In the 1960s, it developed budgets (for 40 urban areas, 4 regional averages and a U.S. urban average) for three levels: lower, intermediate (or moderate) and higher level. Notably, the lower level BLS budget used the USDA Low-Cost Food Plan rather than the unreasonable Thrifty Food Plan used for the official poverty measure. In 1981, when the BLS discontinued the family budgets, recognizing that they were out of date and needed major revision, the lower level budget was 138 percent of the official poverty threshold for a four-person family.[24]

The BLS family budgets were not designed to measure poverty, but to establish minimum wage levels, develop regional cost of living indices and determine program eligibility. As Trudi Renwick points out, "Discussions of a guaranteed income floor in the late 1960's were based on the BLS lower budget and in 1971 the BLS budget was used to define the wages exempted from the Nixon wage and price controls."[25]

The Department of Labor Employment and Training Administration still uses the 1981 BLS family budget, with an adjustment for inflation, to compute a "lower living standard income level" (broken down by region and selected metropolitan areas) to serve as the minimum criteria for determining whether employment leads to "self-sufficiency" under the Workforce Investment Act; some states are using higher standards such as the Self-Sufficiency Standard discussed below. The 2001 lower living standard regional figures for a family of four range from $25,300 in the non-metropolitan South to $30,360 for the metropolitan Northeast, or 144 to 172 percent of the official poverty line.[26]

With their influential "Basic Needs Budget," Trudi Renwick and Barbara Bergmann furthered the approach of creating budgets that were prescriptive (based on adequate expenditures and standards) rather than descriptive (based on actual inadequate expenditures and standards). Simply using actual expenditure figures for low-income people would incorporate the constraints they face in obtaining basic goods and services into public policy rather than use public policy to assure that basic needs are met. The Renwick and Bergmann Basic Needs Budgets were designed to provide an alternative to the poverty thresholds. They account for basic necessities, consider taxes and the value of non-cash benefits in the measure of a family's resources, and vary by family composition, geographic location and whether parents are in the paid labor force.[27]

In recent years, a growing array of family budget studies have been conducted to calculate alternative poverty measures, compute adequate income, determine the number of jobs that pay an adequate wage in a community (e.g., job gap studies) and support living wage campaigns. These studies are similar in that they examine subsistence requirements based on expert standards or actual expenditures for selected categories, including food, housing, health care, child care, transportation and personal expenses, and often include the net effect of taxes and tax credits. Many of these budget studies account for cost-of-living differences due to family composition and location, although they vary in degree of detail. They are mostly focused at the state and local level. In a 2000 review of some 20 family budget studies, the Economic Policy Institute found that most of the recommended levels came to about twice the official poverty line.[28]

In a valuable new report, the Economic Policy Institute (EPI) applies family budget methodology nationwide by calculating basic budgets needed to maintain a safe and decent standard of living for six family types for every metropolitan statistical area (MSA) in the country and one combined rural area per state. In addition, EPI counts the number of working families who fall below these basic budget levels, provides a comparison with the official poverty line, and uses "hardship measures" to explore the basic needs these families are unable to meet. EPI confirms that many families who fall below 200 percent of the official poverty level experience hardships.

EPI concludes with recommendations to expand the social safety net to help families meet their basic needs.[29]

The widely employed "Self-Sufficiency Standard" was developed by Diana Pearce of the University of Washington for the Wider Opportunities for Women (WOW) State Organizing Project for Family Economic Self-Sufficiency. In the words of a WOW report, "The Self-Sufficiency Standard measures how much income is needed, for a family of a given composition in a given place, to adequately meet its basic needs—without public or private subsidies."[30] The Standard allows for a high level of specificity with calculations for 70 family types (accounting for children of different ages)—from a single adult with no children to two adults with three teenagers. Highly variable costs such as housing and child care are calculated at the most geographically specific level available. Already completed for 14 states and cities (with county breakdowns), the Standard will be calculated for at least another 21 states by the end of 2002.

The Self-Sufficiency Standard is being used around the country to raise awareness of the real cost of living; support living wage campaigns; evaluate public policy alternatives; serve as a benchmark to

---

Carol Williams did not need an economic study to prove that her $24,000-a-year job as an administrative assistant could not support three children in New York, even when squeezed into a one-bedroom, $600-a-month apartment in the Bronx.

"By the time I paid my car payments and my car insurance and some bills, I was broke," said Ms. Williams, a widow. "Most of the time we were scrambling to buy food."

There was nothing wrong with her budgeting skills. Though the federal government says poverty in New York City officially ends at $14,150 for a household of three—just as it does in Brooklyn, Miss., or Manhattan, Kan.—Ms. Williams and many residents like her have found that getting by takes tens of thousands of dollars more.

In fact, according to a study [The Self-Sufficiency Standard for the City of New York] that scrutinized basic family expenses in the five boroughs, meeting bare-bones needs in the city costs two to five times more than the national poverty levels for families with children.

Nina Bernstein, New York Times, *September 13, 2000.*

measure welfare and workforce development policy outcomes; challenge the "work first" philosophy of the 1996 welfare law and fight for access to education and training; and change the way welfare and workforce development caseworkers counsel clients regarding jobs.[31] Connecticut now requires calculation of the Standard and legislation has been introduced in Massachusetts to make the Self-Sufficiency Standard an official state tool to measure what families need and help them attain it.

As the *Boston Globe* editorialized, "The Federal poverty level seems like a joke... The standard creates a new policy goal: Don't just push families a few steps beyond official poverty; help the one in four families that can't make ends meet get to self-sufficiency."[32] With welfare reform reauthorization approaching in 2002, WOW is leading an effort to have Congress pass legislation that would require states to use the Standard to measure outcomes for individuals leaving welfare.

RELATIVE POVERTY AND PUBLIC OPINION

In contrast to the detailed budget approaches reviewed above, others advocate a relative approach, defining the poor as those whose incomes fall below half the median income. This "relative poverty" measure is the most commonly used definition among industrialized countries.[33] However, this measure sheds little light on the actual extent of material deprivation.

Other analysts argue for defining poverty based on a subjective measure of the income level individuals think is necessary to sustain a household.[34] Polls typically show that the official poverty line is too low in the eyes of most respondents.

For example, a 2001 NPR/Kaiser/Kennedy School poll asked, "I'd like to know what income level you think makes a family [of four] poor?" The poll provided a range of levels up to $50,000. Among respondents, 88 percent considered a family of four making less than $15,000 a year to be poor; 64 percent considered a family of four making less than $20,000 a year to be poor; 42 percent said those making less than $25,000 a year; and 12 percent said $35,000 (the 2000 poverty line for a family of four was $17,601).[35]

Asking a different question, a 2000 poll by Lake Snell Perry & Associates found an even greater gap between the official poverty line and public perception: "How much income would you say a family of four needs to earn in a year in order to make ends meet?" It takes at least $35,000 a year, 69 percent said, and another 23 percent said it takes at least $25,000 a year.[36] While polls can be very revealing, they are no substitute for more standardized measures of adequate budgets.

The Need for a National Floor

As noted earlier, needs budgets and sufficiency standards typically take into account wide variations in the cost of living across and within regions and states. These are essential tools for advocating state and local policies that provide for living wages, higher minimum wages and higher eligibility thresholds for government support, and for other purposes such as evaluating and improving welfare and workforce development programs.

Our focus is on a national measure applicable to national policies such as the federal minimum wage. Our national minimum needs budget presented in the next chapter is based on an average of costs throughout the nation. It helps us in using the minimum wage and other federal policies such as the Earned Income Tax Credit to set a national floor under wages and living standards.

We emphasize the word floor. Today, many states and localities have higher minimum wages (e.g., California, Oregon, Massachusetts and Vermont), living wage ordinances (discussed in Chapter 3) and higher eligibility thresholds for social services. States should be encouraged to reach higher than the federal standard, but not allowed to engage in a "race to the bottom," by opting out of the federal minimum wage as President Bush has advocated.

In the words of Bush's chief economic adviser Lawrence Lindsey, "The right minimum wage for Manhattan is not the same minimum wage in the Rio Grande Valley."[37] New York state should have a higher state minimum wage as many states do now. Texas should not have a state minimum that is lower than the federal minimum. That's the whole point of a floor. States should be able to opt up, but not out, of the federal standard.

Many of our most significant social and economic policies, including anti-poverty policies, have been legislated, regulated and/or enabled by the federal government. Examples include the successful movements for child labor laws, reduction of working hours, Social Security, Medicare, workers' compensation insurance and establishment of the minimum wage. The most popular policies such as Social Security and Medicare have been universal in scope.[38]

Child Labor Laws: A growing number of states enacted child labor laws in the 19th and early 20th century following the lead of Massachusetts, which passed the nation's first child labor law in 1836—requiring children under the age of 15 employed in manufacturing to spend at least three months each year in school—and then a compulsory school attendance law in 1852. But these laws were seldom enforced and full of exceptions. About 43 percent of 14- and 15-year-old boys were reportedly working full time at the turn of the last century, a figure that probably understates the reality.[39] As the Labor Department notes, "Children as young as 6 or 7 years were recruited to work 13-hour days, for miniscule wages, in hot and dusty factories. Proposals to change these conditions met with stiff opposition."[40] Finally, the federal 1938 Fair Labor Standards Act established a minimum age of 16 for most kinds of work—two years higher than the age of 14, which most existing state laws stipulated.

Labor Hours: In 1840, President Van Buren issued an Executive Order restricting work in Federal Navy yards to ten hours per day. But in the following 70 years few states passed any limitations on working hours except for "protective" limitations on women's working hours, designed primarily to reinforce gender discrimination. Various state laws on working hours were supported and rejected in the Supreme Court in the early 1900s. But, again, it was only with passage of the Fair Labor Standards Act and the overcoming of a challenge in the Supreme Court in 1941 that meaningful time requirements were put on employment hours as employers were required to pay "time and a half" after 40 hours per week (originally 44 hours).

Pensions and Social Security: The history of pension law is interwoven with the role of the federal government because of the place of the Civil War pension system. By the early 20th century "nearly two-thirds of older, white, native-born men in the North received a 'veterans' pension."[41] In the following 20 years, 1915 to 1935, 29 states had some form of welfare assistance for the elderly, but it varied dramatically by location. With passage of the federal 1935 Social Security Act a growing number of seniors were able to retire with some sense of guaranteed economic support. It took many more years to undo various racist and sexist exclusions to Social Security coverage such as agricultural and domestic workers. Before the New Deal "Old Age Insurance" benefits and 1940s federal protection of private pensions, over half of men aged 65 and older were still working. The percentage of men aged 65 and older who worked dropped to 33 percent by 1960 and 17 percent by 1989.[42]

Minimum Wage: Massachusetts enacted the first minimum wage law in 1912. Sixteen more states and the District of Columbia passed minimum wage laws in the following 12 years. Opposition from employers, however, brought repeated legal attacks, which resulted in a Supreme Court ruling in 1923 that claimed minimum wage laws violated the constitutional rights of employers and workers to enter contracts. The Depression of the 1930s saw several states attempt minimum wage laws and continuing battles in the courts. The Supreme Court reversed itself in 1937. The landmark federal 1938 Fair Labor Standards Act established a national minimum wage, applied first to male and female workers involved directly or indirectly in interstate commerce, and then expanded over the years to cover most workers.

2

■ ■ ■ ■ ■

A National Minimum Needs Budget

If we eat, there's no money for clothes. If we buy clothes, there's no money to pay utilities for the house. And there's never enough to pay for insurance for the car.

Maria Guerra, Brownsville, TX,
school food service worker, 2000.[1]

People should not have to choose between eating or heating, health care or child care. Our proposed minimum needs budget covers these kind of necessities. It is designed to help set a national floor under wages and living standards.

The minimum needs budget includes the average cost of minimally adequate housing (including utilities), health care, food, child care, transportation, clothing and personal expenses, household expenses, telephone and taxes—factoring in tax credits. These are core elements in the needs budget literature.

The budget is a floor without a cushion. We exclude the cost of savings, debt, insurance other than health and car insurance, recreation, higher education and so on because they are not typically defined as basic necessities, although few would question their value.[2] In the case of higher education, for example, we advocate that government assistance be adequate enough to make college affordable to everyone.

We present minimum needs budgets for six household compositions: single adult, two adult-no children, single parent-one child, single parent-two children, two adult-one child and two adult-two children. For each of these households, we present budgets with and without some form of employment-provided health coverage.

Together, these six configurations form a majority of households. The average American household size is 2.62 people and the average family size is 3.24. As seen in the table below, one out of four households has one person. Another one out of four is a married couple with children present. One out of eleven is a female-headed household (no husband present) with children. The number of male-headed households (no wife present) with children has grown to about one in six of all single parent households, but is still only 2 percent of all households.[3]

TABLE 2-1
Household Composition, 2000

	NUMBER in thousands	PERCENT OF ALL HOUSEHOLDS
All Households	**104,705**	
1-Person Households	**26,724**	**25.5**
Female Householder	15,543	14.8
Male Householder	11,181	10.7
Family Households	**72,025**	**68.8**
With own children under 18 present*	37,496	35.8
One child	16,221	15.5
Two children	13,949	13.3
Married Couple	**55,311**	**52.8**
With own children under 18 present	25,771	24.6
One child	9,682	9.2
Two children	10,452	10.0
Female Householder	**12,687**	**12.1**
With own children under 18 present	9,681	9.2
One child	5,239	5.0
Two children	2,954	2.8
Male Householder	**4,028**	**3.8**
With own children under 18 present	2,044	2.0
One child	1,300	1.2
Two children	543	0.5

* Includes children by birth, stepchildren and adopted children.
Source: U.S. Census Bureau, *America's Families and Living Arrangements*, June 2001.

Looking at people in the paid workforce, ages 18-64, we see that 63 percent don't have children under 18. Among the 37 percent who are working parents, 30 percent are married and 7 percent are single parents. (See table below.)

TABLE 2-2
Parental Status of Workforce, 2000
age 18-64

	NUMBER *in thousands*	PERCENT
Working parents with children under 18	51,944	37.1
Married couple	42,361	30.3
Single parents	9,583	6.8
Female	7,670	5.5
Male	1,913	1.4
Workers without children under 18	88,014	62.9
Female	39,874	28.5
Male	48,140	34.4

Source: U.S. Bureau of Labor Statistics, *Employment Characteristics of Families in 2000*, April 19, 2001.

Many of the needs budgets we reviewed in the previous chapter are disaggregated by family size, geographic region and other criteria. This is crucial for understanding what particular households actually need to live on in different parts of the country, determining appropriate local and state polices, and assisting particular families. Our national minimum needs budget also reflects different household compositions.

We want to reiterate, however, that a national minimum wage floor is essential. States should be able to opt higher, but not lower, than the federal standard. Similarly, while family size is an important variable for understanding family needs and in setting government program amounts, the minimum wage should be a universal floor for employees. Mandating variable wage floors by family size, for example, could lead to discrimination as employers favored employees without children.

Our budget is based on average national costs, which, by definition, average out higher and lower costs around the country. To provide context, especially for those readers living in atypically high- or low-cost areas, we calculated minimum needs budgets for five sample high-, medium- and low-cost metropolitan areas: New York City; Los Angeles; Des Moines, Iowa; Kansas City, Missouri; and Gadsden, Alabama (see Appendix C). While our minimum needs budgets for Kansas City and

Des Moines are close to the national budgets, Gadsden's budgets are much lower while New York City's are much higher. For example, the minimum needs budget for a two adult-one child household without employment health insurance ranges from $24,865 in Gadsden to $40,247 in New York. Beyond the five sample cities, we do not provide minimum needs budgets for other areas, recommending instead that readers utilize more geographically targeted tools such as WOW's Self-Sufficiency Standard, EPI's family budgets and local living wage studies.[4]

Our minimum needs budget is not intended for use as an alternative poverty measure. It determines the costs associated with meeting minimum needs, but it does not measure the actual resources (wages, cash or in-kind governmental assistance, etc.) households have available for meeting those needs.

While details and sources are provided in Appendix B, we review expenditure categories briefly below.

Budget Categories

HOUSING

Safe, decent housing is a basic necessity. But as we'll see later, housing is a real hardship for many people. Housing costs represent the largest expense in all our needs budgets except for two-adult families without employment health benefits, for whom health care is the largest expense.

HUD Fair Market Rents are used to calculate the cost of housing. HUD Fair Market Rents are defined as "the amount that would be needed to pay the gross rent (shelter rent plus utilities) of privately owned, decent, safe and sanitary rental housing of a modest (non-luxury) nature with suitable amenities."[5] HUD Fair Market Rents represent rent costs at the 40th percentile of area rents and include the cost of all utilities except telephone.

To calculate housing costs, we assumed that no more than two persons share one bedroom and that children do not share a bedroom with their parents. Under these assumptions, a one-bedroom apartment would be sufficient for households without children. Households with children would require at least a two-bedroom apartment.

HEALTH CARE

Health care is a basic necessity and a major factor in well being and standard of living. Health insurance coverage is a crucial factor in access to preventive and acute care and insulates families from catastrophic medical expenses (we discuss health care extensively in Chapter Six). However, even when workers have access to employment-based health insurance coverage, they are increasingly required to contribute toward the cost of the premium and bear substantial out-of-pocket costs, including copayments for services. We include health care expenses (premium contributions and out-of-pocket expenses) in the needs budget.

Most people (nearly 63 percent) are covered by private sector employment-based insurance either through their own employment or a relative's.[6] But the share of workers covered by employer-based health plans drops from 82 percent in the top fifth of wage earners to less than 30 percent in the lowest fifth.[7]

Even among persons with employment-based coverage, the share required to contribute to coverage cost has been increasing. Average employee contributions to health insurance coverage have outpaced the increase in the medical care component of the CPI-U since the mid-1980s. While health care costs doubled, employee contributions were approximately three times higher in 2000 than in 1988.[8]

FOOD

Food is clearly a basic necessity. Adequate nutrition is crucial for survival, health and child development.

To calculate food costs, we used the USDA Low-Cost Food Plan rather than the inadequate USDA Thrifty Food Plan underlying the Census poverty threshold. The Low-Cost Food Plan is still very minimal. It does not incorporate the cost of food purchased and consumed away from home. We made the conservative assumption that all meals are prepared in the home, even if consumed elsewhere, since minimum nutritional needs can be met this way, although it is often more inconvenient and impractical.

CHILD CARE FOR A PRESCHOOL CHILD

Since we assumed that adult members of households work full time, year round, we included child care costs in the minimum needs budget. Child care costs were recognized by the National Academy of Sciences (NAS) poverty panel as a work-related expense that affects a family's resources and they recommended child care be included in the development of a new poverty measure.[9] The inability to afford consistent and secure child care services frequently restricts employment, job training, education, job improvement, job mobility and pay increases.

Low-income families do not differ substantially from higher-income families in their use of multiple nonparental child care arrangements or informal care. However, there is greater variation in the use of multiple arrangements by low-income families compared to middle-income families. These differences often result from lack of funds for child care among low-income households. Children from low-income families are less likely to be cared for in child care centers than children from high-income families (26 percent v. 35 percent); are more likely to be in relative or parent care (56 percent v. 41 percent) and are more likely to be cared for in family child care homes (17 percent v. 14 percent).[10]

While some parents across the economic spectrum strongly prefer good child care with a relative where possible, for others it is a fall-back—a less desirable and less reliable arrangement, necessitated by limited income.

To calculate the average cost of child care services we assumed that families with children have one child 3 or 4 years old in full-time child care provided by a non-relative to reflect the most common age of children in child care and to provide conservative cost estimates (infant care is much more expensive). As high as these expenses are for many families, we should remember they are heavily subsidized by the intolerably low wages paid to child care workers, as discussed in later chapters.

CARE FOR A SCHOOL-AGE CHILD

We also included the cost of school-age care in the minimum needs budget. We assume that all adult members of households work and that school-age children 12 and under will require some form of paid care.

A 2000 U.S. Census Bureau report found that children living in poverty are more likely to be cared for by siblings (19.2 percent v. 13.4 percent) and less likely to be involved in enrichment activities, such as sports, lessons, clubs or before/after-school programs (27.1 percent v. 35.6 percent) and are more likely to have a self-care arrangement (21.0 percent v. 15.4 percent).[11]

To calculate costs for care for a school-age child, we assumed that families with two children have one child in before- or after-school care, and that the school-age child requires care during the summer months.

TRANSPORTATION

Transportation expenses are a standard element in all minimum needs budgets. The NAS Panel also recognized transportation costs as a work-related expense impacting a family's resources, and recommended that transportation costs be included in measuring poverty. Adequate transportation is essential in providing access to employment opportunities and a means to obtain necessary goods and services.

A study based on data from the 1995 National Personal Transportation Survey found substantial differences in the use of transportation by low-income families compared to other families. Low-income families were considerably less likely to own a car (74 percent v. 97 percent) and, if they did, the car was likely to be older (11 years v. 8 years). Low-income workers were less likely to use a car to get to work (84 percent v. 90 percent) and they were more likely than workers in other households to walk to their destination (6 percent v. 3 percent) and to use public transit (5 percent v. 2 percent). In addition, 60 percent of trips made by low-income households are 3 miles or less compared to 50 percent for other households.[12]

Transportation constraints on low-income households limit their ability to take advantage of regional employment opportunities and to obtain goods and services in order to meet their other needs. Lack of transportation often means that low-income families actually pay more for purchases since they have less opportunity to comparison shop, seek out discounts or buy in bulk.

To calculate transportation costs, we assumed that households own a used car. Unfortunately, in many non-metropolitan areas public transit is scarce or nonexistent and many metro areas do not have adequate, reliable public transit systems, especially serving low-income neighborhoods. Moreover, only 8 percent of households do not own a car. However, in large metropolitan areas, 26 percent of low-income households did not own a car and 36 percent of low-income, single parent households were without a car.[13]

A 2000 study looked at the relevance of disproportionately low car ownership rates by blacks and Latinos living in metropolitan areas to employment in the "ever-important suburban employment centers." The report found that given the difficulties of reverse-commuting from city to suburbs by public transit, inadequate public transit schedules and persistent racial housing segregation in metropolitan areas, raising the car ownership rates of blacks and Latinos would help narrow their employment gaps with whites.[14]

Having safe and reliable transportation is critical to finding and keeping a job, and accessing jobs with higher wages and better working conditions.[15] We strongly advocate the expansion of public transit. However, it would be unrealistic to leave out car costs, especially for working families.

CLOTHING AND PERSONAL EXPENSES

The needs budgets reviewed include the cost of clothing and other personal expenses (such as personal care products and services) either as a separate category, as we do, or in the more inclusive category of miscellaneous expenses. We assume that average annual expenditures for clothing and personal expenses by consumers in the first quintile of income are sufficient to meet a household's minimum needs in these categories.

HOUSEHOLD EXPENSES

Most of the needs budget studies we reviewed also included household expenses, although the studies varied as to which expenses were

TABLE 2-3
Annual Minimum Needs Budgets Without Employment Health Benefits*
1999 dollars

EXPENDITURE CATEGORY	SINGLE ADULT	TWO ADULTS	SINGLE PARENT, ONE CHILD	SINGLE PARENT, TWO CHILDREN	TWO ADULTS, ONE CHILD	TWO ADULTS, TWO CHILDREN
Housing	$6,272	$6,272	$7,733	$7,733	$7,733	$7,733
Health Care	3,066	6,376	6,376	6,376	6,376	6,376
Food	1,759	3,557	2,801	4,243	4,649	6,104
Child Care	0	0	4,582	4,582	4,582	4,582
School-Age Care	0	0	0	2,968	0	2,968
Transportation	1,285	1,881	1,726	1,726	2,056	2,056
Clothing and Personal Expenses	610	1,152	904	959	1,142	1,343
Household Expenses	489	489	489	489	489	489
Telephone	550	550	550	550	550	550
Subtotal before taxes	**14,031**	**20,277**	**25,161**	**29,626**	**27,577**	**32,201**
Payroll Tax	1,073	1,551	1,925	2,266	2,110	2,463
Federal Tax (including credits)	1,211	1,369	1,280	631	1,154	511
State Tax (including credits)	234	325	430	476	414	462
TOTAL	**16,549**	**23,522**	**28,796**	**32,999**	**31,255**	**35,637**
Hourly Wage**	7.96	11.30	13.84	15.86	15.03	17.13

* The term "without employment health benefits" refers to workers whose employers do not pay any portion of the employee's health insurance costs. The minimum needs budgets "without employment health benefits" reflect the amount these households would pay to purchase health insurance coverage in the private market.

** The hourly wage necessary for one full-time, full-year worker to earn the respective minimum needs budget or the combined wage for two adult workers.

Source: Solutions For Progress.

included. We assume that average annual expenditures on household expenses and household operations by consumers in the first quintile of income are sufficient to meet a household's minimum needs in these categories.

TELEPHONE SERVICES

Telephone services are considered a necessity, but nearly a fourth (23.3 percent) of low-income households do not have continuous phone service.[16] The lack of a telephone may have serious consequences in an emergency. Telephone services affect the ability to contact employers (and vice versa), make appointments, communicate with children, schools and child care providers, arrange for transportation

---

TABLE 2-4

Annual Minimum Needs Budget
With Employment Health Benefits*

1999 dollars

EXPENDITURE	SINGLE ADULT	TWO ADULTS	SINGLE PARENT, ONE CHILD	SINGLE PARENT, TWO CHILDREN	TWO ADULTS, ONE CHILD	TWO ADULTS, TWO CHILDREN
Housing	$6,272	$6,272	$7,733	$7,733	$7,733	$7,733
Health Care	1,244	2,517	2,517	2,517	2,517	2,517
Food	1,759	3,557	2,801	4,243	4,649	6,104
Child Care	0	0	4,582	4,582	4,582	4,582
School-Age Care	0	0	0	2,968	0	2,968
Transportation	1,285	1,881	1,726	1,726	2,056	2,056
Clothing and Personal Expenses	610	1,152	904	959	1,142	1,343
Household Expenses	489	489	489	489	489	489
Telephone	550	550	550	550	550	550
Subtotal before taxes	**12,209**	**16,418**	**21,302**	**25,767**	**23,718**	**28,342**
Payroll Tax	923	1,256	1,630	1,971	1,814	2,168
Federal Tax (including credits)	889	746	-31	-601	259	-12
State Tax (including credits)	175	194	278	302	285	314
TOTAL	**14,196**	**18,614**	**23,179**	**27,439**	**26,076**	**30,812**
Hourly Wage**	6.83	8.95	11.14	13.19	12.54	14.81

* The term "with employment health benefits" refers to workers who have employer-provided health insurance—that is, workers whose employers pay at least a share of their health insurance premium costs.

** The hourly wage necessary for one full-time, full-year worker to earn the respective minimum needs budget, or the combined wage for two adult workers.

Source: Solutions For Progress.

and contact emergency medical, fire and police services if necessary. To estimate the costs of telephone services, we assumed that average annual expenditures on telephone services by households in the first quintile of income are sufficient to meet a household's minimum needs in these categories.

TAXES

To estimate average taxes for the minimum needs budget, we first assumed that families earn an income sufficient to meet their minimum needs. If the tax calculation seems high, remember that it reflects the actual average tax liability of families with an income just sufficient to meet their minimum needs, not the average tax liability of today's low-income families.[17]

In the tax calculation, we included the employee share of federal payroll taxes, federal income tax, state income taxes, and any tax credits (e.g., EITC, child care credit) for which a family with an income meeting its minimum needs budget would be eligible. Sales taxes are not included in this calculation since they are included in the annual expenditures for specific cost categories, such as clothing and personal expenses, reported in the Consumer Expenditure Survey. For the pur-

---

TABLE 2-5

Minimum Needs Budget Without Employment Health Benefits as Percent of Federal Poverty Threshold

HOUSEHOLD COMPOSITION	MINIMUM NEEDS BUDGET 1999	FEDERAL POVERTY THRESHOLD 1999	DIFFERENCE BETWEEN POVERTY THRESHOLD & NEEDS BUDGET	NEEDS BUDGET AS PERCENT OF THRESHOLD
Single Adult*	$16,549	$8,667	$7,882	191%
Two Adults	$23,522	$11,156	$12,366	211%
Single Parent, One Child	$28,796	$11,483	$17,313	251%
Single Parent, Two Children	$32,999	$13,423	$19,576	246%
Two Adults, One Child	$31,255	$13,410	$17,845	233%
Two Adults, Two Children	$35,637	$16,895	$18,742	211%

* Under 65 years old.

Sources: Solutions for Progress and U.S. Census Bureau, "Poverty Thresholds in 1999, by Size of Family and Number of Related Children Under 18 Years."

pose of tax calculations, we assume all adults are under the age of 65 years and work in the labor force.

We assume in calculating the minimum needs budgets for two-parent households that both parents work full time out of economic necessity. Most Americans do not see this as the "ideal situation for a family in today's society." Only 13 percent told a recent Gallup Poll that it was ideal that both parents work full time outside the home; 24 percent preferred one parent working full time and the other part time, and 41 percent preferred that one parent stays at home to raise children. Support for the stay-at-home parent scenario decreases with age, with only 31 percent of those aged 18 to 29 believing this was ideal. A strong majority, 69 percent, of those preferring that one parent stays home or work part time while the other works full time, said it doesn't matter which parent is the full-time worker (up from 55 percent in 1991).[18]

Below the Minimum Needs Budgets

O ur estimates show that 29 million households (fitting our six categories)—including 14.9 million working households—do not have sufficient income to meet their minimum needs budgets even if they are covered by employment-based health insurance.[19] This represents about 24 percent of all households and 16 percent of working households. A working household is defined as a household

| TABLE 2-6 |

Minimum Needs Budget With Employment Health Benefits as Percent of Federal Poverty Threshold

HOUSEHOLD COMPOSITION	MINIMUM NEEDS BUDGET 1999	FEDERAL POVERTY THRESHOLD 1999	DIFFERENCE BETWEEN POVERTY THRESHOLD & NEEDS BUDGET	NEEDS BUDGET AS PERCENT OF THRESHOLD
Single Adult	$14,196	$8,667	$5,529	164%
Two Adults	$18,614	$11,156	$7,458	167%
Single Parent, One Child	$23,179	$11,483	$11,696	202%
Single Parent, Two Children	$27,439	$13,423	$14,016	204%
Two Adults, One Child	$26,076	$13,410	$12,666	194%
Two Adults, Two Children	$30,812	$16,895	$13,827	182%

Through [the Children Defense Fund's] Community Monitoring Project, which documents the impact of the 1996 welfare changes on poor mothers and children, we learned of a 45-year-old North Carolina mother with an 11-year-old daughter who had left welfare for a job. She was working 38 hours a week at $6 an hour and was proud to have been named employee of the month. After leaving welfare she lost her housing and was living in a transitional homeless shelter with her daughter. She had no health insurance and has been unable to pay medical bills for herself or for her daughter. She earned a few dollars more than the official poverty line but not enough to make ends meet.

Children's Defense Fund,
The State of America's Children Yearbook 2001.

with at least one worker employed full time or part time, whether for the full year or only part of the year.

The minimum needs budget figures substantially exceed official federal poverty thresholds. As seen in the tables above, a single person without employment health coverage would need to have 191 percent of the federal poverty threshold of $8,667 to meet their basic needs (since our minimum needs budgets are in 1999 dollars, we use 1999 poverty thresholds for comparison). Other families would need more than double the official poverty level to meet their minimum needs budgets. Single parent families would need double the poverty threshold even if they had employment-based health insurance coverage.

3

■ ■ ■ ■ ■

Shortchanging The Minimum Wage

Recent clients at a Greenwich, Connecticut food bank included "a cook from a local French restaurant, a construction worker, housekeepers from nearby estates who made the minimum wage, $5.15 an hour, and a woman who cared for the children of housekeepers."
New York Times, *February 26, 1999.*[1]

The minimum wage used to bring a family of three with one full-time worker above the official poverty line. Now it doesn't bring a full-time worker with one child above the line. The minimum wage has become a poverty wage instead of an anti-poverty wage.

The minimum wage is well below our minimum needs budget for even a single person—with or without employment health benefits. A full-time, year-round worker earning the current minimum wage of $5.15 per hour makes $10,712 annually (or $21,424 for a full-time two-earner family). Only households with two adults working full time, no children and employment health benefits can meet their minimum needs budget at this wage. If "minimum wage" doesn't cover necessities, it's no minimum.

The federal minimum wage, enacted in 1938, was meant to put a firm floor under workers and their families, strengthen the economy by increasing consumer purchasing power, create new jobs to meet rising demand, foster economic development in lagging regions of the country—principally the South—and prevent the original "race to the bottom" of employers moving to cheaper labor states in a downward spiral.

In 1933, when "President Roosevelt asked Frances Perkins to become Secretary of Labor, she told him that she would accept if she could advocate a law to put a floor under wages and a ceiling over hours of work and to abolish abuses of child labor."[2] When President Roosevelt sent the Fair Labor Standards bill to Congress in 1937—with its provisions for a minimum wage, overtime pay and restrictions on child labor—he said that America should be able to give working men and women "a fair day's pay for a fair day's work."

Roosevelt continued, "A self-supporting and self-respecting democracy can plead no justification for the existence of child labor, no economic reason for chiseling workers' wages or stretching workers' hours." Further, he said, goods produced "under conditions that do not meet a rudimentary standard of decency should be regarded as contraband and ought not to be able to pollute the channels of interstate commerce."[3]

The minimum wage was not just intended as an anti-poverty wage. As the Economic Policy Institute points out, the minimum wage "is also an important labor market institution, whose purpose is to set a floor on the low end of the labor market. In this regard, it serves to counterbalance the lack of bargaining power suffered by the economy's lowest-paid workers... When the minimum wage is allowed to fall in real terms, it undermines this important labor market protection."[4] And that's just what many minimum wage opponents want.

When workers are not paid a fair day's pay they are not just underpaid—they are subsidizing employers, stockholders and consumers.

The Incredible Shrinking Minimum

As the Depression ended, the economy expanded, worker productivity increased and living standards improved in the post-World War II period, the minimum wage rose 160 percent, adjusting for inflation, in its first 30 years. Since then, it's plummeted. Today's minimum wage is lower than the level of 1950.

The real value of the minimum wage peaked in 1968 at $7.92 per hour (in 2000 dollars), and then declined in the early 1970s to $6.21. Increases in the minimum wage in the mid- to late-1970s brought its real value back up to $7 in 1978. But there were no minimum wage increases between 1982 and 1989, when the minimum reached a modern low of $4.65, adjusting for inflation.

Today's minimum wage workers earn a third less in real wages than their counterparts did a third of a century ago. Now at $5.15, the real

> **"I**f we would have had our druthers," acknowledges Murray Weidenbaum, the chairman of Mr. Reagan's first Council of Economic Advisers, "we would have eliminated it [the minimum wage]." However, because that would have been such "a painful political process," Mr. Weidenbaum says that he and other officials were content to let inflation turn the minimum wage into "an effective dead letter."
> **Rick Wartzman,** Wall Street Journal, *July 19, 2001.*

value of the minimum wage is 35 percent lower than it was in 1968. Profits, on the other hand, are 64 percent higher, as we'll see below.

As anyone who saw the value of their stocks shrivel with the Nasdaq knows, the climb back isn't the same as the fall down (to take the simplest example, it takes a 100 percent gain to make up for a 50 percent loss). Minimum wage workers need a gain of 54 percent just to get back to the level of 1968.

In order to adjust the minimum wage, Congress must pass legislation, which the President must sign. In 1968, congressional pay was 9 times more than the minimum wage. Now, at $145,100, it's nearly 14 times more.[5]

The Fair Minimum Wage Act of 2001 sponsored by Senator Edward M. Kennedy (D-MA) and Representative David Bonior (D-MI) calls for raising the minimum wage by $1.50 in three increments: 60 cents ($5.75) 30 days after enactment; 50 cents ($6.25) on January 1, 2002; and 40 cents to reach $6.65 on January 1, 2003. A Republican alternative calls for the lower figure of $6.15 and a host of business tax breaks. Based on projected inflation rates, a wage of $6.15 in 2003 would be worth only $5.67 in 2000 dollars. A wage of $6.65 in 2003 is equivalent to $6.13 in 2000 dollars.[6]

Raising the minimum wage has great public support. When asked whether they support raising the minimum wage by a dollar, for example, 86 percent of Americans agreed.[7] In fact, many Americans think the current minimum wage is higher than it actually is. A June 2001 survey by the Pew Research Center for the People and the Press found that only 4 percent of Americans thought the minimum wage was less than $5 while 51 percent correctly thought it was about $5; 28 percent thought it was about $6; and 11 percent said about $7 or more.[8]

The Bush administration says that if the federal minimum wage is raised states should be able to opt out and substitute their own lower minimum at or above the current $5.15. That would destroy the national

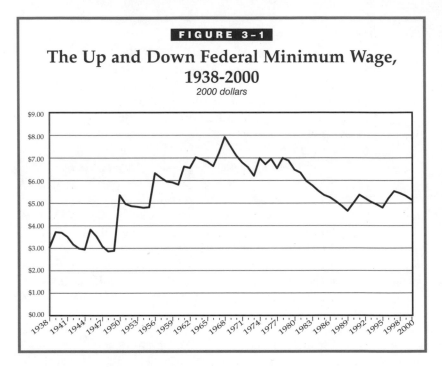

FIGURE 3-1

The Up and Down Federal Minimum Wage, 1938-2000

2000 dollars

floor under workers. Many states would keep the minimum wage at $5.15 as inflation wore it down. By 2003, for example, $5.15 would be worth only $4.75 in 2000 dollars, according to current projections.[9]

Most states have minimum wages that are equal to or less than the federal minimum. Ten states and the District of Columbia have higher minimums than the federal: Alaska ($5.65), California (at $6.25, going up to $6.75 in 2002), Connecticut ($6.40, going up to $6.70 in 2002), Delaware ($6.15), District of Columbia ($6.15), Hawaii ($5.25), Massachusetts ($6.75), Oregon ($6.50), Rhode Island ($6.15), Vermont ($6.25) and Washington ($6.72, with inflation adjustment beginning in 2001). Maine legislation to raise the state minimum wage to $5.65 in January 2002 and $6.15 in 2003 is awaiting action by the governor. Georgia recently raised its minimum wage from $3.25 to $5.15, as did Wyoming, which had a pathetic minimum wage of $1.60. Four states still have lower rates: Kansas ($2.65), New Mexico ($4.25), Ohio ($4.25) and President Bush's state of Texas ($3.35). Where federal and state rates are different, the higher standard applies. The rest either don't have a state minimum wage or set the state rate at the same as the federal rate.[10]

Real world results from the last minimum wage hike directly counter the notion that states should be able to opt out. States with the highest number of workers affected by the last minimum wage raise

TABLE 3-1

Real Value of Federal Minimum Wage, 1938-2000
2000 dollars

YEAR	VALUE	YEAR	VALUE	YEAR	VALUE
1938	$3.05	1959	$5.92	**1980**	**$6.48**
1939	**3.72**	1960	5.82	**1981**	**6.35**
1940	3.69	**1961**	**6.62**	1982	5.98
1941	3.51	1962	6.56	1983	5.79
1942	3.17	**1963**	**7.03**	1984	5.55
1943	2.99	1964	6.94	1985	5.36
1944	2.94	1965	6.83	1986	5.26
1945	**3.83**	1966	6.64	1987	5.08
1946	3.53	**1967**	**7.22**	1988	4.88
1947	3.09	**1968**	**7.92**	1989	4.65
1948	2.86	1969	7.51	**1990**	**5.01**
1949	2.89	1970	7.10	1991	5.37
1950	**5.36**	1971	6.80	1992	5.22
1951	4.97	1972	6.59	1993	5.06
1952	4.87	1973	6.21	1994	4.94
1953	4.84	**1974**	**6.99**	1995	4.80
1954	4.80	**1975**	**6.72**	**1996**	**5.21**
1955	4.82	**1976**	**6.96**	**1997**	**5.53**
1956	**6.33**	1977	6.54	1998	5.44
1957	6.13	**1978**	**7.00**	1999	5.32
1958	5.96	**1979**	**6.88**	2000	5.15

Note: Years with minimum wage hikes are in bold.

Source: U.S. Bureau of Labor Statistics, "Value of the Federal Minimum Wage, 1938-1997," adjusted for inflation using the CPI-U.

did not have higher unemployment rates than other states. Focusing on a subset of workers heavily impacted by the 1996-97 minimum wage hikes—women age 16 to 25 with a high school education or less—the Economic Policy Institute compared the ten states with the largest share of affected workers (Texas, New Mexico, Wyoming, North Dakota, Alabama, Oklahoma, West Virginia, Arkansas, Louisiana and Mississippi) with the ten states with the smallest share of affected workers (Connecticut, New Jersey, Massachusetts, New Hampshire, Washington, District of Columbia, Maryland, Minnesota, Colorado and Delaware). EPI found that between 1995 and 2000, unemployment among women in the most affected states declined 26 percent—from 18.7 percent to 13.8 percent. In the least affected states, unemployment fell 24 percent—from 13.7 to 10.4 percent.[11]

Rosalina Garcia is a single mom who...goes to work every day, cleaning an expensive Sacramento office building and setting an example for her 13-year-old son about the value and dignity of hard work. But in the setting of her wage level, her employer and the state of California send a very different message. She is barely able to scrape by on $5.75 an hour, constantly forced to choose which basic needs of her and her son to neglect...

Worker representatives on the [Industrial Welfare Commission, which sets the state minimum wage] have put forward a modest proposal to increase the state's minimum wage to $8 an hour over three years, but it has run into opposition from corporate lobbyists...

When Garcia got her chance to testify at a hearing in Sacramento, she asked the commissioners, "How would you like to switch jobs and see if $5.75 an hour is enough to raise a family?"

Bill Camp and Julio Quezada, Sacramento Bee, October 4, 2000. (California raised its minimum wage to $6.25, with a step up to $6.75 on January 1, 2002.)

We need to build on the New Deal federal minimum wage, not destroy it. States should be able to opt up, but not out, of the federal standard.

Back in the 1930s, when Southern congressmen asked for setting lower minimum wages for their region, International Ladies Garment Workers Union leader David Dubinsky suggested lower pay for Southern congressmen.[12]

Productivity Outpaces Wages

For decades now, workers have been shortchanged in good times and bad. Government let the minimum wage floor drop, dragging down average worker wages as employers followed—and encouraged—the government's stingy lead.

Productivity went up, but wages went down. Worker productivity is the measure of output produced by an hour of labor. Rising productivity means that the same amount of labor time produces more goods and services—and the cost of producing each unit of output declines. Increases in productivity enable employers to increase wages and sustain profits without raising prices.

In the words of the Department of Labor Wage and Hours Division, "As the productivity of workers increases, one would expect worker compensation [wages and benefits] to experience similar gains." That's not what happened. Instead, since 1969, "profits recorded significant gains, real hourly earnings were flat, and the real value of the minimum wage declined."[13]

Productivity grew 74.2 percent between 1968 and 2000, but the gains were not shared with workers.[14] Despite long-overdue wage growth since 1996, hourly wages for average workers in 2000 were 3 percent lower, adjusting for inflation, than they were during the Johnson administration. Real weekly wages were 11 percent lower than in 1968. Wages for minimum wage workers were 35 percent lower.

What if wages had kept rising with productivity, and were 74.2 percent higher in 2000 than they were in 1973? The average hourly wage would have been $24.56 in 2000, rather than $13.74. That's a difference of nearly $11 an hour—or about $22,000 a year for a full-time, year-round worker.

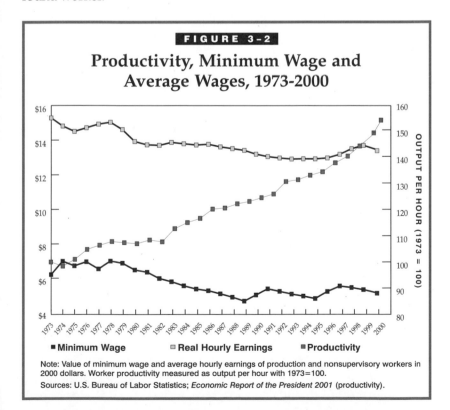

FIGURE 3-2

Productivity, Minimum Wage and Average Wages, 1973-2000

■ Minimum Wage   ▫ Real Hourly Earnings   ■ Productivity

Note: Value of minimum wage and average hourly earnings of production and nonsupervisory workers in 2000 dollars. Worker productivity measured as output per hour with 1973=100.

Sources: U.S. Bureau of Labor Statistics; *Economic Report of the President 2001* (productivity).

TABLE 3-2

Minimum Wage, Average Wages and Business Cycles, 1967-2000

2000 dollars

| | AVERAGE WAGES | | MINIMUM WAGE |
	HOURLY	WEEKLY	HOURLY
1967	$13.82	$525.06	$7.22
1973	15.28	563.88	6.21
1979	14.61	521.66	6.88
1982	13.70	476.91	5.98
1989	13.41	464.16	4.65
1992	12.97	446.28	5.22
1995	12.92	445.57	4.80
1999	13.69	472.13	5.32
2000	13.74	474.03	5.15
	PERCENT CHANGE		
1967-2000	-0.6	-9.7	-28.7
1973-2000	-10.1	-15.9	-17.0
1973-1995	-15.4	-21.0	-22.7
1995-2000	6.3	6.4	7.3
BUSINESS CYCLES*	**ANNUAL GROWTH RATE**		
1967-1973	1.7	1.2	-2.3
1973-1979	-0.6	-1.0	0.8
1979-1989	-1.0	-1.3	-3.6
1979-1981	-2.9	-3.5	-3.2
1981-1989	-0.4	-0.6	-3.6
1989-2000	0.1	0.1	0.6
1989-1995	-0.6	-0.7	-0.1
1995-2000	1.0	0.9	0.8

Note: Hourly and weekly wages for production and nonsupervisory workers on private nonfarm payrolls, accounting for about 80 percent of the civilian workforce. Minimum wage peaked in 1968 at $7.92 and the average hourly wage peaked in 1973 at $15.28 in 2000 dollars. Adjusted for inflation with CPI-U. During 1973-2000, productivity grew 54.2 percent and during 1968-2000, it grew 74.2 percent.

* A business cycle describes the pattern of fluctuations in the economy. A complete business cycle includes an economic downturn followed by an economic expansion. The length of a business cycle is measured from the peak of an expansion to the peak of the next expansion.

Source: U.S. Bureau of Labor Statistics.

The minimum wage would have been $13.80 in 2000—not $5.15—if it had kept pace with productivity. That's a difference of $8.65 an hour, or nearly $18,000 for a full-time year-round worker.

Wages have gone down while education levels have gone up. In 1970, 36 percent of the civilian workforce, ages 25 to 64, were not high

For about four years I had to start work at 5 a.m. at the Holiday Inn and get out at 1 p.m. I had to come home, pick up my kids from school and make dinner for them. Then I had to start my other job at 5 p.m. until 1 a.m., and then I would start all over again at 5 a.m. So I slept for two hours in the morning and for two hours in the afternoon. Your family is what drives you and gives you energy, but you can only continue like that for so long.

> *Gonzalo Gama, Hotel Worker, Hollywood, CA, quoted in*
> *Los Angeles Alliance for a New Economy,*
> *The Other Los Angeles, August 2000.*

school graduates and only 14 percent had four years of college or more. In 1999, only 10 percent were not high school graduates and 30 percent were college graduates.[15]

In the words of union leader Amy Dean, founder of the Silicon Valley-based Working Partnerships USA, "The new economy is an hourglass: it offers more good jobs than ever before, but it's squeezing the middle class into oblivion, and it's creating a massive base of workers struggling desperately, at low-pay, no benefit, dead end, and often temporary service occupations."[16]

Barbara Ehrenreich explores the struggle of low-wage workers to get by in her eye-opening book, *Nickel and Dimed*. She calls it, "A story of how hard you have to work to get nowhere at all."[17]

Profits Outpace Wages

"Two factors can explain the divergence between wage growth and productivity growth," the Economic Policy Institute observes. "Rising wage inequality and a shift of income from workers to business owners. The wage gap between those at the top and the middle has grown steadily, and the returns to capital have soared to historic highs."[18]

When we look at real domestic corporate profits, we see a dramatic rise in profits compared with workers' earnings. Adjusting for inflation, profits increased by 67 percent during the 1990s, while average hourly earnings increased only 4 percent, and the minimum wage rose 3 percent. Looking back to 1968, the minimum wage peak, we see that profits rose 64 percent while average earnings dropped 3 percent and the minimum wage fell 35 percent.

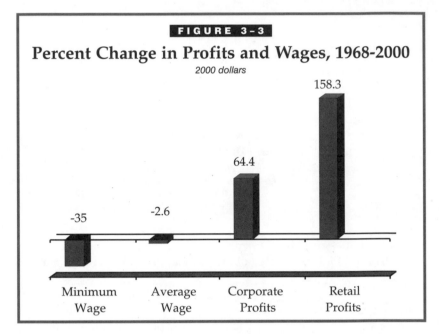

FIGURE 3-3

Percent Change in Profits and Wages, 1968-2000

2000 dollars

158.3

64.4

-35

-2.6

| Minimum | Average | Corporate | Retail |
| Wage | Wage | Profits | Profits |

According to the Department of Labor, the retail trade industry employs more than half the nation's hourly employees paid at or below minimum wage (1.8 million out of 3.3 million minimum wage workers in 1999).[19] Retail profits jumped even higher than profits generally. During the 1990s, retail profits shot up 196 percent. Since 1968, retail profits have risen 158 percent. (See table below.)

Clearly, profits have increased dramatically at the expense of workers. If the minimum wage had kept pace with domestic profits during 1968-2000, it would be $13.02. If it had kept pace with retail profits, it would be $20.46.

CEO Pay Outpaces Wages

In a fireside chat the night before signing the Fair Labor Standards Act, President Roosevelt said, "Do not let any calamity-howling executive with an income of $1,000 a day...tell you...that a wage of $11 a week is going to have a disastrous effect on all American industry."[20]

While workers were mired in quicksand, CEO pay skyrocketed. Many CEOs make more in a year than their employees will make in a lifetime. In 2000, the average chief executive officer (CEO) of a major corporation earned $13.1 million, including salary, bonus and other

TABLE 3-3

Percent Change in Corporate Domestic Profits, Retail Profits, Minimum Wage and Average Wages, 1968-2000

2000 dollars

YEARS	MINIMUM WAGE	AVERAGE HOURLY EARNINGS	DOMESTIC CORPORATE PROFITS	RETAIL PROFITS
1968-2000	-35.0	-2.6	64.4	158.3
1973-2000	-17.0	-10.1	74.8	219.6
1980-2000	-20.5	-1.3	117.1	511.6
1990-2000	2.9	4.2	67.1	195.6

Note: 1968 and 1973 are the respective peak years for the minimum wage and average wages.

Sources: Wages: U.S. Bureau of Labor Statistics. Profits: U.S. Department of Commerce, Bureau of Economic Analysis, "National Income and Product Accounts, Second Quarter 2001 GDP (advance) and Revised Estimates: 1968 through First Quarter 2001," News Release, July 27, 2001.

compensation such as exercised stock options, according to *Business Week's* survey of executive pay at the 365 largest companies. That's nearly $36,000 every day of the year.

The CEO-average worker wage gap has grown ten times wider over the last two decades. In 1980, CEOs made 45 times the pay of average production and nonsupervisory workers. By 1996, CEOs made 236 times as much, and *Business Week's* cover story on 1996 executive pay called it, "Out of control." In 2000, CEOs made 458 times as much.

The gap between CEOs and minimum wage workers has become a grand canyon. In 1980, CEOs made as much as 97 minimum wage workers. In 2000, they made as much as 1,223 minimum wage workers.

"The fast food industry pays the minimum wage to a higher proportion of its workers than any other American industry," writes Eric Schlosser in his extraordinary book, *Fast Food Nation*. "While the real value of the wages paid to restaurant workers has declined for the past three decades, the earnings of restaurant company executives have risen considerably. According to a 1997 survey in *Nation's Restaurant News*, the average restaurant industry corporate executive bonus was $131,000, an increase of 20 percent over the previous year."[21] That's not including salary. Just the average bonus for one executive would cover a year's hike in the minimum wage from $5.15 to $8.00 for 22 workers.

While workers have been denied their fair share of rising productivity, CEOs have taken an unjustifiably higher share. As the *Wall Street*

TABLE 3-4

Pay of CEOs, Average Workers and Minimum Wage Workers, 1980-2000
in 2000 dollars

	1980	1990	1995	1996	1997	1998	1999	2000
CEO*	1,306,120	2,635,042	4,293,701	6,365,583	8,368,598	11,198,282	12,816,807	13,100,000
Average Worker**	28,950	27,432	26,863	26,983	27,404	28,083	28,465	28,579
Minimum Wage Worker	13,475	10,414	9,989	10,843	11,493	11,317	11,072	10,712
Ratio of CEO pay to average worker pay†	45	96	160	236	305	399	450	458
Ratio of CEO pay to minimum wage	97	253	430	587	728	990	1158	1223

* CEO pay: average compensation of CEOs at major corporations including salary, bonus and other compensation such as exercised stock options. *Business Week* annual reports on executive pay. The 2000 survey examined CEO pay at the 365 largest companies.

** Average worker pay: production and nonsupervisory workers on private nonfarm payrolls (about 80 percent of the civilian labor force) working full time based on average hourly wage. U.S. Bureau of Labor Statistics.

† This ratio is not equivalent to past *Business Week* CEO-worker pay ratios, which are based on factory worker pay.

Journal memorably put it in their 1998 survey of executive pay, "Pay for performance? Forget it. These days, CEOs are assured of getting rich—however the company does."[22]

Fortune magazine titled its June 2001 special report on CEO pay: "Inside the great CEO pay heist." *Fortune* reported, "The No. 1 earners in each of the past five years got packages valued cumulatively at nearly $1.4 billion, or $274 million on average. Yet far from delivering the superb results investors might have expected from the world's highest-priced management, four of the five companies have been marginal to horrible performers." Compensation insiders told *Fortune* about how the system is rigged, totally out of control and hurts company shareholders.[23]

In the words of columnist Matthew Miller:

> CEOs who cheerlead for market forces wouldn't think of having them actually applied to their own pay packages… The reality is that CEO pay is set through a clubby, rigged system in which CEOs, their buddies on board compensation committees, and a small cadre of lawyers and "compensation consultants" are in cahoots to keep the millions coming irrespective of performance…

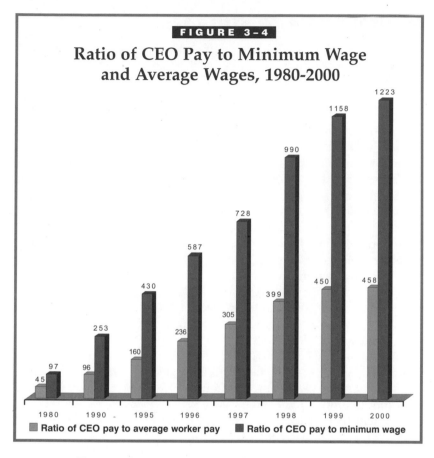

FIGURE 3–4

Ratio of CEO Pay to Minimum Wage and Average Wages, 1980-2000

■ Ratio of CEO pay to average worker pay ■ Ratio of CEO pay to minimum wage

Everyone's incentive is to make sure that every CEO, like the children of Lake Wobegon, gets paid "above average." The result is ever-rising pay packages…

The argument made against policies like a higher minimum wage…is that they represent an unacceptable and even dangerous attempt to tamper with market forces.

Next time Congress takes up these debates, don't let the hypocrites fool you. After all, if the boss wouldn't think about having his paycheck determined entirely by the free market, why should the rest of us?[24]

When CEOs take a disproportionate share of the profits of rising productivity it actually hurts productivity and performance. Studies have found that wide pay gaps are associated with greater dissatisfaction, poorer quality work, higher turnover, and lower individual and group performance.[25]

Minimum Wage Workers

As if to justify miserly pay, minimum wage opponents often claim that most minimum wage workers are teenagers living with their families. In fact, the typical minimum wage earner is an adult woman, not a teenager. Two out of three minimum wage workers are adults. While women make up just under half the total workforce, two out of three minimum wage workers are women. (See table below.)

Nearly four in ten minimum wage workers hold full-time jobs.[26] More workers would hold full-time jobs if they could, but many low-wage employers keep workers part-time to avoid paying benefits and overtime. Looking at the fast food industry, for example, about 90 percent of workers "are paid an hourly wage, provided no benefits, and scheduled to work only as needed... Managers try to make sure that each worker is employed less than forty hours a week, thereby avoiding any overtime payments."[27]

A small but significant number of workers are stuck earning minimum wage for many years. A recent longitudinal study of young workers found that, after ten years in the labor force, nearly one out of seven workers (13 percent)—including one out of six female workers (16 percent)—had spent at least half of their time at jobs that paid at or near the minimum wage.[28] The U.S. Bureau of Labor Statistics reports, "Even among workers in their mid-40s, which are the peak earning years for most workers, approximately 8 percent are in jobs paying less than the minimum plus $1.00." Moreover, "Blacks and women are more likely than white males to spend significant portions of their career in minimum wage jobs."[29]

Only one out of three minimum wage workers is a teenager under age 20—and many of them are already out of school and working for a living. The United States does not provide universal public college education and a significant number of high school graduates cannot afford to go on to college even if they want to. In 1998, more than a third of people who graduated high school within the past year were not enrolled in college.[30]

And if you think that teenagers—whatever their reasons for working—don't deserve a "fair day's pay for a fair day's work," think again.

> **A** person who puts in a fair day's work should be paid a fair day's pay regardless of whether he or she works for a week, a month, a year or 10 years in the job.
> *AFL-CIO, "The Realities Behind the Minimum Wage,"*
> *www.aflcio.org.*

TABLE 3-5

Workers at or below Minimum Wage by Age, Sex, Race and Full Time/Part Time Status, 2000

	EMPLOYED PERSONS in thousands	PERCENT OF EMPLOYED PERSONS	WORKERS AT OR BELOW MINIMUM WAGE in thousands	PERCENT OF WORKERS AT OR BELOW MINIMUM WAGE
Total	135,208	100.0	2,710	100.0
Age 25 and older	100,755	74.5	1,262	46.6
Under 25 years old	34,453	25.5	1,448	53.4
Teenagers (16-19)				31.0
Male	72,293	53.5	954	35.2
Female	62,915	46.5	1,756	64.8
White	113,476	83.9	2,242	82.7
Male	61,696	45.6	752	27.7
Female	51,780	38.3	1,490	55.0
Black	15,334	11.3	361	13.3
Male	7,180	5.3	157	5.8
Female	8,154	6.0	204	7.5
Hispanic	14,492	10.7	318	11.7
Male	8,478	6.3	141	5.2
Female	6,014	4.4	177	6.5
Full-Time	112,291	83.1	1,025	37.8
Male	64,938	48.0	399	14.7
Female	47,353	35.0	626	23.1
Part-Time	22,917	16.9	1,673	61.7
Male	7,355	5.4	550	20.3
Female	15,562	11.5	1,123	41.4

Note: Workers who are paid below minimum wage may be exempt from coverage under the Fair Labor Standards Act or being paid an illegally low amount. See Chapter Five for minimum wage coverage and exemptions. As seen in Chapter Five, a much higher proportion of workers earn under $8 (27.5 million). Numbers may not add up due to rounding. Hispanics may be of any race.

Sources: U.S. Bureau of Labor Statistics; Employment Standards Administration, Wage and Hour Division.

As Eric Schlosser points out in *Fast Food Nation*, employers commonly violate restrictions on teenage work hours during the school week and on the use of hazardous machinery. "The injury rate of teenage workers in the United States is about twice as high as adult workers. Teenagers are far more likely to be untrained, and every year, about 200,000 are injured on the job."

Fast food work is not just low paid compared to other jobs, it is high risk. "Roughly four or five fast food workers are now murdered on the job every month, usually during the course of a robbery... In 1998, more restaurant workers were murdered on the job in the United States than police officers."[31]

Fast food restaurants have done much less than convenience stores, gas stations or banks to make their premises unattractive to armed robbers. In the mid-1990s, the Occupational Health and Safety Administration (OSHA) proposed voluntary guidelines for preventing violence at restaurants and stores that do business at night, such as improving visibility within stores and lighting in parking lots. OSHA was prompted, in part, "by the fact that homicide had become the leading cause of workplace fatalities among women." The National Restaurant Association and other industry groups successfully opposed them. "The restaurant industry has continued to fight not only guidelines on workplace violence, but any enforcement of OSHA regulations." The name of one leading industry group formed to lobby against OSHA regulations is the "Alliance for Workplace Safety."[32]

Minimum wage law allows employers to pay a wage of $4.25 per hour for employees under 20 years of age during their first 90 consecutive days on the job. According to Schlosser, the "typical fast food worker quits or is fired every three to four months." The annual turnover rate in the fast food industry is about 300 to 400 percent.

Taxpayers actually subsidize high turnover in the fast food industry and other low-wage industries through the misuse of so-called "training" subsidies:

> While quietly spending enormous sums on research and technology to eliminate employee training, the fast food chains have accepted hundreds of millions of dollars in government subsidies for "training" their workers. Through federal programs such as...the Work Opportunity Tax Credit, the chains have for years claimed tax credits of up to $2,400 for each new low-income worker they hired. In 1996 an investigation by the U.S. Department of Labor concluded that 92 percent of these workers would have been hired by the companies anyway—and that their new jobs were part time, provided little training, and came with no benefits...
>
> The Workplace Opportunity Tax Credit was renewed in 1996. It offered as much as $385 million in subsidies the following year. Fast food restaurants had to employ a worker for only four hundred hours [just 10 weeks at 40 hours a week, or a little over 3 months at a more typical 30 hours a week] to receive the federal money—and then could get more money as soon as that worker quit and was replaced... The industry front group formed to defend these government subsidies is called the "Committee for Employment Opportunities."[33]

Good Wages Are Good Business

All our businesses pay well above the federal minimum wage. We know that today's minimum wage shortchanges workers and undermines the long-term health of businesses, communities and the economy.

Tim Styer, Judy Wicks and Hal Taussig,
Philadelphia Inquirer, June 21, 2000.

Many economic and political leaders opposed the minimum wage when it was first implemented, and it is still opposed by many today who predictably try to block raises whenever they are proposed. Opponents argue business can't afford higher minimum wages and that they fuel inflation, increase unemployment, harm low-skill, low-wage workers, and aggravate poverty. We've seen how worker productivity and business profits have greatly—and unjustifiably—outpaced minimum wages. We'll look at the affordability issue more closely below. But first let's look at the other points raised by critics.

In the words of the Small Business Survival Committee, Congress should "Reject any increases in the minimum wage. A minimum wage artificially raises the costs of entry-level employment through government fiat, which means fewer jobs will be available for those most in need—individuals with little or no work experience, especially young workers. For good measure, a minimum wage increase tends to hurt the small business community the most."[1]

Minimum Wage Hikes Do Not Cause Unemployment

Real world recent experience shows the critics are wrong: The minimum wage was last raised from $4.25 to $4.75 an hour in October 1996 and to $5.15 in September 1997. Between 1996 and 2000 the economy boomed, with extraordinarily high growth, low inflation, low unemployment and declining poverty rates. In February 2000, the economy broke the record for the longest expansion in U.S. history. (The expansion began in March 1991.) The unemployment rate reached a low of 3.9 percent in September 2000.

In the words of a report by the Clinton administration's National Economic Council, "Since the 1996-97 increase in the minimum wage, the American economy—and labor markets in particular—have continued to perform very strongly. Between September 1996 and February 2000, 10.2 million jobs were created…even stronger growth than in the previous 2 years. In retail trade, which has a large concentration of minimum wage workers, there were 1.4 million new jobs. Over this same period the overall unemployment rate fell from 5.2 percent to 4.1 percent."[2]

Minimum wage hikes have not led to higher unemployment overall, or for people of color, teenagers, or workers in different parts of the country. Quite the contrary. As the Department of Labor *Monthly Labor Review* sums it up, 2000 ended with the overall unemployment rate at

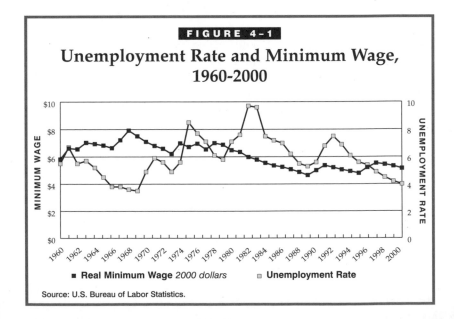

FIGURE 4-1

Unemployment Rate and Minimum Wage, 1960-2000

■ **Real Minimum Wage** *2000 dollars*   □ **Unemployment Rate**

Source: U.S. Bureau of Labor Statistics.

> **M**any economists have backed away from the argument that minimum wage [laws] lead to fewer jobs.
> *Rochelle Sharpe*, **Business Week**, *May 28, 2001*.

4 percent, the lowest rate since 1969. "Every census region and geographic division attained its lowest quarterly unemployment rate on record in 2000." Looking more closely, "The unemployment rates for Hispanics (5.6 percent) and blacks (7.5 percent) declined to record lows in 2000, whereas the rate for whites (3.5 percent) was unchanged from the prior year's 3-decade low." The teenage unemployment rate—12.9 percent in 2000—is the lowest rate since 1969.[3]

Unemployment rates also declined for high school graduates with no college and those with less than a high school education.[4] The most recent minimum wage increase reduced poverty among teenagers and high school dropouts—two demographic groups that opponents assert would be disproportionately harmed by such an increase.[5]

Research on the impact of state and federal minimum wage hikes on particular industries also refutes the critics. In their seminal study of the impact of minimum wage increases in the fast food industry, Card and Krueger found that after the 1992 increase in the state minimum wage in New Jersey, employment increased slightly in New Jersey fast food restaurants compared to fast food restaurants in neighboring Pennsylvania, where the minimum wage was not increased.[6] A study of the impact of the state minimum wage increase in Oregon in 1997 and 1998 found that employment did not decline as a result of the increase, but instead rose by 4 percent in retail trade, the industry most affected by the wage increase.[7]

Before the national unemployment rate dropped below 6 percent (since September 1994), to below 5 percent (since June 1997), to below 4.5 percent (since April 1998) to below 4 percent in September 2000—when rising interest rates intentionally reversed the trend—many economists, businesspeople, bankers and politicians said it couldn't be done without dire inflationary effects. There's a "Natural Rate of Unemployment" (NARU), they said, of about 6 percent. That was as full as "full employment" could get. NARU proponents were wrong. Inflation remained low as unemployment dropped with very positive effects.

The conventional wisdom was also that a 10 percent increase in the minimum wage would result in a 1 to 3 percent decline in the teenage employment rate.[8] Well, as we saw earlier, teenage unemployment has dropped to record lows. In addition, in 2000, 45.5 percent of teenagers (ages 16-19) were employed—a higher rate than before the minimum wage hikes.[9]

It's time to raise the minimum wage... Every time, we've heard the same old gloom-and-doom predictions: A raise would sabotage the economy...hurt the very people it is supposed to help...push small businesses into bankruptcy.

Remember the outcry back in 1996? A chorus of Cassandras called the modest $1 increase (over two years) "a job killer cloaked in kindness" that would trigger "a juvenile crime wave of epic proportions."...

Four years later, we can see that the sky did not fall—but unemployment did (to an historic low)... And, by the way, the crime rate has been going down now for eight years running.

Let's bust the myths, face the facts and give America's minimum wage workers what they deserve...

Alexis M. Herman, U.S. Secretary of Labor,
San Diego Union-Tribune, September 15, 2000.

The critics were wrong about the impact of unemployment going down, and they are wrong about the likely impact of the minimum wage going up.

As a result of the economic expansion and tight labor markets of the 1990s, some traditionally low-wage employers began paying wages above the current minimum wage. Firms found that in order to recruit and retain workers in the tight labor market, they needed to offer higher wages. Even in industries that have typically paid low wages, such as retail and some service industries, the starting hourly wage for unskilled work has risen above $7 per hour in some parts of the country.[10]

We still need a minimum wage hike, of course, because many jobs are still low paying and tight labor markets are typically loosened, unfortunately, by government action (unemployment rates generally continue to climb well after interest rates hit their peak). But the evidence shows that businesses can absorb higher wages.

What About the Economic Slowdown?

At this writing, the economy is in a slowdown. The strong economic expansion would likely have continued if the Federal Reserve had not slammed on the brakes too hard with repeated interest rate hikes in 1999-2000. The Fed acted to purposely slow the supposedly overheated economy to maintain low wages—in the name of fighting inflation. This led to the slowdown in economic growth, upturn in unemployment and subsequent too little, too late interest rate cuts we are experiencing today.[11]

In July 2001, with unemployment rising thanks to Federal Reserve interest rate hikes, Federal Reserve Chairman Alan Greenspan told a congressional hearing that he would abolish the minimum wage if he could. "I'm not in favor of cutting anybody's earnings or preventing them from rising," he said disingenuously, "but I am against them losing their job because of artificial government intervention, which is essentially what the minimum wage is."[12] The Fed's job-destroying interest rate hikes were natural phenomena apparently.

What if the slowdown becomes a recession of significant duration? (The shorthand definition of a recession is two consecutive quarters of negative real GDP growth.)

Minimum wage critics who said that raising the minimum wage would end the boom are now saying the minimum wage can't go up because the boom is over. The reality is that the minimum wage can go up—recession or not. Let's look at recent evidence.

The inflationary threat against which Alan Greenspan and the Federal Reserve purport to protect us is a scenario in which rising demand in a peacetime economy bursts through the limits of capacity to set off a wage-price spiral that compels the government to bring it down by engineering a recession. But, in fact, since 1914, when the U.S. began to measure consumer prices with a comprehensive index, a demand-driven peacetime boom has never generated the kind of inflation with which Greenspan frightens policy makers and the public...

[Looking back to 1914] the first two bouts of inflation were the products of World Wars I and II. The inflation episode of the 1950s was fueled by the Korean War, and the culprit in the 1960s was Lyndon Johnson's refusal to raise taxes to pay for the Vietnam War. The inflation of the 1970s was not a result of an overheated economy but was generated by world oil and grain price shocks, and the brief price spike in 1990 was a result of a sharp, short run-up in oil prices during the Gulf War.

Economic Policy Institute,
"Overinflated peacetime inflation threat," 2000.

The minimum wage was raised during the last recession in 1990-91 (from $3.35 to $4.25). An important 1992 analysis of the impact of that increase by David Card, "which controlled for overall economic conditions, showed no negative effects on employment generated by the increase. [The negative effects were generated by the recession.] The study found that, 'although the 1990 and 1991 minimum wage increases led to significant earnings gains for teenagers and retail-trade workers in many states, these wage increases were not associated with any measurable employment losses.'"[13]

Recessions have lagging effects. "Unemployment tends to lag behind rising interest rates and declining GDP growth, peaking one to two years after GDP has bottomed out."[14] If we do pass a minimum wage hike while the economy is in or recovering from a downturn, don't let critics blame continued rising unemployment on the minimum wage. The real culprits will be the Federal Reserve's 1999-2000 interest rate hikes, sharp hikes in energy prices and the collapse of the speculative stock market bubble. If the past is a guide, a minimum wage hike is part of the solution, not the problem.

Living Wage Evidence

Areas with living wage laws provide more evidence that the minimum wage can be raised significantly. The modern living wage movement had its first victory in Baltimore where "clergy members running food pantries noticed that many regular visitors were working full time but still couldn't feed their families."[15] Baltimore's 1994 living wage ordinance led the way for a fast-growing living wage movement in communities and on campuses around the country. As a Tennessee child care teacher puts it, "What is a living wage? It is a sufficient amount to maintain one's self and one's children in health and safety."[16]

Living wage ordinances typically require that businesses subcontracting with the city, county or university pay their employees a living wage, but some ordinances include city workers and/or businesses receiving economic development subsidies. As Jeane Russell, cochair of the Providence, Rhode Island, Jobs With Dignity Coalition, puts it, "The city gives tax credits and loans to different businesses, such as the Providence Place Mall. These businesses should be creating jobs that pay a living wage for people who live here." She adds, "And, it's not just about wages; it's about getting health benefits, sick days, things like that. We want the people of the community to benefit from all of these tax credits."[17]

> **I**n another era, city dwellers trying to work their way out of poverty might plausibly have looked to government employment to provide the wages and job stability needed to attain an adequate standard of living... This path was especially useful for those groups who experienced considerable discrimination in the labor market. But...since the 1980s, the privatization of urban services has become a well-established trend. Driven by the desire to reduce costs, cities have contracted for a wide range of municipal functions, including car towing and storage, legal services, street light operation, labor relations, solid waste disposal, and ambulance services. Baltimore, which has been more aggressive than many other cities, has privatized bus services, airports, parking lots, billing, day care, and even building inspections... As a consequence, many city jobs that once provided steady, full-time work with benefits at adequate pay have been spun off to the private sector where low wages, part-time and seasonal work, and the lack of benefits is increasingly the norm.
>
> *Economic Policy Institute*, The Effects of the Living Wage in Baltimore, *February 1999.*

Despite strong opposition from many of the same people who oppose a higher minimum wage, some 70 living wage ordinances have been enacted around the country and campaigns are going on in about 80 communities and universities. Most living wage ordinances require or encourage employers to pay some form of health benefits. Among enacted ordinances, the wages required now range from $6.50 an hour in Duluth, Minnesota to $11 in Santa Cruz, California with employment health benefits to $12.25 in Santa Monica, California without employment health benefits. Most of the current ordinances mandate wages over $8 an hour. (For a review of living wage actions see Appendix D.) In a growing backlash against the powerful living wage movement, state laws banning local living wage ordinances have passed in Arizona, Colorado, Louisiana, Missouri, Utah and Oregon.[18]

The proposed Federal Living Wage Responsibility Act, sponsored by Rep. Luis Gutierrez (D-IL), would require firms holding a federal contract or subcontract worth at least $10,000 to pay employees working on that contract a living wage, defined as the federal poverty level for a family of four ($8.20 an hour). Some 162,000 federal contract workers (out of 1.4 million) earn below that living wage.[19]

> **I**n Broward County [Florida], one in five families lives in poverty...
>
> Sub-poverty wages do not serve a public purpose. Broward County should not contract with or subsidize employers who pay poverty-level wages... The living wage ordinance I have proposed... would set a living wage standard for county service employees, as well as companies which have service contracts with the county exceeding $100,000 per year...
>
> A recent review of cities ranked "best for business" by *Fortune*, *Entrepreneur* and *Inc.* magazines, describes almost half the cities listed as having a living wage law on the books...
>
> *Kristin Jacobs, vice chair, Broward County Commission, Sun-Sentinel, July 23, 2001.*

Robert Pollin and Stephanie Luce, authors of *The Living Wage*, and a growing number of researchers have examined the real and potential impact of living wage ordinances on workers, businesses and communities. The results are quite positive.[20] For example, a study of Baltimore's living wage found that companies did not reduce staffing and reported higher worker morale and productivity. Indeed, "contractors interviewed about the living wage gave generally positive responses. From bus companies to temporary agencies to janitorial services, the prevailing opinion offered was that the living wage 'levels the playing field' and relieves pressure on employers to squeeze labor costs in order to win low-bid contracts."[21]

As Jared Bernstein points out, "It is essential to recognize that any policy or regulation that affects all firms puts no single firm at a competitive disadvantage." With a living wage ordinance in place, all firms who bid for contracts "would face the same wage floor; no firm could underbid the wage floor set by the living wage. This no more creates a competitive disadvantage within the locality than any other regulation such as a requirement that firms may not practice discriminatory hiring."[22]

A *Business Week* article asked, "What's So Bad About a Living Wage? Paying above the minimum seems to do more good than harm." Studies find that "employers learn to live with them by trimming profit margins and finding efficiency gains from improved morale and lower turnover." Living wage laws "have imposed little, if any, cost" to the cities that have passed them and "have lifted many families out of poverty."[23] As cited in a later *Business Week* article, "David Neumark, a visiting Fellow at the

Public Policy Institute of California and a leading minimum wage opponent, found that when living wage laws raise pay by 50%, say from $5.15 an hour to $7.73 an hour, poverty declines by 1%."[24]

Living wage laws are typically limited in scope and the number of workers or sectors covered is relatively small. They are an important supplement, not a substitute, for a decent federal minimum wage for all workers—regardless of where they live or who they work for.

Business Volatility

Opponents of minimum wage increases are quick to blame any adverse occurrence on the minimum wage and ignore the inherent volatility of U.S. businesses. The reality is that businesses have a high attrition rate. For example, a Small Business Administration (SBA) study found that more than half of businesses started in 1992 ceased operations within 5 years.[25]

A National Bureau of Economic Research study on job creation and destruction reveals a constant level of business volatility in the U.S. economy. This volatility cannot be attributed to the increased cost of labor over time. It is driven by the voluntary choices business owners make as well as by business failure. Research economists at the

> **We think providing fair wages and benefits for good performance makes good business sense.**
> *Les Cappetta, vice president for business development, Host Marriott Services, which runs the food courts and concession stands at Los Angeles International Airport, People, March 30, 2000.*

> **Juana Zatarin lives in a one-bedroom apartment that rumbles whenever a jumbo jet lands at Los Angeles International Airport. But life is looking up for the 44-year-old mother of three, who works as a baggage screener at the airport. Thanks to Los Angeles' so-called living wage law, which requires city contractors to pay employees a minimum of $8.97 an hour, Zatarin's salary has jumped nearly 50% in the past year... This summer, Zatarin took her family on vacation for the first time since 1994. "I'm more relaxed now that I can make our payments," she says.**
> *Steven V. Brull, Business Week, September 4, 2000.*

SBA report that only one out of seven businesses ceasing operations actually fails. They cite a broad range of factors to explain why firms cease operations, including entrepreneurial preferences, new opportunities, retirement, and personal and health reasons.[26] These factors are far more significant in explaining business volatility than increased labor costs.

Even among businesses that fail, the reasons for dissolution vary. In a survey of businesses that filed for bankruptcy, more than one-fifth of debtors cited a variety of reasons reflecting outside business conditions, e.g., new competition, increases in rent, insurance or other costs of doing business, declining real estate values, etc. (38.5 percent); financing, e.g., high debt service, loss of financing or the inability to get financing (28 percent); inside business conditions, e.g., mismanagement, a decline in production, a bad location, the loss of major clients and the inability to collect accounts receivable (27.1 percent); and tax obligations (20.1 percent) as reasons for filing.[27]

Looking at a decade of data—and oversimplifying like many minimum wage opponents do—you could make a stronger case that minimum wage hikes lowered business closing and failure rates than raised them. Neither would be accurate since so many factors come into play, but let's look at the record. The business failure rate fluctuated from 82 per 10,000 in 1995, before the 1996-97 minimum wage hikes, to 80 in 1996 and 89 in 1997 and dropped to 76 in 1998, a lower rate than before the minimum wage hikes began.[28]

Employer closing rates measure businesses that existed in the beginning of a year, which were terminated during the course of the year. As noted above, most business closings are not failures, but rather indicate retirement and other changes. The SBA recommends the use of the "employer closing rate" as the best indicator of small business failure. The SBA states that although the rate includes large businesses, the ratio and number of small business is so large that the rate remains "essentially the same" when large businesses are removed. After the earlier minimum wage increase in 1991, the employer closing rate fell from 10.8 percent in 1991 to 10.3 percent in 1992 and 9.4 percent in 1995. It stood at 9.7 for 1996 and 1997 and then fell again to 9.4 percent in 1998. An estimated 9.3 percent of employer firms existing in 1999 closed that year.[29]

When they aren't looking for a rationale to argue against minimum wage increases, traditional economists and business leaders view business closures as a natural selection process in which less efficient firms will not survive precisely because they are less efficient. Business competition is generally touted as a great public good, even if it means some businesses driving others out of business.

Businesses operate with widely varying degrees of savvy, efficiency and flexibility. Weaker businesses will be more vulnerable to any change in expenses, such as the cost of rent, electricity, fuel, supplies or borrowing money (which goes up when the Federal Reserve raises interest rates). Yet, for the most part, firms seem to bear many of these other increases in factor costs without resorting to the same ideological rhetoric that surrounds discussions of the minimum wage. And unlike higher rent, for example, higher wages generally lead to increased productivity and reduced turnover. Unlike a higher electric bill, the money paid out in higher wages recycles in the community and economy in the form of increased consumer spending.

Firms can and do respond in a variety of ways to wage increases—just as they do to other increases—without laying off workers. For example, they can increase the productivity of workers through greater investment in training, reduce operating expenses in other areas, forego raises at the top and narrow the gap between top and bottom, or increase prices.

Even if some firms do raise prices, passing on some or all of the minimum wage increase to consumers, this doesn't mean inflation goes up. Inflation is the pervasive and sustained rise in the aggregate level of prices measured by an index of the cost of various goods and services.[30] When consumers have higher wages and greater purchasing power under conditions of low inflation—as we have experienced in recent years—they can consume more, stimulating economic growth.

Research has shown that recent minimum wage increases have not contributed significantly to an increase in the price level (i.e., inflation), although some firms may have raised prices to offset wage increases. For example, Pollin, Luce and Brenner found that the impact of the 1997-1998 California minimum wage increase on changes in the overall price level in selected California metropolitan areas was insignificant.[31] *Business Week* reports that the inflationary impact of an increase in the minimum wage to $6.15 per hour would likely be minimal if productivity remains strong.[32]

Evidence also comes from areas with living wage laws. The Economic Policy Institute study of the impact of the Baltimore living wage ordinance found that among 26 contracts that could be compared to pre-living wage contracts, the total price increased just 1.2 percent—an amount below the inflation rate for the period.[33]

Even *if* some rise in inflation were to occur, it would be much less harmful than the continuation of low wages. A USDA report observes, "The literature consistently finds inflation has a relatively minor effect on the incidence of poverty and on the well-being of poor and near-poor households."[34]

"Increasing the federal minimum wage by a dollar would add about two cents to the cost of a fast food hamburger," Eric Schlosser writes in *Fast Food Nation*.[35] Even if employers passed on the full two cents—or perhaps six cents in a rise in the minimum wage to $8—that's a price well worth paying for improving worker livelihoods and the health and safety of workers and consumers. The cheap mass production practices, in which low wages play a central role, lead to more injuries on the job and the spread of food borne pathogens such as *Salmonella*, *Listeria* and *E.coli* 0157:H7. Food poisoning in the United States sickens about 200,000 people (sometimes with lasting damage) and kills 14 people a day. Other countries have enacted much tougher food safety laws and inspection systems to successfully combat food poisoning. As Schlosser writes, when it comes to low wages, health and safety, "The real price never appears on the menu."[36]

We expect businesses to observe certain standards, such as not dumping toxic waste into an adjacent stream even if it's cheaper than disposing of it safely. We should expect businesses to pay a minimum wage that even the lowest paid workers can live on.

Businesses Benefit With Higher Wages

All around the country, successful business owners have shown that businesses benefit from a higher-paid, highly motivated workforce. Higher wages make it easier for employers to recruit and retain entry-level workers, leading to reduced turnover and

> The market is a tool, and a useful one. But...many of America's greatest accomplishments stand in complete defiance of the free market: the prohibition of child labor, the establishment of a minimum wage, the creation of wilderness areas and national parks, the construction of dams, bridges, roads, churches, schools and universities. If all that mattered were the unfettered right to buy and sell, tainted food could not be kept off supermarket shelves, toxic waste could be dumped next door to elementary schools, and every American family could import an indentured servant (or two), paying them with meals instead of money.
>
> *Eric Schlosser*, Fast Food Nation, *2001.*

> **W**hat is often referred to as the "free" market often isn't free at all. Government plays a rule-setting role, seeking to promote market efficiency, while also containing the social costs stemming from a completely unfettered market... Federal, state, and local governments consistently provide billions of dollars in subsidies, tax breaks, and other forms of corporate welfare to businesses in the name of economic growth. Given the degree to which many businesses already benefit from market interventions, it is inconsistent and even spurious for businesses to selectively argue that the market should be left to its own devices in the case of determining wage levels. Additionally, businesses that pay poverty wages indirectly rely on government assistance programs to make up the difference between these wages and what it costs their employees to live. Without the intervention of government and private charities, paying poverty wages wouldn't be a sustainable business practice.
>
> *Responsible Wealth,* **Choosing the High Road: Businesses That Pay a Living Wage and Prosper, 2000.**

absenteeism as well as lower costs associated with training and recruitment. Moreover, businesses report improvements in the quality of products and services delivered to customers.[37]

As the Responsible Wealth report, *Choosing the High Road*, points out:

> The cost of employee turnover is no small matter for many businesses. In 1999 Bliss & Associates and Gately Consulting developed a method that precisely measures the business costs and impacts of employee turnover. Bliss and Gately determined that turnover costs at least 150% of the employee's base salary. For example: If a company of 50 employees has an average base salary of $15,000 and a turnover rate of 10%, it will spend at least $112,500 to replace those employees when such costs as training, lost productivity, new hires and recruitment costs are calculated. Therefore, having a motivated and stable workforce not only creates a work environment that supports increased productivity, but it reduces the significant expense of recruitment and training. Such business benefits can go a long way toward offsetting higher wage and payroll tax costs associated with paying a living wage.[38]

Other studies highlighting the efficiency gains from legislated wage increases examine the impact of prevailing wage laws, which require firms with federal (and some state) government contracts to pay wages comparable to jobs in the private-sector (often the average area wage or union wage for the comparable private sector job). As Jared Bernstein notes, "The motivation for this legislation was both to insure that workers on government projects could earn a living wage, and to insure against low-quality work by low-bidding contractors." Research on prevailing wage laws shows that "training of employees increased substantially and as a result, occupational injuries fell. Contracts were completed more efficiently and with fewer delays." A study of the effect of repealing Utah's prevailing wage law found that total cost overruns on state highway construction tripled after repeal.[39]

TABLE 4-1
Median Wage and Job Tenure by Industry

INDUSTRY	MEDIAN WAGE	AVERAGE TENURE in years
Private Households	$7.00	2.9
Agriculture	7.50	3.1
Retail Trade	8.00	2.0
Personal Services	8.35	2.7
Entertainment/Recreation	9.00	2.3
Social Services	9.23	2.6
Medical Services, excluding Hospitals	11.00	3.2
Business, Auto & Repair Services	12.00	2.7
Manufacturing–Non-Durable Goods	12.46	5.1
Wholesale Trade	12.50	3.9
Construction	13.00	2.8
Transportation	13.33	3.9
Finance, Insurance and Real Estate	13.68	3.6
Educational Services	13.72	3.3
Manufacturing–Durable Goods	13.94	4.9
Hospitals	14.40	5.2
Other Professional Services	15.00	2.8
Public Administration	15.00	7.2
Mining	15.38	6.5
Communications	17.00	5.2
Utilities/Sanitary Services	17.60	5.2
TOTAL	12.00	3.5

Note: Half the workers are paid less than the median wage, half are paid more.

Sources: Solutions for Progress analysis of U.S. Census Bureau Current Population Survey Outgoing Rotation Group Files, July 1999–June 2000; Bureau of Labor Statistics, *Employee Tenure in 2000*.

The Strategic Rewards survey of 551 large employers by Watson Wyatt Worldwide, a leading global consulting firm, found, "Employers that view their people strategy as a source of competitive advantage are outperforming companies that don't, by a margin of two to one." Study coauthor Rick Beal says, "It appears that companies that take seriously the truism 'your people are your most important asset' are winning." A majority of top-performing employees surveyed said "paying above market" was very effective in attracting workers along with stock options, learning new skills in current job, opportunities for advancement, career development and flexible work schedules.[40]

Industries with lower hourly wages generally experience lower than average job tenure, as seen in the table above. In other words, workers in industries with low pay do not stay in their jobs as long as workers in industries paying above the median. The impact of an increase in the minimum wage on payroll would be muted by the reduction in turnover and recruitment costs.

A higher minimum wage also means that workers will have more disposable income to spend on products and services. Increased demand for goods and services may result in increased employment, generating additional purchasing power. This "multiplier effect" is assumed to be stronger among lower-income families, who need to consume a greater proportion of their income. Thus higher payroll costs from a mandated minimum wage increase may be offset by an increase in business revenues.[41]

Small Business Can Raise Wages

Opponents of minimum wage increases typically claim that small businesses will be unable to compete and they will have to lay off workers and maybe close their doors. Big businesses use supposed concern for small businesses as camouflage for their self-interested opposition to the minimum wage.

When's the last time you heard a chain store executive worry that their new store would drive the local mom and pop store out of business? Driving independent local entrepreneurs out of business is the name of the game in the "malling" of America.

President Bush's supposed concern for small business is belied by his attempt to cut the Small Business Administration budget by 40 percent. Among other things, the Bush administration would hike the fees paid by businesses that tap the 7(a) loan guaranty program, designed to aid small businesses that can't get financing through normal market channels.

As Philadelphia business owners who pay a living wage, we believe that no one who works full time should live in poverty. We know from personal experience that profitability and economic fairness can go hand in hand...

The three of us built successful businesses in traditionally low-wage industries. We know that companies can make the sometimes seemingly difficult choice to pay a living wage and prosper.

Founded just two years ago, Urban Works is a profitable employee-owned contract cleaning company, which pays a minimum of $7.90 an hour plus benefits. Employees are productive and morale is high, which has reduced turnover and absenteeism, as well as recruitment expenses, and enhanced customer satisfaction.

Now 17 years old, the White Dog Café is a very successful business with 100 employees. Although the restaurant industry has a reputation for paying low wages and running people into the ground, the White Dog Café pays a minimum of $8 an hour within three months, plus benefits, including a 401(k) retirement plan. With higher pay and benefits, and lower turnover, the staff is more experienced and committed to their work, which is key to the restaurant's success.

Idyll, Ltd., a specialty travel business, also pays employees a living wage, as well as providing health insurance and a 401(k) plan

In reality, small businesses can absorb and benefit from a minimum wage increase just as big businesses can. Every year the Small Business Administration honors state and national businesspeople. Cindy McEntee, owner of Mo's Enterprises, is the SBA's 2001 Oregon Small Business Person of the Year and first runner-up to the national award. Mo's Enterprises, started by McEntee's grandmother in Newport, Oregon, consists of three restaurants and a chowder factory, which produces Mo's famous clam chowder for retail stores.

"In its 50 years in business, Mo's has always paid more than the required minimum wage and offered major medical health insurance. Of the 45 full-time year-round employees, 17 have worked at Mo's for 10 years or more. Some have worked over 15 and some over 20 years. Cindy is a supportive employer and cares very much about her employees' quality of life."[42] Cindy considers Mo's employees to be the company's greatest asset. She learned that from her grandmother. "Mo taught me how to treat employees not as interchangeable units, but as family, to make them all feel like they're part of a with a 50 percent match by the company. With profit margins above the industry norm, Idyll, Ltd. has found that it makes good business sense to pay decent wages and good benefits to sustain a productive and dedicated group of employees.

All our businesses pay well above the federal minimum wage. We know that today's minimum wage shortchanges workers and undermines the long-term health of businesses, communities and the economy...

A low minimum wage makes it harder to resist the seeming competitive pressures to pay low wages but, as our businesses show, higher wages can help build more profitable businesses even in traditionally low-wage industries.

Tim Styer CEO of Urban Works, Judy Wicks, owner of the White Dog Café, and Hal Taussig, CEO of Idyll, Ltd., "In industries large and small, living wage is good for business," Philadelphia Inquirer, June 21, 2000.

It made a big difference in my life. First I paid off a credit loan I had been worrying about. I have three children and now I can afford to buy them some things they have always wanted. But the best thing is that I'm talking with a realtor about buying a house.

White Dog Café employee Oliver Collins, on earning a higher wage, quoted in Responsible Wealth, Choosing the High Road.

joint effort, part of the business." As a result, she says, "We have a very low turnover. One of our employees has worked for the business since 1950."[43]

Our data show that small businesses would not be disproportionately affected by a minimum wage increase. Across most sectors, the cost of the wage increase relative to total receipts minus total payroll and benefits did not vary significantly by firm size. As illustrated in the table below, the variation in the relative cost of an increase in the minimum wage to $8 per hour to firms varied by less than 1 percentage point across size categories in 11 industries. For retail trade sectors the variance ranges from 1 percent to 1.3 percent.

Within a few industries, such as educational services, a minimum wage increase would affect firms differently across size categories. However, in the sectors in which there were variations in the relative impact of a wage increase by firm size, small firms were not necessarily the most affected. For example, in the social services and forestry and fisheries sectors, a wage increase would have a greater

Small Business Owners of Washington State (SBOWS) is a 100-plus member network of small business owners who believe workers should be paid livable wages, provided benefits, and treated with respect.

In 1998, Washington State had a ballot initiative to increase the state's minimum wage from $5.15 to $6.15 per hour. Krishna Fells, co-owner of a high technology consulting business, believed full-time workers should not live in poverty and began to build a coalition of businesses that would publicly support the initiative... In eight days, SBOWS was up to 100 members...

SBOWS used their collective voice to educate other small businesses about the impact of NOT raising the minimum wage. Since small businesses don't get the tax breaks given to large businesses, they pay fairly high taxes. As a result, small businesses and other taxpayers often end up paying for government subsidies (medical and food assistance, EITC) to employees who aren't earning enough at their jobs to support themselves and their families. Not raising the minimum wage would be detrimental to small business.

Responsible Wealth, Choosing the High Road.

impact on the operational costs of the larger firms (firms with more than 500 workers) and on medium-sized firms in the personal services, entertainment and recreational services, medical services and educational services sectors. These findings clearly indicate that sector is far more significant than firm size when it comes to absorbing a minimum wage increase.

Higher Wages Benefit Low-Income Urban Communities

Millions of low-wage workers live in low-income urban communities. Low wages hurt low-income communities, compounding the damage done by public and private disinvestment and discrimination. They need both higher wages and public and private reinvestment.

Often, local businesses are pillars of their communities—through good times and bad—providing not just products and services but

TABLE 4-2

Cost of Minimum Wage Increase to $8 as Percent of Net Receipts* by Industry and Firm Size

INDUSTRY	ALL	<20	NUMBER OF EMPLOYEES 20-49	50-99	100-499	>=500
Agriculture	n.a.	n.a.	n.a.	n.a.	n.a.	n.a.
Mining	0.2	0.2	0.3	0.3	0.3	0.2
Construction	0.5	0.3	0.5	0.6	0.6	0.5
Manufacturing	0.4	0.2	0.5	0.6	0.4	0.3
Transportation	1.0	0.6	0.9	1.2	1.2	1.0
Communications	0.2	0.2	0.3	0.3	0.2	0.2
Utilities/Sanitary Services	0.1	0.1	0.1	0.1	0.1	0.1
Wholesale Trade	0.1	0.1	0.1	0.1	0.1	0.1
Retail Trade	1.2	1.0	1.2	1.2	1.1	1.3
FIRE**	0.2	0.2	0.3	0.3	0.2	0.2
Private Households	n.a.	n.a.	n.a.	n.a.	n.a.	n.a.
Business, Auto & Repair	1.5	0.7	0.9	1.6	2.0	1.8
Personal Services	4.4	2.5	3.6	5.0	4.6	4.6
Entertainment/Recreation	1.7	2.0	1.8	2.3	2.9	1.2
Hospitals	1.4	0.8	0.7	1.1	1.6	1.4
Medical Services, excluding Hospitals	2.4	1.3	2.0	3.5	3.0	2.3
Educational Services	8.9	5.1	7.5	15.2	10.7	7.7
Social Services	7.9	4.5	6.2	7.6	8.7	10.1
Other Professional Services	0.8	0.6	0.7	0.9	0.9	0.8
Forestry and Fisheries	2.7	1.0	1.6	4.1	5.2	5.2
Public Administration	n.a.	n.a.	n.a.	n.a.	n.a.	n.a.
TOTAL	0.6	0.6	0.7	0.8	0.8	0.6

n.a. Company statistics were not available for these sectors.

* Total receipts minus total payroll and benefits.

** Fire, Insurance and Real Estate.

Sources: Solutions for Progress, analysis of Current Population Survey Outgoing Rotation Group files, July 1999–June 2000; U.S. Census Bureau, *Statistics of U.S. Businesses, 1997;* U.S. Bureau of Labor Statistics, *Employer Costs for Employee Compensation,* March 2000.

running tabs for customers juggling more bills than income, donating time and resources to neighborhood efforts, and serving as unofficial community centers.

When business costs are higher in low-income neighborhoods because banks and insurance companies deny services or overcharge for them, workers should not have to pay with lower wages—these discriminatory practices should end. Government should support business development in low-income areas with the kinds of mass transit, road repair, public services and infrastructure development higher-income areas are accustomed to.

Higher wages are good for business in low-income communities. Three years ago *Inc.* magazine and the Initiative for a Competitive Inner City (ICIC) began publishing the annual ICIC-Inc. Magazine Inner City 100, a national listing of 100 successful, fast-growing companies located in low-income urban areas. The 2001 Inner City 100 have increased their number of jobs by 120 percent over the past five years. Their average hourly wage, excluding benefits, is $11.81, more than double the minimum wage. Their benefits for full-time employees are well above average: 98 percent offer health insurance, 81 percent offer a bonus plan, 72 percent offer a 401(k) retirement plan, 41 percent have profit sharing for employees and 13 percent offer employee stock ownership programs.

The Inner City 100 have lower than average turnover and most frequently cite customer service as their principal competitive advantage. Looking at ownership, 40 percent are minority owned, compared to the 11 percent national average, and 21 percent are women owned, as compared to the 6 percent national average.[44]

Dancing Deer Baking Company is ranked number 7 in the Inner City 100. "Boston's available inner-city workforce is one of the primary factors for Dancing Deer Baking Company's high growth, says CEO Trish Kartner. Without her dedicated employees, the quality, taste and presentation of Dancing Deer products would not have been possible, Kartner says. Dancing Deer provides its [40] employees with health insurance, paid lunches and paid overtime—benefits uncommon in the food service industry, according to Kartner... As a result of employee treatment, Dancing Deer has never been short-handed since it opened in 1994, and its turnover rate remains low year after year."[45]

The Dancing Deer Baking Company is located in the Dudley Street neighborhood of Boston. Long Boston's most impoverished and disinvested neighborhood, Dudley is being transformed by the residents, businesses, nonprofits and partners of the Dudley Street Neighborhood Initiative (DSNI) into a dynamic Urban Village. In 2000, the Fannie Mae Foundation selected Dudley as one of 10 "Just Right" emerging neighborhoods across the nation for increasing affordable homeownership

---

If the bakers are happy, it shows in the food.
Trish Kartner, CEO, Dancing Deer Baking Company,
Inner City 100.

while attracting capital investment. "The Dudley Street Neighborhood Initiative is legendary among community organizing groups," says *City Limits* magazine. DSNI "is the rare community organizing group that can take credit for rebuilding a neighborhood."[46]

In the words of DSNI's Economic Development committee, "There is one inescapable fact. The incomes of those who live in the neighborhood must rise for the neighborhood to experience greater economic vitality. The key to economic renewal for the neighborhood is ultimately neighborhood residents who have greater access to a wide range of opportunity (education, jobs, small businesses) both within and outside of the neighborhood, and who see the wisdom of spending their time, energy and money locally."[47]

Al Lovata is the chair of DSNI's Economic Power Committee and the CEO of Be Our Guest, a highly successful party equipment rental company, which won the Greater Boston Chamber of Commerce Small Business of the Year Award in 1997. He says, "I absolutely buy the case for the $8 minimum wage. It's good for the Dudley Street neighborhood and it's good for the country."[48]

When it comes to customer buying power, low-income neighborhoods have lower income, on the one hand, but often have higher density on the other. For example, a study of 100 neighborhoods in Ohio central cities found that in virtually every sector relating to retail trade—laundries, cleaning enterprises, beauty shops, automotive repair shops, furniture repair and upholstery enterprises, video stores, legal services and accounting enterprises—a larger population base of potential customers is required to offset the lower per capita buying power of neighborhood-based consumers.[49]

The Business Case for Pursuing Retail Opportunities in the Inner City, a report by the Boston Consulting Group in partnership with the Initiative for a Competitive Inner City, finds that "a concentrated consumer base of shoppers is cited as *the* primary competitive advantage in the inner city, according to a survey of retail store managers around the country." There is high buying power per square mile despite the lower household incomes. To take some profitable examples from chain stores, the Super Stop & Shop located at the South Bay Center in Boston adjacent to the Dudley neighborhood is the highest grossing store in the large chain. Pharmacies in inner city Boston, New York, Miami, Chicago, Atlanta and Oakland "can generate average store sales of up to 45 percent higher than the regional average, and in some areas pharmacies average more than twice the regional average." A "leading apparel retailer reports that its inner-city stores generate twice the sales volume of the typical store within the division and higher profits."

At the turn of the last century, Edward A. Filene appeared to fit, almost perfectly, every popular stereotype of the business tycoon. But this Boston merchant, unlike most of his similarly gruff, cigar-smoking, wealthy contemporaries, is still remembered today, more than 60 years after his 1937 death.

Most Americans who recognize Filene's name know him from the popular Boston-based chain of retail stores that still bears his name. Students of American business practice know Filene from his gloriously innovative approaches to merchandising. But there's another side of Edward Filene that deserves to be remembered, especially today, a time when communities across the United States are debating whether or not to mandate that employers pay a "living wage."

Nearly a century ago, Edward Filene laid out a compelling *business* case for paying decent wages. Higher pay, for Filene, wasn't a matter of sentimentality. Paying good wages was good business.

Filene's business philosophy evolved over years of pragmatic business decision making. At the start of his career, notes one Filene biographer, the overwhelming majority of merchants accepted, as an absolute truth, "that it is better to sell an article at a profit of one dollar than to sell it at a profit of one cent." Filene understood, long before his peers, that selling an article at a one-cent profit is *always* better than selling that article at a far higher profit — if the lower profit margin multiplies your sales by one hundred and one.

The report found, "The revenue and profit potential in the inner-city is enormous. The estimated 7.7 million households…possess over $85 billion in annual retail buying power… This amounts to nearly 7 percent of total retail spending in the U.S…. In many inner-city areas, more than 25 percent of retail demand is unmet… Unmet demand approaches 30 percent in Boston, 40 percent in many areas of Chicago's inner city, and 60 percent in Harlem." Unmet demand points to job creation. "Filling the unmet inner-city retail demand could create up to 250,000 new direct retail jobs and more than 50,000 indirect jobs in these communities." This includes up to 8,000 jobs in Harlem, for example.[50]

The best community redevelopment displaces neither longtime residents nor local businesses. Rather, local residents and businesses share in the revitalization they helped create.

Filene was absolutely confident that his approach made eminent business sense, but he acknowledged that his success depended on one other critical variable: Before people could get their money's worth, they had to have money. True mass production, Filene explained, is not production *of* masses of goods, but production *for* masses of people. Commercial success, Filene believed, rested ultimately on the average customer's power to purchase. Given that reality, Filene understood, sound business policy would seek to expand the average consumer's purchasing power, and Filene spent his business career working to do just that. Within his own enterprise, he bargained collectively with employees, instituted a profit-sharing plan, and put in place a then-novel assortment of fringe benefits.

Filene's vision extended far beyond the shelves of his showcase store. He realized early on that credit was as important to average working people as to the biggest corporations. His solution was to found the American credit union movement. But Filene left behind much more than the modern credit union. He helped create the US Chamber of Commerce, to encourage community-mindedness among business leaders. He later went on to launch the first significant 20th century consumer cooperatives.

A businessman who really knows his business, Filene believed, must necessarily be a worker for the "common good." That "common good"— for business and society—is what the living wage movement is all about.

Responsible Wealth, Choosing the High Road.

An ICIC report on inner city shoppers finds, "Significant opportunities exist for specialty and independent retailers to serve unmet inner-city demand. Independents often maintain an edge on their competition because of a greater familiarity with the marketplace, more unique merchandise, and tailored customer service."[51]

While some dollars from a higher minimum wage will be spent outside the local community, many dollars will recycle within the community. There would be greater income and economic security for residents and a stronger customer and sales base for local business.

5

■ ■ ■ ■ ■

$8 Minimum— Make It A Living

It is but equity...that those who feed, clothe and lodge the whole body of the people, should have such a share of the produce of their own labour as to be themselves tolerably well fed, clothed and lodged.
Adam Smith, **The Wealth of Nations, 1776.**

Your paycheck should keep you out of poverty, not keep you in it. The federal minimum wage can and should be increased to $8 per hour. Why $8?

- $8 is the amount needed for a single full-time worker to meet their minimum needs budget—without employment health benefits, which most low-income workers don't have;

- $8 matches the 1968 minimum wage peak, adjusting for inflation.

The primary objective of the Fair Labor Standards Act was "eliminating labor conditions detrimental to the maintenance of the minimum standard of living necessary for health, efficiency, and general well-being of workers...without substantially curtailing employment or earning power."[1]

The $8 minimum wage meets that objective. Once set at a reasonable minimum, the minimum wage should be protected from erosion by indexing it to inflation.

We have had major shifts in wages and working conditions in the

[In-N-Out Burger] was the nation's first drive-through hamburger stand. Today there are about 150 In-N-Outs in California and Nevada, generating more than $150 million in annual revenues... [The owners] have succeeded by rejecting just about everything the rest of the fast food industry has done...

The chain pays the highest wages in the fast food industry. The starting wage of a part-time worker at In-N-Out is $8 an hour. Full-time workers get a benefits package that includes medical, dental, vision, and life insurance. The typical salary of an In-N-Out restaurant manager is more than $80,000 a year. The managers have, on average, been with the chain for more than thirteen years. The high wages at In-N-Out have not led to higher prices or lower quality food. The most expensive item on the menu costs $2.45... The ground beef is fresh, potatoes are peeled every day to make the fries, and the milk shakes are made from ice cream, not syrup.

In March of 2000, the annual *Restaurants and Institutions Choice in Chains* survey found that among the nation's fast food hamburger chains, In-N-Out ranked first in food quality, value, service, atmosphere, and cleanliness. In-N-Out has

past, all to the benefit of our nation. We abolished slavery, the horrendous system in which workers were not only unpaid, they were brutally treated and traded as commodities. We outlawed using young children as cheap labor. We passed laws affirming workers' right to organize and better their wages and working conditions by bargaining collectively. We said our elders should be able to stop working and still have an income to live on, and enacted Social Security. We said it was against the law to use race or gender as a basis for paying people lower wages. Many of these changes had deep opposition. But our economy and society progressed greatly with these landmark advances.

It's time now to take the next step and abolish poverty wages. We would be shocked to hear someone argue today that we can't afford to end race and gender discrimination in the workplace and therefore we should keep it. Yet employers regularly make that baseless argument against raising the minimum wage.

Paying poverty wages is a form of economic discrimination. It compounds gender and race discrimination, which has shaped who is disproportionately paid low wages. Paying poverty wages is a form of ranked highest in food quality every year that the chain has been included in the survey.

Eric Schlosser, Fast Food Nation.

In-N-Out Burger continues to draw raves from burger aficionados. In its latest coup, the Irvine chain ranked No. 1 in overall customer satisfaction, topping 70 other chains in a new nationwide survey of 87,600 fast-food consumers.

Customers gave In-N-Out their highest rating in such categories as flavor, quality, friendly employees and cleanliness, according to the survey, released Thursday by Sandelman & Associations, a Villa Park firm that tracks trends in the fast food industry. [In-N-Out Burger was No. 1 again in 2001.]

Greg Hernandez, Los Angeles Times, *May 26, 2000.*

When the Valley's first In-N-Out opened November 2 in Scottsdale, it was to lines so long that people waited up to two hours just to place their orders... Is a basic burger worth all this fuss?... The answer, actually is yes...

There are never any surprises, just consistent high quality every time we visit. All this for less than $5 bucks? No wonder this fad has flourished since 1948.

Carey Sweet, Phoenix New Times, *December 28, 2000.*

discrimination against the children of low-wage workers, who face impoverishment and deprivation just because their parents work hard at jobs that are underpaid.

It's time to abolish poverty wages. Certainly, employers can pay a minimum wage equivalent to what their counterparts paid more than three decades ago when nearly half the U.S. population wasn't born yet, Lyndon Johnson was in the White House, disco was in the future, measles was common, computers had their own room—and it wasn't in your home, calling long distance was a really big deal, and webs were spider wide, not world wide.

Recall, as we saw earlier, that the minimum wage, adjusting for inflation since the 1968 peak year, would be:

- $13.80 if it had kept pace with productivity;

- $13.02 if it had kept pace with domestic profits;

- $20.46 if it had kept pace with profits in the retail industry, which employs more than half the nation's hourly employees paid at or below minimum wage.

Where Work Does Not Pay

O ne out of ten workers makes less than $6.15 an hour; one out of seven makes less than $6.65 and one out of four makes less than $8. Of the more than 27.5 million workers who make less than $8 per hour, 16.8 million are adults 25 and over. More than 16 million workers making less than $8 are women; 22 million are white and 4.2 million are black. More than 17 million worked full-time. (See tables below.)

About a fourth of the workforce would benefit directly from an increase in the minimum wage to $8. This does not include those workers currently making $8 or somewhat above who would benefit from the "ripple effect" from a new minimum wage as wage scales were adjusted to the new floor.[2]

TABLE 5-1

Workers Paid Less Than $8 Per Hour, by Age, Sex, Race and Full Time/Part Time Status

	EMPLOYED PERSONS* in thousands	PERCENT OF EMPLOYED PERSONS	WORKERS BELOW $8 in thousands	PERCENT OF WORKERS BELOW $8
Total	119,191	100.0	27,537	100.0
Age 25 and older	99,428	83.4	16,844	61.2
Under age 25	19,763	16.6	10,693	38.8
Male	62,074	52.1	11,381	41.3
Female	57,117	47.9	16,156	58.7
White	99,294	83.3	22,049	80.1
Male	52,603	44.1	9,198	33.4
Female	46,691	39.2	12,850	46.7
Black	14,365	12.1	4,231	15.4
Male	6,580	5.5	1,627	5.9
Female	7,785	6.5	2,604	9.5
Full-Time	99,591	83.6	17,110	62.1
Male	55,963	47.0	7,687	27.9
Female	43,628	36.6	9.423	34.2
Part-Time	19,600	16.4	10,427	37.9
Male	6,111	5.1	3,694	13.4
Female	13,489	11.3	6,733	24.5

* Includes persons who are not self-employed and who earn between 50 cents and $100 an hour.

Source: Solutions for Progress, analysis of July 1999-June 2000 Current Population Survey Outgoing Rotation Group files.

TABLE 5-2

Jobs Paying Less Than $9 Per Hour, 1999

Occupation	Median hourly wage	Occupation	Median hourly wage
Textile cutting machine setters, operators & tenders	$8.98	Cooks, institution & cafeteria	$7.89
Helpers—painters, paperhangers, plasterers & stucco masons	8.95	Crossing guards	7.70
		Funeral attendants	7.70
Telemarketers	8.91	Agricultural equipment operators	7.67
Barbers	8.91	Retail salespersons	7.66
Skin care specialists	8.87	Sewing machine operators	7.57
Bakers	8.82	Hotel, motel & resort desk clerks	7.54
Pharmacy aides	8.76	Personal & home care aides	7.50
Mail clerks & mail machine operators, except postal service	8.76	Nonfarm animal caretakers	7.50
		Pressers, textile, garment & related materials	7.49
Laborers & freight, stock & material movers, hand	8.75	Farmworkers, farm & ranch animals	7.40
Floral designers	8.66	Laundry & dry-cleaning workers	7.25
Tellers	8.60	Food preparation workers	7.23
Demonstrators & product promoters	8.56	Packers & packagers, hand	7.20
		Counter & rental clerks	7.16
Library assistants, clerical	8.49	Cooks, short order	7.14
Landscaping & groundskeeping workers	8.48	Service station attendants	7.11
		Food servers, nonrestaurant	7.09
Tour guides & escorts	8.46	Maids & housekeeping cleaners	7.03
Preschool teachers, except special education	8.41	Child care workers	6.91
		Parking lot attendants	6.89
Helpers, roofers	8.41	Baggage porters & bellhops	6.84
Ambulance drivers & attendants, except EMTs	8.40	Graders & sorters, agricultural products	6.76
File clerks	8.38	Hosts & hostesses, restaurant, lounge & coffee shop	6.73
Couriers & messengers	8.36		
Stock clerks & order fillers	8.35	Farm labor contractors	6.71
Hairdressers, hairstylists & cosmetologists	8.33	Manicurists & pedicurists	6.70
		Cashiers	6.68
Nursing aides, orderlies & attendants	8.29	Dishwashers	6.57
		Amusement & recreation attendants	6.55
Home health aides	8.21		
Forest & conservation workers	8.21	Bartenders	6.52
Meat, poultry & fish cutters & trimmers	8.08	Counter attendants, cafeteria, food concession & coffee shop	6.46
Security guards	8.07	Farmworkers & laborers, crop, nursery & greenhouse	6.42
Sewers, hand	8.06		
Cooks, restaurant	8.05	Combined food preparation & serving workers, including fast food	6.30
Shoe & leather workers & repairers	8.04		
		Ushers, lobby attendants & ticket takers	6.26
Janitors & cleaners	7.90		
Recreation workers	7.90	Cooks, fast food	6.24
Taxi drivers & chauffeurs	7.89	Waiters & waitresses	6.07

* Half the people in the occupation make less than the median wage; half make more.

Source: U.S. Bureau of Labor Statistics, News Release, "Occupational Employment and Wages in 1999 Based on the New Standard Occupational Classification System," December 20, 2000.

Hierarchical job structures in manufacturing resemble pyramids. A small number of managerial and administrative jobs sit at the top of the structure; progressively wider layers of professional, technical, and supervisory jobs lie below but near the top; and large numbers of production and maintenance jobs comprise the base. In the post-World War II decades, basic manufacturing jobs were associated with high wages and compressed differentials, good benefits and income security. These jobs were considered "men's work" because of the products and tasks involved and because sole wage earners could support families at middle-income levels...

By contrast, jobs in light manufacturing industries usually were associated with women's work and therefore commanded lower pay and social status.

Service industry jobs are characterized by wide pay disparities and are best pictured as hourglasses. Large numbers of high-status professional and managerial jobs requiring formal credentials and qualifications occupy the top half of the structure and equally large or larger numbers of uncredentialed, low-status occupations inhabit the bottom half, with relatively small

Low-wage jobs are not distributed evenly throughout the economy. Low-wage workers are disproportionately concentrated in comparatively few industries—primarily agriculture, private household services, retail trade, personal services, social services (including child care, for example) and entertainment/recreation services.[3] Tables below and in Appendix A show the number and percentage of workers making less than $5.15, $6.15, $6.65 and $8. A disproportionate share of low-wage workers is employed in the large retail trade industry.[4] Approximately 17 percent of all workers are employed in retail trade, and nearly half of retail workers make less than $8 an hour.

The Labor Department's list of the ten occupations predicted to produce the most new jobs by 2008 include such low-paid jobs as retail salespersons, cashiers, office clerks, and personal care and home health aides. (See table.)

numbers of technical jobs in between. Wage dispersion is large, union representation scarce, and market performance uneven, resulting in the labor force being polarized between highly valued employees and generally devalued workers.

Finally, job structures in retail establishments resemble a wide, flat pin cushion with a single pin protruding from the top. The pin represents the good jobs and the cushion the bad ones. Management and supervisory jobs pay below comparable jobs in goods-producing and support industries but proportionately much more than those of the clerks, cashiers, and restaurant workers, who also have few if any benefits and slim chances for advancement. In addition, hourly retail jobs are increasingly part-time, whether or not employees prefer such arrangements. The average fastfood restaurant worker in the early 1990s, for example, worked 30 hours a week, had six months or less on the job, received no benefits, and got a pay raise only when the legal minimum wage rose. Union representation is rare outside large northern and coastal cities. Retail jobs thus epitomize contingent employment.

Charles Craypo and David Cormier, "Job restructuring as a determinant of wage inequality and working-poor households," Journal of Economic Issues, *March 2000.*

TABLE 5-3

Occupations Producing the Most New Jobs, 1998-2008
in descending order

OCCUPATION	1998 EMPLOYMENT	2008 EMPLOYMENT	CHANGE
	jobs in thousands		
Systems analysts	617	1,194	577
Retail salespersons	4,056	4,620	563
Cashiers	3,198	3,754	556
General managers and top executives	3,362	3,913	551
Truck drivers	2,970	3,463	493
Office clerks, general	3,021	3,484	463
Registered nurses	2,079	2,530	451
Computer support specialists	429	869	439
Personal care and home health aides	746	1,179	433
Teacher assistants	1,192	1,567	375

Source: U.S. Bureau of Labor Statistics, Employment Projection, "The 10 occupations with the largest job growth, 1998-2008," February 9, 2000.

TABLE 5-4

Percent of Workers in Industries by Wage Category

Industry	Employment	Wage* <$5.15	Wage <$6.15	Wage <$6.65	Wage <$8.00
			percent		
Agriculture	1,769,623	7.9	27.6	35.3	52.2
Mining	526,232	1.4	3.2	4.7	8.3
Construction	6,869,113	1.2	4.5	6.5	13.1
Manufacturing–Durable	11,758,075	0.7	3.9	5.6	11.8
Manufacturing–Nondurable	7,524,397	1.4	7.4	10.3	18.5
Transportation	5,706,469	1.9	4.7	6.4	13.0
Communications	1,867,969	0.5	2.6	3.6	7.5
Utilities/Sanitary Services	1,522,206	0.4	2.5	3.0	6.6
Wholesale Trade	4,661,886	1.3	5.8	8.6	17.0
Retail Trade	20,115,539	4.4	24.7	32.4	48.1
FIRE**	7,666,247	1.7	4.5	6.2	12.8
Private Households	940,044	28.5	42.7	48.0	63.3
Business, Auto and Repair Services	7,501,674	2.2	9.3	12.3	21.4
Personal Services	2,762,989	5.9	21.1	28.3	43.3
Entertainment &. Recreation Services	2,197,442	3.9	21.0	26.4	38.6
Hospitals	5,030,321	1.0	4.1	5.8	12.9
Medical Services	5,803,431	1.7	9.1	12.3	23.2
Educational Services	10,837,605	2.8	9.0	11.2	18.0
Social Services	2,889,308	5.3	18.7	23.8	36.8
Other Professional Services	5,189,227	2.4	5.3	7.1	12.7
Forestry and Fisheries	93,128 ·	4.0	10.8	13.1	21.2
Public Administration	5,958,354	1.2	3.4	4.5	8.6
TOTAL	119,191,280	2.6	10.6	14.0	23.1

For example, 48.1 percent of workers in retail trade make less than $8.

* Workers paid less than $5.15. Workers paid exactly $5.15 are included in the next wage category. With these wage categories we can see who will be affected by proposed minimum wage increases because we show the workers who make less than a given wage rather than equal to or less than a given wage.

** Fire, Insurance and Real Estate.

Source: Solutions for Progress, analysis of Current Population Survey Outgoing Rotation Group files, July 1999-June 2000.

TABLE 5-5

Percent of Workers in Wage Category by Industry

INDUSTRY	INDUSTRY EMPLOYMENT	WAGE <$5.15	WAGE <$6.15	WAGE <$6.65	WAGE <$8.00
Agriculture	1.5	4.5	3.9	3.7	3.4
Mining	0.4	0.2	0.1	0.1	0.2
Construction	5.8	2.7	2.5	2.7	3.3
Manufacturing-Durable	9.9	2.6	3.6	3.9	5.1
Manufacturing-Nondurable	6.3	3.3	4.4	4.7	5.1
Transportation	4.8	3.5	2.1	2.2	2.7
Communications	1.6	0.3	0.4	0.4	0.5
Utilities/Sanitary Services	1.3	0.2	0.3	0.3	0.4
Wholesale Trade	3.9	1.9	2.1	2.4	2.9
Retail Trade	16.9	28.6	39.3	39.1	35.1
FIRE	6.4	4.3	2.7	2.8	3.6
Private Households	0.8	8.7	3.2	2.7	2.2
Business, Auto and Repair Services	6.3	5.2	5.5	5.5	5.8
Personal Services	2.3	5.3	4.6	4.7	4.3
Entertainment & Recreation Services	1.8	2.7	3.6	3.5	3.1
Hospitals	4.2	1.6	1.6	1.7	2.4
Medical Services	4.9	3.2	4.2	4.3	4.9
Educational Services	9.1	9.8	7.7	7.3	7.1
Social Services	2.4	4.9	4.3	4.1	3.9
Other Professional Services	4.4	4.0	2.2	2.2	2.4
Forestry and Fisheries	0.1	0.1	0.1	0.1	0.1
Public Administration	5.0	2.3	1.6	1.6	1.9

For example, 16.9 percent of the workforce is in the retail trade industry; 35.1 percent of workers who are paid less than $8 are in the retail trade industry.

Source: Solutions for Progress, analysis of Current Population Survey Outgoing Rotation Group files, July 1999–June 2000.

Women's Work

Women are more likely than men to be paid low wages. Women account for 48 percent of the labor force, but 59 percent of workers making less than $8. Women hold a disproportionate share of the jobs in low-wage industries and a disproportionate share of the low-wage jobs in higher paid industries. (See tables below and in Appendix A.)

For example, women are 92 percent of private household workers, an industry in which 63 percent of workers are paid less than $8 an hour. Women are only 28 percent of the durable manufacturing workforce, but 46 percent of those paid less than $8. Women are 41 percent of the communications workforce, but 58 percent of those paid less than $8. Women are 52 percent of retail trade workers and 59 percent of those paid less than $8. Women are the great majority of workers paid less than $8 in medical services (88 percent), social services (84 percent) and educational services (74 percent).

An increase in the minimum wage to $8 is crucial for women workers and their families.

Jobs traditionally seen as "women's work" often mean low wages. Take child care. Child care workers typically make about as much as parking lot attendants and much less than animal trainers. The Center for the Child Care Workforce reports that in 1999, family child care providers made an average $4.82 an hour; center-based child care workers, not including preschool teachers, made $7.42; and preschool teachers made $9.43. Parking lot attendants made $7.38 and animal trainers made $12.39. Out of 700 occupations surveyed by the Department of Labor Occupational Employment Statistics program only 15 occupations have lower average wages than child care workers.[5] Looking at median wages in 1999, child care workers made $6.91, parking lot attendants $6.89 and preschool teachers $8.41.[6]

In 1960, women who worked full time, year round made 61 cents for every dollar earned by men. In four decades women closed the gap by just 11 cents. Full-time working women made 72 cents for every dollar earned by men in 1999 (latest figure available). That's down from the all-time high of 74 cents in 1996.[7]

Do women pay 72 cents on the dollar for food, health care, housing or child care?

Full-time working women earned a median income of $26,324 in 1999. Men earned $36,476—a difference of $10,152 a year. That's not pocket change. It's enough to pay rent of $846 a month. It's nearly the total wages of a full-time minimum wage worker.

TABLE 5-6

Percent of Female Workers Within Industries by Wage Category

INDUSTRY	TOTAL EMPLOYMENT	WAGE <$5.15	WAGE <$6.15	WAGE <$6.65	WAGE <$8.00
			percent		
Agriculture	460,141	4.1	22.1	30.5	45.5
Mining	59,017	1.2	3.2	4.5	6.4
Construction	668,922	2.8	7.6	9.8	18.5
Manufacturing– Durable	3,324,825	0.9	6.5	9.1	19.2
Manufacturing– Nondurable	3,000,137	2.1	11.3	15.6	26.9
Transportation	1,572,541	2.1	5.8	8.0	16.4
Communications	756,331	0.3	3.2	5.1	10.7
Utilities/Sanitary Services	327,614	0.1	2.4	2.8	6.8
Wholesale Trade	1,503,508	1.4	8.2	12.4	20.8
Retail Trade	10,411,962	5.0	28.0	37.2	54.8
FIRE	4,715,283	1.8	4.9	6.9	15.1
Private Households	862,981	28.0	42.1	47.4	62.9
Business, Auto & Repair Services	2,837,453	2.2	10.4	14.3	24.8
Personal Services	1,772,014	6.8	24.4	33.4	49.7
Entertainment & Recreation Services	926,816	4.7	24.0	30.5	43.3
Hospitals	3,843,648	1.0	3.9	5.6	13.3
Medical Services	4,886,487	1.7	9.2	12.5	24.1
Educational Services	7,533,098	3.1	9.3	11.9	19.2
Social Services	2,327,633	5.0	19.0	24.8	38.5
Other Professional Services	2,666,057	2.4	6.2	8.5	16.0
Forestry and Fisheries	22,128	9.8	23.2	26.3	35.2
Public Administration	2,638,359	1.4	4.3	5.9	11.0
TOTAL	57,116,957	3.2	13.0	17.3	28.3

For example, 54.8 percent of women retail trade employees are paid less than $8.

Source: Solutions for Progress, analysis of Current Population Survey Outgoing Rotation Group files, July 1999-June 2000.

> **W**hen someone works for less pay than she can live on—when, for example, she goes hungry so that you can eat more cheaply and conveniently—then she has made a great sacrifice for you, she has made you a gift of some part of her abilities, her health, and her life. The "working poor," as they are approvingly termed, are in fact the major philanthropists of our society... To be a member of the working poor is to be an anonymous donor...to everyone else. As Gail, one of my restaurant coworkers put it, "you give and you give."
>
> *Barbara Ehrenreich*, Nickel and Dimed.

The average 25-year-old woman who works full time until retiring at age 65 will earn $523,000 less than the average working man, according to the Institute for Women's Policy Research. That's a gap of more than half a million dollars.

The discriminatory pay gap remains going up the education ladder. The typical full-time working woman with a high school degree makes less than a male high school dropout. The typical woman with a college bachelor's degree makes a few thousand more than a man with only a high school degree, but the typical woman with a master's degree makes less than a man with only a college bachelor's. Women with a doctorate make less than men with a master's.[8]

While most minimum wage workers are women, the top of the wage pyramid looks quite different. Women hold just 4 percent of top-earner spots at the Fortune 500 largest U.S. companies, according to Catalyst's latest survey. The Fortune 500 has only four CEOs who are women and women hold only 6 percent of the positions "with clout," such as chairman, CEO, president and executive vice president. Women hold 12 percent of the seats on Fortune 500 company boards. For 90 companies, zero is the number of corporate officers who are women; 71 companies have no women on their boards.[9]

Fortune magazine has observed, "At the same level of management, the typical woman's pay is lower than her male colleague's—even when she has the exact same qualifications, works just as many years, relocates just as often, provides the main financial support for her family, takes no time off for personal reasons, and wins the same number of promotions to comparable jobs."[10]

Most Americans see that discrimination still exists. For example, a December 1999 CBS News Poll asked, "What about salaries? These days, if a man and a woman are doing the same work, do you think the

TABLE 5-7

Percent of Female Workers to Total Employment by Industry and Wage Category

INDUSTRY	FEMALE EMPLOYMENT	WAGE <$5.15	WAGE <$6.15	WAGE <$6.65	WAGE <$8.00
Agriculture	26.0	13.6	20.8	22.4	22.6
Mining	11.2	9.9	11.1	10.7	8.6
Construction	9.7	22.8	16.2	14.6	13.8
Manufacturing-Durable	28.3	36.1	46.5	45.7	45.8
Manufacturing-Nondurable	39.9	61.3	60.9	60.1	57.8
Transportation	27.6	30.8	34.2	34.7	34.6
Communications	40.5	24.5	50.7	56.6	57.9
Utilities/Sanitary Services	21.5	3.4	21.1	20.1	22.3
Wholesale Trade	32.3	35.1	45.7	46.3	39.5
Retail Trade	51.8	58.5	58.6	59.3	59.0
FIRE	61.5	62.4	66.8	68.9	72.4
Private Households	91.8	90.4	90.4	90.8	91.3
Business, Auto and Repair Services	37.8	38.8	42.2	44.1	43.7
Personal Services	64.1	73.8	74.4	75.8	73.6
Entertainment & Recreation Services	42.2	51.6	48.2	48.8	47.4
Hospitals	76.4	75.8	72.0	73.7	78.5
Medical Services	84.2	82.5	85.7	85.9	87.5
Educational Services	69.5	76.9	71.9	73.3	74.0
Social Services	80.6	76.9	81.9	84.0	84.4
Other Professional Services	51.4	50.7	60.1	61.8	64.8
Forestry & Fisheries	23.8	58.5	51.0	47.6	39.5
Public Administration	44.3	53.7	55.9	58.1	56.6
TOTAL	47.9	59.1	58.8	59.3	58.7

For example, 51.8 percent of retail trade workers are women and women are 59 percent of retail trade workers paid less than $8.

Source: Solutions for Progress, analysis of Current Population Survey Outgoing Rotation Group files, July 1999-June 2000.

man generally earns more, the woman generally earns more, or that both earn the same amount?" In response, 65 percent said the man earns more (70 percent of women said this as did 59 percent of men). Only 30 percent said they earn the same and 1 percent said the woman earns more.[11]

Pay discrimination hurts two-income families and is a major cause of poverty for single mothers and their children. Back in 1977, a U.S. Labor Department study found that if working women were paid what similarly qualified men earned, the number of poor families would decrease by half.[12]

What about today? "If married women were paid the same as comparable men, their family incomes would rise by nearly 6 percent," according to a study by the AFL-CIO and the Institute for Women's Policy Research. "If single working mothers earned as much as comparable men, their family incomes would increase by nearly 17 percent, and their poverty rates would be cut in half." In sum, "working families lose a staggering $200 billion of income annually to the wage gap."[13]

Raising the minimum wage is a crucial tool in helping women and their families escape poverty.

A Closer Look at $8 by Industry

The share of workers affected directly by an increase in the minimum wage to $8 varies substantially by industry. For example about two-thirds of private household workers, half of agriculture and retail workers, and a third of social service workers would directly benefit from an $8 minimum wage. By contrast, less than a tenth of workers would benefit directly in mining, communications, utilities and public administration.

To determine the impact of a wage increase to $8 per hour, we calculated the direct cost of raising the current minimum wage, the indirect effect of increasing the wages of workers paid at or slightly more than our recommended minimum wage, and the additional costs to the employer of employee benefits and taxes within each industry. We then compared the total cost of the wage increase to total payroll, total receipts minus total payroll and benefits, and the cost of goods sold.[14] The cost of goods sold consists of "the direct costs incurred...in producing goods and providing services. Included were costs of materials used in manufacturing; costs of goods purchased for resale; direct labor; and certain overhead expenses, such as rent, utilities, supplies, maintenance and repairs."[15]

About a fourth of the workforce would see their wages rise if the minimum wage were increased to $8 per hour. Remember that when the minimum wage is raised from $5.15 to $8, for example, most workers affected are not getting an extra $2.85 an hour (or more in the case of workers now paid less than the minimum), they are getting a portion of it. A worker earning $6 would get $2 more. A worker earning $7.90 would get only another 10 cents to reach the new minimum wage.

The direct cost of an increase to $8 totals about $69 billion across all major sectors of the economy—assuming too that there are no exemp-

TABLE 5-8

Workers Paid Less Than $8 by Industry

MAJOR INDUSTRY	INDUSTRY EMPLOYMENT	WAGE <$8.00 Number of Workers	WAGE <$8.00 % of Workers
Agriculture	1,769,623	923,984	52.2%
Mining	526,232	43,750	8.3%
Construction	6,869,113	900,465	13.1%
Manufacturing–Durable	11,758,075	1,391,698	11.8%
Manufacturing–NonDurable	7,524,397	1,394,425	18.5%
Transportation	5,706,469	743,223	13.0%
Communications	1,867,969	139,321	7.5%
Utilities/Sanitary Services	1,522,206	100,132	6.6%
Wholesale Trade	4,661,886	793,097	17.0%
Retail Trade	20,115,539	9,677,149	48.1%
FIRE	7,666,247	980,938	12.8%
Private Households	940,044	594,916	63.3%
Business, Auto & Repair	7,501,674	1,605,873	21.4%
Personal Services	2,762,989	1,196,582	43.3%
Entertainment/Recreation	2,197,442	847,333	38.6%
Hospitals	5,030,321	649,030	12.9%
Medical Services, excl. Hosp.	5,803,431	1,347,052	23.2%
Educational Services	10,837,605	1,953,938	18.0%
Social Services	2,889,308	1,063,495	36.8%
Other Professional Services	5,189,227	656,870	12.7%
Forestry and Fisheries	93,128	19,741	21.2%
Public Administration	5,958,354	514,205	8.6%
TOTAL	119,191,280	27,537,214	23.1%

Source: Solutions for Progress, analysis of Current Population Survey Outgoing Rotation Group files, July 1999–June 2000.

tions to the minimum wage as there are now. The total cost, including the "ripple effect"—as firms increase the wages of workers currently making $8 and a little above to maintain their wage hierarchy (see explanation in wage methodology appendix)—is about $96 billion, which is not a large amount when you put it in context.

Keep in mind that a trillion is a thousand billion. Now let's compare the cost of an increase in the minimum wage to $8 with other relevant costs of business operations, including total payroll and benefits ($4.1 trillion), the total cost of goods sold ($10.5 trillion), and receipts minus payroll and benefits ($14.9 trillion).[16]

The cost of an increase in the minimum wage to $8 per hour represents less than 1 percent of receipts minus payroll and benefits, less than 1 percent of the cost of goods sold, and about 2 percent of total payroll and benefits. These figures actually overstate the cost.

Our cost calculation assumes that there are *no exemptions* from the minimum wage and that all wage and salary workers are paid at least $8 per hour. More than one-fourth (28.5 percent) of wage and salary workers—33.9 million workers—were exempt from the minimum wage provisions of the Fair Labor Standards Act in 1999. More than 70 percent of exempt workers were executive, administrative or professional employees, many of whom earn far more than the minimum wage. However, about a third of workers in agriculture, forestry and fisheries, and nearly half of private household workers are exempt from minimum wage law.[17]

To isolate the cost of raising the minimum wage from removing exemptions and expanding eligibility, we estimate that if the minimum wage were increased to $8 per hour, but current exemptions applied, the total cost of the wage increase would be reduced by more than $20 billion to $75 billion—an even more negligible amount when compared to receipts minus payroll and benefits, the cost of goods sold, and total payroll and benefits.

Moreover, our estimate of the cost of increasing the minimum wage to $8 does not include an analysis of the benefits of increased wages. As discussed earlier, higher wages can reduce turnover and training costs, enhance productivity and increase worker purchasing power, which in turn can increase sales. For these and other reasons, the net cost of the wage increase could be significantly lower than the cost indicated in our calculations.

An increase in the minimum wage to $8 per hour represents a small increment of receipts minus payroll and benefits: less than 1 percent in the mining; construction; manufacturing; communications; utilities and sanitary services; wholesale trade; and the finance, insurance and real estate industries (FIRE); and less than 2 percent of receipts minus payroll and benefits in retail trade; transportation; business, automobile and repair services; and entertainment and recreation services.

An increase to $8 also represents a small increment of the cost of goods sold: less than 1 percent in the mining; construction; manufacturing; communications; utilities; wholesale trade; and the finance, insurance and real estate industries; and less than 2 percent of the cost of goods sold in the retail; transportation; business, auto and repair services; hospitals and other professional services. (See tables in Appendix A.)

For business generally, an $8 minimum wage can be managed just like modest changes in prices for rent, insurance, goods and services. The essential difference is that an increase in the minimum wage allows millions of individuals and families to work their way out of poverty

Meatpacking is now the most dangerous job in the United States. The injury rate in a slaughterhouse is about three times higher than the rate in a typical American factory. Every year about one out of three meatpacking workers in this country...suffer an injury or a work-related illness that requires medical attention beyond first aid... Thousands of additional injuries and illnesses most likely go unreported...

One of the leading determinants of the injury rate at a slaughterhouse today is the speed of the disassembly line. The faster it runs, the more likely that workers will get hurt. The old meatpacking plants in Chicago slaughtered about 50 cattle an hour... Today some plants slaughter up to 400 cattle an hour—about half a dozen animals every minute, sent down a single production line, carved by workers desperate not to fall behind...

Some of the most dangerous jobs in meatpacking today are performed by the late-night cleaning crews... They are considered "independent contractors," employed not by the meatpacking firms but by sanitation companies. They earn hourly wages that are about one-third lower than those of regular production employees. And their work is so hard and so horrendous that words seem inadequate to describe it. The men and women who now clean the nation's slaughterhouses may arguably have the worst job in the United States. "It takes a really dedicated person," a former member of a cleaning crew told me, "or a really desperate person to get the job done."

Eric Schlosser, Fast Food Nation.

and provides more dollars to workers, which are then recycled back in the form of greater purchasing power.

A few sectors of the economy would be disproportionately affected by an increase in the minimum wage to $8 per hour, namely agriculture, household services and some service sectors: personal services, educational services and social services.[18] Retail trade is a large employer of low-wage workers, but as seen earlier, retail profits have outpaced general domestic corporate profits and dramatically outpaced worker's wages in the past three decades. The cost of raising the minimum wage to $8 in the retail industry would be less than 2 percent of receipts minus payroll and benefits and of the cost of goods sold. Again, that isn't accounting for the benefits of lower turnover, higher productivity and greater consumer purchasing power, for example. Moreover, retail is a highly competitive industry. Raising the federal minimum wage makes it easier to pay higher wages because competitors have to do the same.

The relative cost of a wage increase in some sectors is higher than average because the proportion of payroll to receipts is higher. Service industries have relatively high ratios of payroll (including estimated benefits) to receipts. While the average proportion of payroll to receipts across industries is roughly 21 percent, the proportion of payroll to receipts is 38.8 percent in the personal services sector, 44.5 percent in the educational services sector and 46.2 percent in the social services sector.[19] In contrast, the proportion of payroll to receipts in the retail trade sector is only 15.1 percent, which sheds light on why the cost of the wage increase is not high, despite the large number of low-wage workers employed in this sector.

The personal and social services industries provide many services historically provided by unpaid female labor in the home. The social services sector includes the child care industry and the residential care industry, for example. The personal services sector includes, for example, laundry and cleaning services, and beauty and barber shops. Like retail, this is a highly competitive industry and raising the minimum wage makes it easier to pay higher wages because competitors have to do the same. Moreover, these businesses benefit when current and potential customers have higher wages and, therefore, more money to spend on their services, many of which are the kind of services that people cut back on or use more depending on their incomes. The market value assigned to wages in these sectors has been shaped by a history of gender and race discrimination. To tolerate the continued low pay in these sectors means legitimizing past and present discrimination.

EDUCATIONAL AND SOCIAL SERVICES

The educational and social services sectors provide public goods financed in large part with public dollars at a price heavily subsidized by the low pay of workers. It's in the public interest to mandate a minimum wage that will attract and retain workers and improve services. Government has a crucial role to play as the dominant payer for services in these sectors. Instead of being a major part of the problem, government has to be a major part of the solution.

As the Paraprofessional Healthcare Institute points out in a recent study, "The single largest funder of health care, the federal government has in essence created an entire labor market of paraprofessional health care workers—a labor market that would not exist without its funding, a labor market that keeps low-income women in the ranks of the working poor. And yet our government has yet to accept responsibility for creating and maintaining literally thousands of poverty-level jobs."[20]

Medicare and Medicaid finance about 60 percent of long-term care. As Joan Fitzgerald observes about nursing homes and other long-term care facilities:

> Nobody is happy with the nation's nursing homes. Too many patients are receiving substandard care. Workers, particularly nurse's aides who provide the majority of direct care, suffer from low wages, lack of benefits, understaffing, inadequate training, and limited career opportunities...
>
> Government, in effect, sets wages and career paths by setting reimbursement rates. Government also regulates the conditions of care and subsidizes training programs for nursing assistants and other paraprofessionals...
>
> On an average eight-hour shift, a nurse's aide is expected to assist as many as 20 residents with bathing, dressing, eating, exercising, and eliminating. It is impossible to complete all the tasks in a cursory manner, let alone to take time to talk to residents or individualize their care. Both workers and residents feel frustrated. The work is hard, the pay is low, and aides are not treated with respect. It is not surprising that more than 40 states have critical shortages of direct-care staff.
>
> The annual turnover rate (the percentage of staff who have to be replaced annually due to quitting or firing) for nurse's aides is higher than 90 percent. A study of job leavers by the National Network of Career Nursing Assistants found that even those who like their jobs often resign because they cannot earn a sufficient income to support their families.[21]

Wage pass-throughs are an important tool for improving pay and services. A wage pass-through may be legislated in industries that rely largely on government funding in order to target increased funds, including higher reimbursement levels, to increase compensation of low-wage workers in these industries. These pass-throughs have been developed based on absolute dollar amounts of wages and benefits as well as percentages of increased reimbursement rates.

Numerous states have used wage pass-throughs to increase wages, decrease job turnover and enhance the quality of services. Eighteen states have enacted state-sponsored wage pass-throughs for direct service, low-wage workers in the non-hospital medical services sector, resulting in wage increases of $0.50 to $2.14. Some states have

> California offers an illustration of what is possible through its home-care workers who have made the most progress to date. There, a drive organized by the SEIU (Service Employees International Union) led to a change in state policy that will transform home-care workers from poverty-wage freelancers into paraprofessionals who will earn as much as $11.50 an hour. Home-care workers in California are paid for by various state and local agencies... The SEIU promoted a policy change in which California's largest counties took on the home-care workers as direct employees and the state guaranteed higher wages.
>
> Joan Fitzgerald, The American Prospect, May 21, 2000.

developed wage pass-throughs for home care workers. Arkansas, Maine, Michigan, California and other states have targeted pass-through support for nursing facilities workers.[22] In Massachusetts, for example, a $42 million nursing-home-quality initiative "includes a $35 million pass-through, plus $5 million to create career-ladder programs for direct-care workers, $1.1 million for training scholarships, and $1.1 million for training and post-employment supports for people moving off welfare. The legislation is the result of the efforts of the Coalition to Reform Eldercare (CORE), a group of labor, advocacy organizations and nursing home operators."[23]

A substantial part of building the political commitment and will to utilize wage policy to combat poverty is to align the interests of multiple stakeholders. As a major payer, government can help to meet the overlapping needs and priorities of many groups through a wage pass-through: Employees benefit from higher wages and the opportunity to advance professionally. Employers benefit from lower staff turnover, reduced recruiting and training costs and increased consumer satisfaction. Consumers benefit from higher quality services. We address the low-paid, high-turnover child care industry in the next chapter.

AGRICULTURE

Agriculture and private household services epitomize industries of hard work at poverty wages. More than half the workers employed in agriculture make less than $8 per hour and more than a fourth make less than $6.15 an hour.

Agriculture represents a special sector because Americans have traditionally had the cost of our food production heavily subsidized by low-wage workers. At the same time, taxpayers have heavily subsidized agriculture. It's time for us to include decent wages for agricultural workers as a goal of agricultural policy.

Hired farmworkers are less than 1 percent of wage and salary workers, but they account for about 30 percent of farmworkers (farm operators and unpaid family members are the other 70 percent). As a U.S. Department of Agriculture report makes clear, their importance to agriculture is not reflected in their wages. In 1998, 22 percent of full-time farmworkers were paid less than the minimum wage of $5.15 an hour. "Many farm employers (including those employing 500 or less mandays of labor in a calendar quarter and those employing workers primarily in the range production of livestock) are not required to pay the Federal minimum wage."[24]

In 1999, 42 percent of all farms received government payments, averaging $16,751.[25] An individual farmer can get more than $280,000 a year from various payments. As summed up in an eye-opening 2000 article in the *New York Times*:

> The big harvest of government checks usually happens in the fall—$40,000 for just being a farmer, another $40,000 for emergencies like bad market conditions, more than $100,000 for not making any money on what is grown, and $50,000 for taking other land out of production...
>
> This year, the government distributed a record $28 billion in direct payments, accounting for half of all the money made by farmers. In eight states, including Montana, government assistance made up 100 percent of overall farm income...
>
> The departing agriculture secretary, Dan Glickman, says farming has "become largely an income transfer program," with the government underwriting rural business and requiring very little in return...
>
> Over the last four years, the top 1 percent of farmers in this country—about 15 farmers—received an average of $616,000 each from the government. The top 10 percent—about 150 farmers—were paid an average of $308,000 per farmer over the last four years. These numbers do not include the record payout for 2000...
>
> [Mr. Glickman] added, "It's important enough for this country to keep rural communities going. And while I don't like the large payments going to some farmers—that's an outright embarrassment—many of these payments are keeping large sections of rural America from folding up and going down.[26]

Government payments go disproportionately to large farms. About 80 percent of farms categorized as occupation farming/high sales and large family farms (averaging payments of $85,208) received government payments. These two groups, combined, received 46 percent of total government payments to farm operators in 1999.[27] Critics charge that program rules favoring large farms have helped drive smaller farms out of business. In 1999, the USDA settled a class-action lawsuit with thousands of black farmers who had been denied loans and other subsidies in a long pattern of racial discrimination.

In 2000, a team of USDA researchers explored options for reshaping farm policy to establish a more effective safety net for farmers "so that people have enough resources to maintain a minimum standard of living. Current direct government payments to farmers do not generally benefit the lowest income farmers but instead go to the most well-off... Unlike the present safety net programs, which generally target producers of major field crops, this alternative set of safety nets targets farm households that fall below certain income- and earnings-based criteria."[28]

Unfortunately, the USDA safety net report focuses only on farmers, not farmworkers. Farmworkers are concentrated on higher-production

The shepherd was deep in the desert, eight miles from the nearest road... It was midafternoon, 110 degrees... Two years and eight months into a three-year contract as a shepherd under a federal guest worker program, the 40-year-old Peruvian said he was still waiting for a day off. He lives in a 6-by-12 foot trailer with no running water, no electricity, no phone, no toilet...

The man, who would not let his name be used for fear of angering his employer, is typical of shepherds in the United States...

Shepherds are excluded from minimum wage regulations. Until July 1, when California's Industrial Welfare Commission, which regulates working conditions, ordered sheep ranchers to increase herders' wages by $150 a month, shepherds, who are essentially on duty 90 hours a week, made $900 a month... [California shepherds] make the most money. In other states, the pay is anywhere from $600 to $800 a month.

Evelyn Nieves, New York Times, *July 11, 2001.*

farms, with 70 percent of paid labor on farms with $500,000 or more in sales.[29] Certainly, big profitable agricultural businesses should pay workers a decent wage without government subsidy.

We can build on the USDA safety net report and redesign government farm policy so that it meets the multiple goals of maintaining a high level of domestic production—because it is good for the country in the long run even if market conditions on their own would force many U.S. farmers out of business; keeping small family farms in business; and maintaining an adequate living standard for both farmers and farmworkers.

HOUSEHOLD EMPLOYMENT

Two-thirds of private household workers make less than $8 an hour and 43 percent make less than $6.15 an hour. As with agriculture, any effort to provide a viable wage will have a significant impact—as well it should.

We simply cannot exempt household workers who take care of children, clean, cook, garden and maintain other peoples' homes from a decent minimum wage. It is unconscionable for those with higher incomes to be subsidized by impoverished workers. The employment of household help has grown along with the employment of women outside the home and as people put in longer hours on the job.

The Long Island, NY-based Workplace Project, an organization of over 400 Latina and Latino immigrants, founded UNITY Housecleaners, a domestic workers' cooperative, in 1999. UNITY members provide a full range of housecleaning services and set fair wages and decent working conditions. Lilliam Araujo, women and cooperatives coordinator for the Workplace Project, makes well above minimum wage at $60 per four-hour housecleaning job. She says the women used to feel their jobs were not appreciated. "Now, they know they have the right to say 'no.' There have been employers who asked them to do double the work for no pay, no rest periods and no food. There have been employers who asked that their floors be polished by hand, for us to get on our knees."[30] They treated the floors better than the housecleaners.

It should be obvious that if you want someone else to do your cleaning, you should pay them a decent wage. Where child care is involved, government also has a role to play. Child care subsidies, which we return to in the next chapter, should adequately cover child care in the home as well as outside it so child care providers no longer subsidize child care with low wages.

Wage Policy and Poverty

espite current policy rhetoric, work is not a sure way out of poverty. Most poor families—by official count—include at least one worker. More than one-fourth of minimum wage workers and more than 15 percent of low-wage workers are below the official poverty line.[31] Many more cannot meet their basic needs.

A USDA Economic Research Service report underscores the importance of higher wages in reducing poverty: "Although considerable antipoverty rhetoric has emphasized work, a key to permanently reducing poverty is to improve the returns to labor. While the economy has generated many jobs, wages and benefits are often insufficient to lift a family out of poverty."

The report finds that "low real wage rates and not the unemployment rate are the most important determinant of poverty in the long run." Although unemployment plays an important role, the real wage rate is "the most effective mechanism for decreasing poverty." The report observes:

> From 1959 until the late 1970's, fluctuation in the poverty rate paralleled changes in the performance of the macroeconomy. Business cycle upswings significantly reduced poverty while busi-

TABLE 5-9

Difference Between Minimum Needs Budget and Annual Pay for Full-Time Work Without Employment Health Benefits

HOUSEHOLD COMPOSITION	MINIMUM NEEDS BUDGET 1999	DIFFERENCE BETWEEN PAY & BUDGET AT $5.15/HOUR	DIFFERENCE BETWEEN PAY & BUDGET AT $6.15/HOUR	DIFFERENCE BETWEEN PAY & BUDGET AT $6.65/HOUR	DIFFERENCE BETWEEN PAY & BUDGET AT $8.00/HOUR
Single Adult	$16,549	-$5,837	-$3,757	-$2,717	$91
Two Adults, No Children	$23,522	-$2,098	$2,062	$4,142	$9,758
Single Parent, One Child	$28,796	-$18,084	-$16,004	-$14,964	-$12,156
Single Parent, Two Children	$32,999	-$22,287	-$20,207	-$19,167	-$16,359
Two Adults, One Child	$31,255	-$9,831	-$5,671	-$3,591	$2,025
Two Adults, Two Children	$35,637	-$14,213	-$10,053	-$7,973	-$2,357

Note: We assumed that both adult members in two-adult households are employed full-time, year-round.

ness cycle troughs increased poverty. Since the late 1970's, the relationship between economic performance and poverty is less clear...

If the historical relationship between economic expansion and poverty prevailed during [the 1980s] then the prolonged expansion observed from 1983 to 1989 would have reduced poverty to about 9.3 percent, the lowest in U.S. history. By 1989, however, the measured poverty rate was 12.8 percent, higher than in 1979.[32]

The shrinking minimum wage set the tone for falling real wages and increased poverty among workers. It has also contributed to an increase in inequality. One study of wage inequality found that the decline in the real value of the minimum wage throughout the 1980s was responsible for nearly a fourth of the increase in wage inequality among men and nearly one-third of the increase in wage inequality among women.[33] An increase in the minimum wage to restore its value would reduce poverty and inequality.

Americans believe that work should be the major avenue out of poverty. This view was reinforced by the passage of the Personal Responsibility and Work Opportunity Reconciliation Act of 1996 (PRWORA), which placed work requirements and stringent time limits on beneficiaries of public assistance programs. For millions of Americans, however, the simple fact is that work does not provide

---

TABLE 5-10

Difference Between Minimum Needs Budget and Annual Pay for Full-Time Work With Employment Health Benefits

HOUSEHOLD COMPOSITION	MINIMUM NEEDS BUDGET 1999	DIFFERENCE BETWEEN PAY & BUDGET AT $5.15/HOUR	DIFFERENCE BETWEEN PAY & BUDGET AT $6.15/HOUR	DIFFERENCE BETWEEN PAY & BUDGET AT $6.65/HOUR	DIFFERENCE BETWEEN PAY & BUDGET AT $8.00/HOUR
Single Adult	$14,196	-$3,484	-$1,404	-$364	$2,444
Two Adults, No Children	$18,614	$2,810	$6,970	$9,050	$14,666
Single Parent, One Child	$23,179	-$12,467	-$10,387	-$9,347	-$6,539
Single Parent, Two Children	$27,439	-$16,727	-$14,647	-$13,607	-$10,799
Two Adults, One Child	$26,076	-$4,652	-$492	$1,588	$7,204
Two Adults, Two Children	$30,812	-$9,388	-$5228	-$3,148	$2,468

Note: Most low-income workers do not have employment health benefits. We assumed that both adult members in two-adult households are employed full-time, year-round.

sufficient income to protect themselves and their children from the devastating effects of poverty.

A minimum wage of $8 is necessary, but not sufficient. It would meet the minimum needs budget for a single adult without health insurance. A full-time, year-round worker earning a wage of $8 per hour makes $16,640 annually (or $33,280 for a two-earner family). That's nearly enough to lift a family of four with one full-time, year-round worker above the official poverty threshold. An $8 minimum wage would substantially improve the lives of millions of working households. But it has limitations. It would not be sufficient to fully meet the minimum needs of single parent families with children. It would also not enable working families of four without health insurance to meet their minimum needs budgets, even if both adults work full time, year round. Moreover, families with part-time or part-year workers would continue to have difficulty making ends meet.

In the next chapter, we examine government policy options to fill the gap between wages and minimum needs.

6

■ ■ ■ ■ ■

Policies To Make Ends Meet

WE THE PEOPLE of the United States, in Order to form a more perfect Union, establish Justice, insure domestic Tranquility, provide for the common defense, promote the general Welfare, and secure the Blessings of Liberty to ourselves and our Posterity, do ordain and establish this Constitution for the United States of America.
Constitution of the United States, 1787.

Throughout our history, generations of Americans have reshaped government policy to better "promote the general welfare." Our legacy from the last century includes the New Deal, with its landmark policies of the minimum wage, 8-hour day, curtailment of child labor and Social Security. What legacy will we build in the 21st century?

The $8 minimum wage is a long overdue companion to the 8-hour day. It will end poverty for millions of workers and their families. With better wages more people will be able to meet their needs without government assistance. But government must do more to assure that everyone can meet their basic needs, whatever their wage.

The United States has universal Social Security for seniors, but not universal child care. We have universal Medicare for seniors, but not for all Americans. Public policy in the United States does much less to reduce poverty, especially for children, than policy in other industrialized nations.[1]

We cannot be content, no matter how high [the] general standard of living may be, if some fraction of our people—whether it be one-third or one-fifth or one-tenth—is ill-fed, ill-clothed, ill-housed, and insecure...

We have come to a clear realization of the fact that true individual freedom cannot exist without economic security and independence... We have accepted, so to speak, a second Bill of Rights under which a new basis of security and prosperity can be established for all—regardless of station, race, or creed.

Among these are:

The right to a useful and remunerative job in the industries or shops or farms or mines of the nation;

The right to earn enough to provide adequate food and clothing and recreation;

The right of every farmer to raise and sell his products at a return which will give him and his family a decent living;

The right of every businessman, large and small, to trade in an atmosphere of freedom from unfair competition and domination by monopolies at home and abroad;

The right of every family to a decent home;

The right to adequate medical care and the opportunity to achieve and enjoy good health;

The right to adequate protection from the economic fears of old age, sickness, accident, and unemployment;

The right to a good education.

All of these rights spell security.

President Franklin D. Roosevelt introducing an Economic Bill of Rights, *annual message to Congress, 1944.*

The largest social programs in the United States, Social Security and Medicare, cost over $640 billion per year and represent more than 35 percent of all federal spending.[2] Neither program is means-tested. A much smaller share of government spending—13 percent—is allocated for means-tested benefits that go to the impoverished or low-income workers exclusively. And many of these programs have become leaner and meaner. The largest means-tested program is Medicaid, which accounts for nearly 7 percent of federal spending. The largest single program in Medicaid pays for long-term care for formerly middle-class people who become poor because of their need for expensive continuing care.

The Bush tax cuts are built into a tax code that already favors the wealthy. High-income households can afford to buy or build larger houses to take advantage of the tax deductions for mortgage-interest payments. The top 20% of earners receive more than two-thirds of the benefits from tax deductions for private retirement savings. About three-quarters of these earners also enjoy employer-provided pension plans, and more than 80% are covered by employer-provided health insurance, both of which receive generous tax breaks. In contrast, fewer than 20% of workers in the bottom fifth of the wage spectrum enjoy employer-provided pension coverage, and fewer than 30% enjoy employer-provided health coverage. Since more than 80% of high school graduates from the richest 20% of families attend college, compared with less than 50% of those from the poorest 20%, upper-income families who would send their children to college anyway also benefit disproportionately from generous tax credits and deductions for college tuition.

Laura D'Andrea Tyson, former chair, Council of Economic Advisers in the Clinton administration, Business Week, July 2, 2001.

Other means-tested programs, including the Earned Income Tax Credit, Food Stamps, Supplemental Security Income and so on account for 6 percent of the federal budget.[3] (See Appendix A for federal expenditures serving low-income people.) We can certainly afford additional social spending targeted to eliminating poverty and assuring basic needs, especially if we don't squander tax revenues and misappropriate public spending, a subject we'll return to later.

In this chapter, we will focus on the Earned Income Tax Credit, health care, child care and housing, and briefly review other key policies such as labor rights. In designing policies, it is crucial to recognize that different households have different problems and preferences in meeting minimum needs. One family may need child care while another may need housing assistance. Another family may not have access to employment-provided health insurance or have the means to purchase family coverage on the private market. Policies and programs must be substantial enough to enable all people to meet their minimum needs and yet sufficiently flexible to allow people to utilize those programs that best suit their needs and preferences.

Expand the Earned Income Tax Credit

The Earned Income Tax Credit (EIC) was enacted in 1975 to help offset rising payroll taxes and make work pay, and has strong bipartisan support. The EIC is a refundable tax credit—even if tax filers have no income tax liability, they receive a refund check for the amount of the credit.

The Earned Income Credit raises more families with children above the poverty line than any other government program. According to the Center on Budget and Policy Priorities, the EIC raised more than 4.7 million people—including 2.6 million children—above the official poverty line in 1999. More than 19 million families and individual workers received credits worth about $31 billion in 2000. The EIC has a strong impact in reducing poverty because it is refundable and well targeted to working households with low wages and disproportionately high payroll taxes. Moreover, "Since most EIC benefits are spent locally, the EIC is an economic development tool for low-income neighborhoods."[4]

The EIC should be a supplement to an $8 minimum wage, not a substitute for it. The $8 wage is set to assure that single adults can meet their minimum needs budget. Employers should be required to pay "a fair day's pay for a fair day's work." The EIC should fill the gap between the $8 minimum wage and the minimum needs budgets for all workers and their families.

The EIC fills the wage-needs gap only partly now. EIC payments gradually increase (phase in) for workers with income up to a certain level and then gradually decrease (phase out) until zeroing out when income passes the highest eligibility level allowed. In 2000, workers who were raising one child in their home and had adjusted gross income up to $27,413 could get an EIC maxing out at $2,353 for those with incomes up to $12,690. Workers who were raising more than one child and had income of up to $31,152 could get an EIC maxing out at $3,888 for those with incomes up to $12,690. (Married couples must file taxes jointly to be eligible for the EIC.) Parents of full-time students under age 24 may also be eligible for the EIC.

Workers who were not raising children in their home but were between ages 25 and 64 on December 31, 2000 and had income below $10,380 could get a small EIC maxing out at $353 for workers with incomes up to $5,765. The EIC for workers without children first took effect in 1994.

A full-time minimum wage worker with no children, making $10,712, is over the 2000 EIC eligible limit. This makes no sense. Even with EIC many families remain below the official poverty line and well below their respective minimum needs budgets.

The 2001 tax cut bill contains several EIC provisions taking effect in 2002, among them expanded EIC eligibility and an increase in benefits for married couples with children and authorization for the IRS to deny claims by noncustodial parents required to pay child support. The income level at which EIC benefits for married filers begins to phase down is being increased to provide so-called marriage penalty relief. The level will increase by $1,000 in 2002, $2,000 in 2005 and $3,000 in 2008. From that point on it will be adjusted each year for inflation.[5] The legislation did not expand the EIC (except for adjustments in the cost of living) for individuals and families without children or for single parents.

REDESIGN EIC TO MEET MINIMUM NEEDS

We propose a substantially more generous EIC, designed to enable individual workers and working families to meet their minimum needs budgets, assuming that adults work full time, year round. The EIC

TABLE 6-1

EIC Benefits for Tax Year 2000 at Selected Income Levels

ADJUSTED GROSS INCOME	EIC FOR WORKERS NOT RAISING A CHILD	EIC FOR WORKERS RAISING ONE CHILD	EIC FOR WORKERS RAISING TWO OR MORE CHILDREN
$500	$40	$179	$210
2,000	155	689	810
4,615	**353**	1,709	2,010
5,765	353	2,049	2,410
6,921	264	**2,353**	2,810
9,721	50	2,353	**3,888**
10,000	27	2,353	3,888
10,379	0	2,353	3,888
10,712	0	2,353	3,888
12,690	0	2,353	3,888
16,640	0	1,724	3,059
21,424	0	957	2,048
27,414	0	0	785
31,153	0	0	0
33,280	0	0	0

Note: Maximum EIC benefits appear in bold. $10,712 = full-time, year-round pay at the $5.15 minimum wage; $21,424 = full-time pay for two minimum wage workers; $16,640 = full-time pay at an $8 minimum wage; $33,280 = full-time pay for two $8-an-hour workers. The other income amounts given in the table include the levels where the EIC reaches the maximum credit level and begins to phase out.

Sources: Internal Revenue Service, 2000; Center on Budget and Policy Priorities, *The Earned Income Credit Campaign 2001 Outreach.*

should be restructured in order to benefit those workers and families who need it most.

Workers eligible for the EIC should have their earned income matched up to a maximum benefit amount, rather than having the credit phase in and phase out in a manner that shortchanges many households. The direct dollar-for-dollar match would benefit workers and families with very low earned income more than the current EIC.

We also propose that workers across a wider income range be eligible for the maximum benefit amount so that workers earning $16,640 per year (annual full-time income at $8 an hour) and households with two minimum wage workers earning $33,280 can meet their minimum needs budgets (as defined in Chapter Two), taking into account any other public subsidies such as child care and housing assistance.

The size of the EIC credit and the income threshold at which work- ers and their families would become ineligible would depend on what other policies existed to assure adequate health care, child care, hous- ing and other basic needs. The expanded EIC would be bigger, for example, in the absence of universal health care.

A drawback of the EIC is that most eligible workers and their families receive it in a lump sum payment once a year. Thus, it does not neces- sarily assist them in meeting their day-to-day needs. The IRS does offer an Advance Earned Income Credit (AEIC) option allowing eligible work- ers to receive partial EIC payments in their paychecks. But it has limita- tions. AEIC payments are available to workers with at least one qualify- ing child who expect 2001 income of less than about $28,245. Workers such as self-employed consultants who do not receive paychecks with tax withholding are not eligible, nor are farmworkers paid on a daily basis. Workers who are not raising children in the home are not eligible.

The Center on Budget and Policy Priorities observes,

> For many workers getting part of their EIC in each paycheck can make a difference in paying the rent, buying groceries, and meeting other day-to-day needs. A worker earning between $490 and $1,000 a month, for example, can get about $50 extra in each bi-weekly pay- check. Employers also benefit from promoting Advance EIC pay- ments—they can help employees increase their take-home pay at no cost to business. This can decrease turnover in the workplace…
>
> The advance payment procedure has built-in protections against overpayment. Normally, workers who choose advance payment can get about half, or less, of the EIC amount they're entitled to for the year. They get the rest as a refund when they file their tax return.[6]

Only about 1 percent of EIC recipients have historically used the advance payment option.[7] Many workers are ineligible or don't know about it. Others fear overpaying and needing to owe the government money at tax time; others prefer a large year-end tax refund. To strengthen the EIC, workers who are not raising children should be eligible for the advance payment option and the government should do a much better job about educating workers and employers about the availability of this option.

The EIC, while the strongest current program that can be used to make work pay for everyone, is still insufficient. Working families without all adults working full time, year round would not be able to meet their needs, even after an increase in the minimum wage and a generous EIC expansion. Programs like universal health care are a more democratic and effective way to meet some crucial needs.

Toward Universal Health Care

For most families, health care is the second highest cost in our minimum needs budgets. About 43 million Americans have no health insurance of any kind, putting their health, lives and livelihoods in jeopardy (as discussed initially in the Overview). That's up from 31 million in 1987. Nearly one out of six people (15.5 percent) were uninsured in 1999 (latest data available). One out of eight people (12.9 percent) were uninsured in 1987.

One out of three people below the official poverty line and one out of four people in households with incomes less than $25,000 are uninsured. More than one out of six workers are uninsured, including nearly half of all full-time workers below the official poverty line.

For many people, a health crisis is also an economic crisis. Indeed, more than half a million families who filed for bankruptcy in 1999 had medical problems, "and more than 300,000—or one in four filers— identified an illness or injury as a reason for filing."[8] A comprehensive study of 1999 bankruptcy filings found that "women heads of household, who are already overrepresented in bankruptcy overall, are particularly hard hit by the financial consequences of medical problems." Moreover, "a household's vulnerability to medical related financial problems increases as the head of the household ages, so that by the time they are 65 nearly half of older Americans in bankruptcy gave a medical reason for their filings."[9]

Most people and their families rely on work-based health insurance. Six out of ten people are covered by private sector employment-based insurance either through their own employment or a relative. (See Table 6-2.) But the share of workers covered by employment health plans drops from 82 percent in the top fifth of wage earners to 69 per-

TABLE 6-2

People With and Without Health Insurance, 1999

COVERED BY PRIVATE OR GOVERNMENT HEALTH INSURANCE*

| | | PRIVATE | | GOVERNMENT | | | | |
	TOTAL COVERED	TOTAL PRIVATE	EMPLOYMENT BASED	TOTAL GOV.	MEDICAID	MEDICARE	MILITARY CARE**	NOT COVERED
In Millions	231.5	194.6	172.0	66.2	27.9	36.1	8.5	42.6
In Percent	84.5%	71.0%	62.8%	24.1%	10.2%	13.2%	3.1%	15.5%

PERCENT OF PEOPLE WITHOUT ANY HEALTH INSURANCE (PRIVATE OR GOVERNMENT)

	ALL	AMONG PEOPLE UNDER OFFICIAL POVERTY LINE
People	15.5	32.4
Men	16.5	35.0
Women	14.6	30.4
AGE		
Under 18 years	13.9	23.3
18 to 24	29.0	45.4
25 to 34	23.2	51.9
35 to 44	16.5	44.8
45 to 64	13.8	36.0
65 years and over	1.3	3.4
RACE AND ETHNICITY		
White, non-Hispanic	11.0	28.0
Black	21.2	28.1
Asian and Pacific Islander	20.8	41.7
Hispanic†	33.4	43.7
HOUSEHOLD INCOME		not applicable
Less than $25,000	24.1	
$25,000 to $49,999	18.2	
$50,000 to $74,999	11.8	
$75,000 or more	8.3	
WORK EXPERIENCE		
Worked during the year	17.4	47.5
Worked full time	16.4	47.5
Worked part time	22.4	47.3
Did not work	26.5	40.8

* Note: The estimates by type of coverage are not mutually exclusive. People can be covered by more than one type of health insurance during the year. Employment-based health insurance is coverage offered through one's own employment or a relative's.

** Includes CHAMPUS (Comprehensive Health and Medical Plan for Uniformed Services)/Tricare, Veterans' and military health care.

† Hispanics may be of any race.

Source: U.S. Census Bureau, *Health Insurance Coverage 1999*, September 2000.

TABLE 6-3

Private Sector Employment-Provided Health Insurance, Percent Covered, 1979-1998

	1979	1989	1995	1998
All workers*	70.2	63.1	59.1	62.9
Men	75.1	66.8	61.6	66.0
Women	62.2	57.9	55.5	58.6
White	71.6	65.8	62.3	66.4
Black	64.1	56.9	53.3	58.4
Hispanic	60.9	46.3	42.3	44.6
WAGE FIFTH				
Lowest	40.7	29.4	27.7	29.6
Second	62.8	54.7	51.3	56.4
Middle	75.9	69.4	63.6	69.0
Fourth	84.0	78.6	74.2	77.6
Top	87.9	83.7	79.1	82.3

* Private sector, wage and salary workers age 18-64, who worked at least 20 hours per week and 26 weeks per year.
Source: Economic Policy Institute, *The State of Working America 2000/2001*, Table 2.15.

cent in the middle fifth to less than 30 percent in the lowest fifth—down from about 41 percent in 1979. (See Table 6-3.)

As summed up by the Employee Benefit Research Institute, "The working uninsured are heavily concentrated in certain segments of the population. In 1998...nearly 90 percent had not received a college diploma, 78 percent worked full time, 20 percent worked in the service industry, 60 percent were employed in small firms or were self-employed, 42 percent earned $7 or less per hour, and 99 percent earned less than $50,000 per year... Health insurance makes a difference in health status and access to health care services. Data show that uninsured workers are more likely than insured workers to report that their health status is fair or poor."[10]

Health coverage differs significantly by firm size. In a study of employment coverage in 2000, the Kaiser Family Foundation finds that 60 percent of firms with 3-9 workers offered health benefits compared with 79 percent of those with 10-24 workers, 87 percent of those with 25-49 workers, 97 percent of those with 50-199 workers, and 99 percent of large firms with 200 or more workers. The report observes, "Firms with many low-wage workers are significantly less likely to offer coverage than companies that pay higher wages. Only a third (35%) of small firms [defined here as firms with less than 200 workers] where more than 35% of the workforce earns less than $20,000 per year offer health insurance."[11]

Unlike the past, when most employers providing health insurance paid the full cost, now workers are expected to pay a large share. By 1997, 69 percent of full-time employees with health benefits in medium and large establishments were required to contribute to the cost of individual coverage (up from 26 percent in 1980) and 80 percent contributed to the cost of family coverage (up from 46 percent in 1980). As of 1996, 52 percent of full-time employees paid part of the individual coverage cost at small establishments and 75 percent did so for family coverage. Employee contribution requirements tend to be higher in low-wage firms. A disproportionate number of low-income workers forgo health insurance due to cost.[12]

Health coverage is good for workers and businesses, including small businesses. As the Employee Benefit Research Institute study of small employers with 2 to 50 workers notes, ".Most employers offer sound business reasons for offering health benefits to workers. Many have found that it helps with employee recruitment and retention, increases productivity, and reduces absenteeism."

Unfotunately, many small employers "are making decisions about whether to offer health benefits to their workers without being fully aware of the tax advantages that can make this benefit more affordable. Fifty-seven percent of small employers did not know that they can deduct 100 percent of their health insurance premiums."[13] Indeed, the deductibility of employer contributions for medical insurance and medical care is the second-largest federal tax expenditure (after employer pension contributions), with a price tag of over $80 billion for Fiscal Year 2001.[14]

FALLING THROUGH THE CRACKS

In recent years, there have been significant state and federal initiatives to expand coverage for low-income children through Medicaid and the State Children's Health Insurance Program (SCHIP), established in 1997. States can use SCHIP funds to increase Medicaid income eligibility limits, establish a separate insurance program for children whose families have incomes somewhat above the state Medicaid limit or combine both approaches. According to the Center on Budget and Policy Priorities, the overwhelming majority of low-income children (defined as those with family income below 200 percent of the official poverty line, which comes to about $28,300 for a family of three) are now eligible for health insurance. Among the 7.1 million uninsured low-income children as of 1999, 6.7 million (94 percent) are eligible for child health insurance using current state eligibility standards.

The problem is that many eligible children remain unenrolled and uninsured because of inadequate outreach and other barriers, and many of their parents are ineligible for public health insurance. Despite recent gains, "Among poor children, Medicaid coverage has fallen since 1995, the year before the federal welfare law was enacted, and the proportion of children who are uninsured has increased. This drop is largely a result of the sharp reductions in welfare caseloads and the ensuing problems in assuring that low-income children and families leaving welfare retain the insurance coverage for which they qualify." Moreover, an additional 3.5 million uninsured children live in families with incomes exceeding 200 percent of the official poverty line.[15]

While one out of four children under the official poverty line lacked any health insurance, one out of two officially poor working parents lacked coverage. Officially poor adults under 65 years old have very low rates of health coverage, ranging from 36 percent to 52 percent uninsured, depending on age. (See Table 6-2.)

Low-income workers without employment-based insurance are not eligible for Medicaid or other publicly funded coverage in most states. The eligibility requirement for Medicaid coverage in many states is well *below* the official poverty level. According to the Center on Budget and Policy Priorities, "Half of all states provide coverage to a working parent with two children only if the parent's earnings fall below roughly $10,000 a year [less than the annual income of a full-time worker at minimum wage], an amount that leaves the family nearly $5,000 below the poverty line... In some states, the eligibility cutoff for parents is lower than this. In Alabama, a parent with two children is ineligible for Medicaid if the parent's earnings exceed $3,048 a year, an amount that leaves the family more than $11,500 below the poverty line."[16]

Many former welfare recipients work in low-wage jobs, precisely those jobs in which employer-based health coverage is not regularly offered. Indeed, early evidence from studies of individuals who have left welfare shows that in at least two states approximately one-third of women leaving welfare were uninsured in the first six months after leaving welfare and one-half of women were uninsured after a year.[17]

Pointing to the coverage and eligibility gaps between parents and their children, the Center on Budget and Policy Priorities highlights "the importance of initiatives under consideration in many states and at the federal level to transform child health programs into family-based programs, that is, into programs that cover parents from low-income working families alongside their children. Although a growing number of states have adopted this strategy, using options under existing Medicaid law, many states are likely to remain unable to do so unless the federal government provides additional funding."[18]

DOING HARM

As noted earlier, the United States spends more of its gross domestic product on health care than any other country. Yet unlike many other nations we leave millions of our people with little or no health care protection. The World Health Organization's *World Health Report 2000* ranks the United States 37th in national performance out of 191 countries.[19] Our system is an unhealthy, inadequate, inefficient patchwork of private and public insurance that wastes billions of dollars in the administration of countless private and public eligibility regulations, incompatible time-consuming forms and procedures, and second-guessing of doctors by insurance gatekeepers trained in cost-cutting, not medicine.

In the words of Physicians for a National Health Insurance Program:

> The United States spends more than twice as much on health care as the average of other developed nations, all of which boast universal coverage. Yet over 42 million Americans have no health insurance whatsoever, and most others are underinsured, in the sense

---

Most of the public, and many policymakers and opinion leaders, believe that Medicaid offers a health care safety net for all low-income people. Not only is this myth grossly inaccurate, it also discourages corrective action...

In 40 states, non-parent adults...are ineligible for Medicaid—even if they are penniless—unless they are severely disabled.

FamiliesUSA, The Health Care Safety Net: Millions of Low-Income People Left Uninsured, *July 2001.*

that they lack adequate coverage for all contingencies (e.g., long-term care and prescription drug costs).

Why is the U. S. so different? The short answer is that we alone treat health care as a commodity distributed according to the ability to pay, rather than as a social service to be distributed according to medical need. In our market-driven system, investor-owned firms compete not so much by increasing quality or lowering costs, but by avoiding unprofitable patients and shifting costs back to patients or to other payers. This creates the paradox of a health care system based on avoiding the sick. It generates huge administrative costs, which, along with profits, divert resources from clinical care to the demands of business. In addition, burgeoning satellite businesses, such as consulting firms and marketing companies, consume an increasing fraction of the health care dollar...

Our private health insurers and HMOs now consume 13.6 percent of premiums for overhead, while both the Medicare program and Canadian [National Health Insurance] have overhead costs below 3 percent. Our multiplicity of insurers forces U.S. hospitals to spend more than twice as much as Canadian hospitals on billing and administration, and U.S. physicians to spend about 10 percent of their gross incomes on excess billing costs.[20]

It defies common sense and decency to have a health care system that assures universal coverage for our elders, but not our children: The uninsured rate is just 1.3 percent for people over 65, but 13.9 percent for children. And, while an improvement, it's no solution to build a system for insuring all children, but not young adults and the middle-aged.

The old saying, "An ounce of prevention is worth a pound of cure," couldn't be truer when it comes to health care. Yet our government allows millions of people to fall through the cracks of preventive and acute care when they are young and middle-aged, ensuring they will be unhealthier and more dependent (and costly) when they reach eligibility for Medicare.

One person's health can affect many others. Yet in this highly mobile era of increased vulnerability to epidemics, we have economic disincentives for people to seek and obtain early diagnosis and treatment of contagious diseases. When people don't finish full-course antibiotic treatments it promotes the growth in drug-resistant bacteria, yet antibiotics are often very expensive, causing people to cut doses or stop treatment early.

In the words of the American College of Physicians, "The lack of health insurance has important health and financial consequences for

> The remuneration provided to top-level executives of the largest managed health care companies—in terms of both annual compensation and unexercised stock options—is extraordinarily high. This report examines compensation in the year 2000 for the highest-paid executives of the 10 for-profit, publicly traded companies that own health plans serving multiple states. These include: Aetna, Inc.; CIGNA Corporation; Coventry Health Care, Inc.; Health Net, Inc.; Humana, Inc.; Oxford Health Plans, Inc.; PacifiCare Health Systems, Inc.; Sierra Health Services, Inc.; UnitedHealth Group Corporation; and WellPoint Health Networks...
>
> The highest-paid health plan executive in each of the 10 companies received average compensation *exclusive of unexercised stock options* of $11.7 million... The health plan executive with the largest value of unexercised stock options in each of the 10 companies had stock options worth, on average, $68 million in 2000...
>
> While managed care and insurance companies claim that patient protections will be too costly for consumers, they demonstrate a double standard about costs when it comes to top executives' compensation.
>
> *FamiliesUSA*, Healthy Pay for Health Plan Executives, *June 2001.*

individuals and the nation. Millions of Americans are unable to receive the care they need, which endangers the health and lives of all patients, adds cost to the health care system, and reduces productivity."[21]

Behind all the policy debate, the reality is that people suffer and die for lack of health coverage. We shouldn't lose sight of that. Members of Congress have publicly financed health care—everyone should.

"Living without health insurance," says Sandra Adamson Fryhofer, president of the American College of Physicians-American Society of Internal Medicine, "is a serious health risk that needs to be treated with the same sense of urgency as...drunk driving."[22]

SHORT-TERM AND LONG-TERM SOLUTIONS

Most Americans believe that everyone should have health insurance coverage whatever their income or job. Health care is an area where government policy can provide a humane and cost-effective solution to a terrible problem. We propose options to expand health coverage now to all low-income Americans while working towards the universal coverage we need.

Expand Medicaid: Health care coverage should be provided without delay to low-income single adults and families through an expansion of the Medicaid program. Expanding Medicaid builds on the existing Medicaid and SCHIP programs and national and state initiatives to transform children's health programs into family health programs serving low-income parents and children.

We need to improve Medicaid as we expand it. As a physicians' group observes: Today's Medicaid "offers second-class coverage. Programs like Medicaid that segregate the poor virtually assure poor care, and are more vulnerable to funding cuts than public programs that also serve affluent constituencies. In most states, Medicaid payment rates are low and many doctors resist caring for Medicaid patients."[23]

Medicaid expansion and improvement would cost money initially, but it would save money in a variety of ways. There are efficiencies from having more individuals and families with adequate health care coverage. For example, people would benefit from timely and appropriate primary and preventive care practices, reducing their need for acute care. With adequate access to other medical care, there would be less reliance on hospital emergency rooms. Government support for health care for low-income workers would also benefit small businesses, which pay higher premiums and have less bargaining power with insurance companies.

Universal Health Insurance: Expanding Medicaid is a practical partial solution, but not a cure to our health care problems. The cure is universal health care, a reality in every major industrialized nation besides the United States.

Universal health care takes many different forms in countries around the world—e.g., publicly financed multi-payer insurance systems in France and Germany, national health services in Great Britain and Spain, and single-payer systems in Sweden and Canada. Different proposals have been made for universal coverage here.[24]

Universal health coverage won't come easy in this country, but neither did Social Security or Medicare, upon which so many Americans depend today. Medicare faced years of determined opposition before being enacted. In the words of Dr. Marcia Angell, spokesperson for the Physicians' Working Group for Single-Payer National Health Insurance and former editor of the *New England Journal of Medicine*, it is a "self-fulfilling prophecy" to say that "a single payer system is a good idea, but politically unrealistic." With that kind of defeatism we never would have had Social Security, the minimum wage or many other advances.

Many proposals for universal health care build on Medicare, which now covers about one out of seven Americans, and call for expanding it to the entire population. In recommending "Medicare for All," the Economic Policy Institute notes that the Medicare benefits package would "need to be fully modernized to include prescription drugs, preventive care, improved mental health and substance abuse services, and better cost sharing."[25]

One of the major current proposals for universal coverage is the *Proposal of the Physicians' Working Group for Single-Payer National Health Insurance.* In addition to Doctor Angell, the Physicians' Working Group also includes, among others, Doctors Quentin Young, national coordinator for Physicians for a National Health Program (which has over 9,000 members) and past president of the American Public Health Association; Joel Alpert, past president of the American Academy of Pediatrics; Ron Anderson, CEO of Parkland Health & Hospital System; Christine Cassell and Gerald Thompson, past presidents of the American College of Physicians; Elinor Christiansen, president of the American Medical Women's Association; Rodney Hood, president of the National Medical Association, representing black physicians; and Peter Beilenson and Walter Tsou, respectively commissioners of the Baltimore and Philadelphia Health Departments.

The Physicians' Working Group proposal calls for the creation of a comprehensive National Health Insurance (NHI) Program "that builds upon the strengths of the current Medicare system... A single public plan would cover every American for all medically-necessary services including: acute, rehabilitative, long term and home care, mental health, dental services, occupational health care, prescription drugs and supplies, and preventive and public health measures." Under the Working Group plan:

> Most hospitals and clinics would remain privately owned and operated, receiving a budget from the NHI to cover all operating costs. Investor-owned facilities would be converted to not-for-profit status, and their former owners compensated for past investments. Physicians could continue to practice on a fee-for-service basis, or receive salaries from group practices, hospitals or clinics.
>
> A National Health Insurance Program would save at least $150 billion annually by eliminating the high overhead and profits of the private, investor-owned insurance industry and reducing spending for marketing and other satellite services. Doctors and hospitals would be freed from the concomitant burdens and expenses of paperwork created by having to deal with multiple insurers with different rules—often rules designed to avoid payment. During the transition to an NHI, the savings on administration and profits would fully offset the costs of expanded and improved coverage.[26]

> A universal health system is not "socialized" medicine. It is a financing mechanism. Physicians and hospitals would still be in the private market and patients would have the freedom to choose their physician or hospital... Calling this "socialism" is comparable to saying we have "socialized" parks, streets, police, fire departments, schools, courts and mail delivery.
>
> *Center for Policy Alternatives, 1999.*

Care Giving

While many other countries have reshaped their child care policies to reflect changing realities, our child care policies are stubbornly rooted in the past. They are a relic of two historical phases: the long period of time when most Americans lived and worked on the farm and relatively short period during the 20th century when most children lived in families with "breadwinner" fathers and "homemaker" mothers. As Jody Heymann writes:

> From the founding of the United States until the mid-1800s, most children were raised in farm families in which both parents worked at home. In 1830, 70 percent of children lived in farm families, and only 15 percent had a father who was a wage earner. As the industrial revolution progressed, the number of families in which the father was a wage earner began to rise. In the 1880s, for the first time in U.S. history, being raised in a family in which the father earned a wage or salary outside the home and a mother did not was more common than being raised in a family in which two parents worked on a farm. By the 1920s, the majority of children were growing up in families in which the father worked outside the home, and by 1930, only 30 percent lived in farm families.
>
> Although women had been among the first Americans to work in factories when the industrial revolution got under way in the early 1800s, unmarried women made up the majority of the women's labor force... While women of color had begun working in the paid labor force before white women had, they too showed significantly different work patterns for single and married women...
>
> The limited labor force participation by married women in the 1800s and early 1900s was neither an accident nor a result of women's choices. Openings for men and women were advertised separately, many jobs barred women, many others explicitly barred married women, and employers could legally discriminate against women in

hiring [and doubly so against women of color]. It was not until World War II—when large numbers of women were needed to fill the jobs held by men who had gone to war—that a dramatic decline in discrimination against married women occurred in hiring.[27]

In recent decades, women have joined the paid workforce in larger numbers, propelled by wider opportunity forged by the feminist movement, a rise in single motherhood and the decline of real wages that saw the single-earner "family wage" give way to the two-career household. Work requirements under welfare reform mean that even more mothers of very young children are joining the labor force.

In 1960, 38 percent of women were in the paid workforce. Now, 60 percent of women are in the paid workforce. For women with children under 6, the labor force participation rates are 68 percent for single women and 62 percent for married women. For women with children ages 6 to 17, the rates are 83 percent for single women and 77 percent for married women. About 85 percent of mothers employed before childbearing now return to work before their child's first birthday. Only 29 percent of married-couple families and 21 percent of all families with children under 18 fit the stereotypical 1950s family of a breadwinner father and a homemaker mother who cares for the children and does not work outside the home.[28]

Looking at child care, parental leave and school policies, you would think working mothers were still a minority. You would also think kids have three parents: two parents with jobs to pay the bills, and another parent to be home in mid-afternoon when school lets out. After-school programs are scarce, as are affordable summer programs. This is harmful to children and to society.

When society needed a sudden influx of women into the workforce during World War II, government put its weight behind child care and industry adapted. Societal images of women quickly changed to reinforce their role in wartime industry—and changed again to undermine their role in postwar industry and society. As Susan Faludi writes in *Backlash*: "Rosie the Riveter was revered and, in 1941, Wonder Woman was introduced." Women protested for equal pay and expanded child care, and overwhelmingly voiced their intention to keep their jobs in peacetime. When the war ended, so did the supportive images of women workers. Women were abruptly purged from higher-paid industrial jobs and the government shut down wartime child care centers and eliminated federal funding for child care.

"Employers who had applauded women's work during the war," says Faludi, "now accused working women of incompetence or 'bad attitudes'—and laid them off at rates that were 75 percent higher than men's... The rise in female autonomy and aggressiveness, scholars and government officials agreed, was causing a rise in juvenile delinquency and divorce rates—and would only lead to the collapse of the family. Child-care authorities...demanded that wives stay home."[29]

Judging by government policies today, child caring is not in the public interest. The government does have one highly successful child care policy however—for families serving in the military. Uncle Sam Wants Rosie the Riveter in the military and the factory, but he treats civilian Rosie's children quite differently.

In the late 1980s, the military's child care system was considered a disaster. In recognition of the impact poor quality child care had on recruiting, motivation, productivity and retention—and hence military readiness—the military turned its system around, following passage of the Military Child Care Act of 1989 mandating improvements. In the words of the National Women's Law Center report, *Be All That We Can Be: Lessons from the Military for Improving our Nation's Child Care System*, "The military runs what it calls the 'largest employer-sponsored child care program in the country,' serving over 200,000 children daily at over 300 locations in the world... More impressive than the sheer scale...is its success in offering a comprehensive approach that, according to a variety of analyses and accounts, provides high quality, affordable care."[30]

A key element in improving quality was increased staff compensation and training. The Military Child Care Act requires that the rates of pay for child care workers be equivalent to other employees at the same installation with comparable training, seniority and experience. Staff turnover went from 300 percent annually to less than 30 percent.[31]

Outside the military, child care policy is rooted in the belief that choosing to become a parent is a private matter, and that addressing child care needs is primarily an individual responsibility. Most working families are on their own. The lack of adequate public child care assistance inevitably means that for many children, child care is of poor quality. Conservatives justify their objections to government-financed child care programs by saying that children are better off with their mothers, while simultaneously insisting that poor single mothers receiving public assistance have paid jobs.[32]

In the modern economy, Ann Crittenden observes, two-thirds of wealth is created by human capital—human skills, creativity and enterprise. Raising children, when viewed through this lens, is "the most important job in the world," and certainly something worthy of government support.[33] The societal good of raising children is embedded in family-friendly social policies in many other countries. "The United States...stands out among industrialized countries for its paucity of public child care assistance."[34]

> The writers and scholars and politicians who wax most rhapsodic about the need to replace welfare with work make their harsh judgments from the comfortable and supportive environs of offices and libraries and think tanks. If they need to go to the bathroom midsentence, there is no one timing their absence. If they take longer than a half-hour for lunch, there is no one waiting to dock their pay. If their baby sitter gets sick, there is no risk of someone having taken their place at work by the next morning. Yet these are conditions that low-wage women routinely face, which inevitably lead to the cyclical nature of their welfare histories.
>
> *Rosemary L. Bray*, New York Times Magazine, *November 8, 1992.*

A number of important proposals are being advocated to address the child care needs of working parents and support the nurturing and education of the next generation of Americans. In the long run, we advocate the development of a universal child care and early childhood education system that allows all families to have access to affordable, high quality child care, combined with paid family and medical leave following birth or adoption. Current child care subsidies include tax credits—which are mostly nonrefundable and therefore don't benefit low-income families—and direct subsidies. We examine existing policies and make recommendations for improvements, recognizing that some solutions may be politically easier to implement than others.

PAID FAMILY AND MEDICAL LEAVE

In 1993 Congress passed the Family and Medical Leave Act (FMLA), under which firms with at least 50 employees were required to allow employees 12 weeks of unpaid, job-protected leave each year for childbirth, adoption or to care for a seriously ill family member. For most Americans, the Act is a pipe dream. Many workers cannot afford to take unpaid leave, and about half the workforce isn't covered because they are employed in small firms.

The United States is one of the few countries in the entire world without a national paid maternity leave program. The Nordic countries have the strongest programs; Norway and Sweden provide 80 to 100 percent wage replacement for up to a year following the birth of a child. One hundred and thirty countries have leave policies, according to a study by Sheila Kamerman, director of the Institute for Child & Family

Policy. Just three of those countries—Ethiopia, Australia and the United States—provide only unpaid leave.[35]

Recent Labor Department regulations allow states to pay unemployment benefits to workers who have babies or adopt children and five states provide limited public Temporary Disability Insurance (TDI) programs. About half the states are currently considering family leave benefits legislation.[36] As a vehicle for paid family leave, unemployment insurance will be of little or no benefit to many low-wage workers who don't work enough hours during the year or earn enough to qualify for benefits, a subject to which we'll return. Under the Pregnancy Discrimination Act, "If an employee is temporarily unable to perform her job due to pregnancy, the employer must treat her the same as any other temporarily disabled employee; for example, by providing disability leave or leave without pay."[37] A study by the Institute for Women's Policy Research found that TDI benefits average only $170 to $200 per week and the duration of benefits ranged from 5 to 13 weeks.[38]

We need to work towards a universal system of paid family leave. A 2000 survey found that 84 percent of adults, including 89 percent of parents of young children, support expanding disability or unemployment insurance as a vehicle for paid family leave. The National Partnership for Working Families' Campaign for Family Leave Benefits has brought together a wide range of experts and organizations to take a closer look at options. In addition to unemployment insurance and state and private disability insurance policies, they are looking at the possibility of subsidies for new parents who take time off, or offering tax credits to make family leave more affordable.[39]

IMPROVE THE CHILD TAX CREDIT

The Child Tax Credit is available for taxpayers raising dependent children under 17 years old. It is not directly related to child care expenses. In most cases, if a family's income is so low they don't owe

Instead of slogans about family values, we need policies that value families. No one should have to choose between caring for family members and being able to support them. Yet many people face that dilemma—and will continue to do so until family leave is available and affordable for every worker.

Ellen Bravo, codirector of 9 to 5, National Association of Working Women, author correspondence, March 19, 2001.

federal income taxes, they won't receive a Child Tax Credit—no matter what they may have paid in payroll taxes.

Under the recent tax-cut bill, the child tax credit is going up from $500 per child to $600 in 2001, $700 in 2005, $800 in 2009 and $1,000 in 2010. The credit should be raised immediately to $1,000. The tax credit is becoming partly refundable in 2001 for families earning more than $10,000 a year. This will help about 15 million children (who would have received nothing without the refundable provision) and lift 500,000 children above the official poverty line.[40]

For 2001-2004, the child tax credit is refundable up to 10 percent of the amount by which the family's earnings for the year exceed $10,000. In 2005 and later years, this increases to 15 percent. In 2001, when the credit is $600 per child, a family with two children making $15,000 would be entitled to a credit of $500 (10 percent of $5,000). A single parent making the full-time minimum wage of $10,712 would get a refundable credit of only $71. Someone making less than $10,000 would get zero. The maximum credit is currently available to single parents with incomes up to $75,000 and married parents filing taxes jointly with incomes up to $110,000; the credit gradually phases out above those amounts.

Why should families who earn $110,000 get a credit, but not families earning $9,999, whether or not they have federal income tax liability? Why shouldn't families who earn the least and need the credit the most get it? The credit should be fully refundable for all low-income families. If the credit was made fully refundable for families with little or no income tax liability, more than 2 million children would be lifted above the official poverty line.[41] The Caregivers Credit Campaign is advocating making the credit fully refundable, increasing the amount so it more closely resembles the actual cost of giving care and expanding eligibility to include caregivers of those who are disabled, elderly, or suffering from a serious illness.[42]

RAISE THE DEPENDENT CARE TAX CREDIT

Child care is a big expense for working families with children. For our minimum needs budgets we found that child care costs average about $4,600 annually for a child under 5 (1999) and accounts for roughly 15 to 20 percent of the budget for families with children. Care for school-age children accounts for an additional 8 to 10 percent of the needs budgets for families with children 5 and older. The cost of school-age care inhibits its use by low-income families. Low-income families may not have the income to afford the fees charged for school-age care and subsidy programs for school-age care are limited.[43]

For many families, child care is as expensive as a community or state college—and child care expenses make saving for higher education that much more daunting. In Boston, for example, annual child care costs average $8,121; tuition at a public college averages $4,012.[44]

Current government efforts to subsidize child care costs through tax policy are modest. The Dependent Care Tax Credit (DCTC), which subsidizes families who need care for a child or dependent adult incapable of caring for themselves in order to work or look for work, received a modest increase as part of the recent tax cut package—the first increase, even for inflation, since 1981.[45] The DCTC is not refundable.

Child care credits always sound bigger than they actually are. They turn into the incredible shrinking tax credit when you sit down to do your taxes because taxpayers receive fractions of qualifying expenses, not the full amount. Beginning in 2003, the credit will increase from a maximum percentage of qualifying expenses of 30 percent to 35 percent, and the limits on qualifying expenses will increase from $2,400 to $3,000 for one dependent and from $4,800 to $6,000 for two or more dependents. Thus the maximum credit will increase from $720 for one child to $1,050 (35 percent of $3,000) and from $1,440 for two or more children to $2,100 (35 percent of $6,000). At the same time the income at which the maximum credit can be claimed will be increased from $10,000 to $15,000. For families with incomes above $43,000, the credit will be based on 20 percent of their child care expenses up to the qualifying limits, just as it is now.

Why should the Dependent Care Tax Credit be capped at 35 percent of $3,000 for one child while the mortgage interest deduction isn't capped until the amount of the home or vacation-home mortgage reaches $1 million? Are vacation homes more important to society than children? Why should businesspeople be able to write off much more on their taxes for meals and entertainment than parents can deduct for child care? It makes no sense.

Current DCTC amounts don't come close to covering private child care costs, but they can ease the burden on families. Because the DCTC is nonrefundable, the benefits accrue largely to middle- and high-income taxpayers and not to low-income families who may have little or no income tax liability. In 1998, families in the bottom fifth received just 8 percent of the $2.5 billion in DCTC tax assistance while families in the top fifth received 21 percent. In 1997, less than one-fifth of the benefits went to families with adjusted gross incomes below $25,000.[46]

The maximum allowable expenditures on child care for the purpose of claiming the Dependent Care Tax Credit should be increased, with a cap high enough to accommodate reasonable child care expenses in high-cost urban areas (minus any other child care subsidies). Recall that in Boston, for example, the average was $8,121 for one child. We propose that families earning less than 250 percent of the official poverty line receive a maximum credit (depending on their actual child care expenses) of 100 percent of the maximum child care benefit (varying by number of children). After that the maximum benefit would scale down as incomes rose.

Child care costs should be regularly evaluated and the maximum benefits adjusted accordingly. This is especially important because we must support higher wages for child care workers. The Dependent Care Tax Credit should be fully refundable so that low-income working families fully benefit from the credit. Ten states have refundable dependent care tax credits: Arkansas, California, Colorado, Hawaii, Iowa, Maine, Minnesota, Nebraska, New Mexico and New York.[47] There should be an adequate advance DCTC option to help parents make child care payments throughout the year, complementing an improved Advance EIC.

EXPAND THE CHILD CARE AND DEVELOPMENT FUND

The Child Care and Development Fund (CCDF) was established under the Personal Responsibility and Work Opportunity Reconciliation Act of 1996 (PWRORA). This Fund combined four pre-existing federal child care programs into one funding stream, the Child Care and Development Block Grant (CCDBG). In FY2001, CCDF made $4.5 billion available to states for child care assistance to low-income families.[48] Under PRWORA, states are no longer required to guarantee child care assistance for welfare recipients needing child care to accept or retain employment or participate in education or training activities. But the 1996 law does prohibit states from reducing or terminating assistance to single parents with children under 6 if the parent is unable to comply with work requirements due to the unavailability of child care.

Typically, child care subsidies are available through certificates or vouchers that permit families to purchase child care from a provider of their choice from an approved list. States set the rates at which providers are reimbursed and establish sliding fee scales to determine a family's contribution to the cost of care. Providers in 24 states are permitted to charge parents an additional amount above the copayment if their rates exceed the state reimbursement level. States are also required to set aside funds to improve quality of care and to ensure that providers meet health and safety requirements.[49] In many states, these health and safety requirements are terribly inadequate.

States have broad discretion in implementing child care subsidies under PRWORA. States may use CCDF Funds for families with incomes up to 85 percent of state median income, but only nine states have done so. In seven states, the maximum eligibility level is less than half of state median income. Families with incomes above $20,000 are ineligible in ten states and families with incomes above $25,000 are ineligible in half of the states.[50] The maximum subsidy levels are set too low.

We spend about $10 billion a year in federal and state funds (not including tax credits) to assist low-income families in paying for child care. This includes vouchers for parents to pay for child care, and contracts for spaces in child care facilities that are set aside for low-income children. This level of appropriations covers only 12 percent of the children eligible for such help (despite costs being subsidized by the paltry pay of child care workers). An estimated $15 billion a year would be needed to fund care for all children currently eligible under CCDF rules—a simple and modest goal. However, many families whose incomes are above the eligibility guidelines would remain in need.[51] The income eligibility thresholds should be raised.

UNIVERSAL CHILD CARE OPTION

Even as we recommend immediate steps be taken to improve existing child care assistance policies, in the longer run we advocate universal affordable child care through a more comprehensive system. For example, Barbara Bergmann recommends replacing the Child Care and Development Fund and the Child and Dependent Care Tax Credit with a comprehensive federal plan for universal, high-quality care. Utilizing a sliding scale, low-income parents would pay little or nothing for child care, while others would pay a fraction of the amount their income exceeds the poverty line. She recommends that the program offer after-school care for children up to 12 years old.[52]

The two-phase system of child care developed in France and Belgium provides an interesting model to draw on. Care for younger children is provided in full-day child care centers and some publicly supervised family child care programs. Starting at age $2\frac{1}{2}$ or 3, children typically attend full-day preschool programs, which are part of the educational system. Enrollment of young children in child care centers is 30 percent in Belgium and 24 percent in France; preschool attendance is nearly universal.[53]

OFFER UNIVERSAL PRE-KINDERGARTEN FOR 3- AND 4-YEAR OLDS

Universal pre-kindergarten, like universal public school, can provide quality early childhood education while simultaneously helping working parents in need of child care. Numerous studies have demonstrated the positive impact of early intervention programs on later

> Other nations have demonstrated that economies can thrive while basic family benefits are universally provided... Belgium, Denmark, and Finland all guarantee child-care coverage for infants to 2-year olds. Sweden guarantees a long parental leave period and then offers child care for those children 18 months and older; France for those 2 years old and older. As a result, while only 14 percent of American 3-year-olds are in publicly funded child care, 95 percent are in Belgium, as are 85 percent in Denmark, 95 percent in France, 78 percent in Germany, 88 percent in Italy, and 79 percent in Sweden...
>
> We can afford the needed changes; what we cannot afford is to continue our current practices.
>
> *Jody Heymann*, The Widening Gap.

school success.[54] In 1998, only 42 percent of children between the ages of 3 and 5 living in families earning less than $15,000 were enrolled in pre-K, compared with 65 percent of children in families earning more than $50,000.[55]

The well known Head Start program provides quality education and health check-ups for over 900,00 children. But it reaches only half of all eligible children and is only part day, a problem for working parents. It also requires parents to attend some sessions. While parent involvement is good for everyone, many low-income working parents don't have employers that allow them the time it requires.[56]

Edward F. Zigler and Matia Stevenson suggest linking child care and public education as in their Schools for the 21st Century program. Under this program, the public education system would offer full-day child care for children 3 and 4 years old as well as before-school, after-school and vacation care for school-age children. The concept has been implemented in over 400 schools in 13 states. Zigler and Stevenson estimate that the program costs states between $26 million and $54 million for start-up and $3.7 billion in ongoing operation support.[57]

We support moving towards universal pre-K for all children beginning at age 3. Universal pre-K extends our society's commitment to public education. Delivery mechanisms could include public schools, existing preschools and other child care providers that meet quality standards.

Public pre-K programs, primarily aimed at 4-year-olds, are becoming more available but generally are not universal. Georgia has the most comprehensive full-day program, financed through a state lottery. Forty-two states now have some form of pre-K initiative, with the majority open to a broad range of providers, including child care programs and Head Start agencies.[58] Universal pre-K would ensure that all working families have access to affordable, quality education and care for young children.

CARE FOR SCHOOL-AGE CHILDREN

There is an increasing need for child care services for school-age children, including before- and after-school care as well as summer care, as more adult family members enter the labor market. Research shows that quality school-age care positively impacts children's academic performance, socialization and development. After-school programs also enhance community safety and well-being. No parents should have to leave their preteen children home unsupervised for lack of income. According to the Children's Defense Fund, "In 2000, about 31.6 million children between the ages of 6 and 17 lived in families where the mother was in the labor force. Nearly 7 million children are left home alone each week."[59]

Federal funding for after-school programs is now part of the inadequate Child Care Development Fund. President Bush's proposed CCDF budget for FY2002 contains $400 million for an After School Certificate Program.[60] This amount is woefully inadequate and should be increased significantly.

The average cost of care for school-age children is about $3,000 per year, a significant amount for working families, especially those who struggle to meet their minimum needs. Public financing of before- and after-school programs as well as vacation care could be developed as an expansion of the public education system—as in the Schools for the 21st Century program, for example. Again private providers should not be crowded out, but quality, affordable care would be available to all working families who need it.

> On school days, 3-6 p.m. are the peak hours for teens to commit crimes [and] kids to become crime victims... Experts note the importance of after-school programs to reducing teen crime; a recent survey of police chiefs showed that nine out of ten chiefs said America could greatly reduce crime by expanding educational child care programs and after-school programs.
>
> *U.S. House Democratic Policy Committee,* The Bush Budget Shortchanges Programs Important to Women, *May 10, 2001.*

RAISE CHILD CARE WAGES

Child care teachers, entrusted with the physical, intellectual and emotional development and well-being of our nation's children, are grossly underpaid. As we saw earlier, child care workers typically earn about as much as parking lot attendants and much less than animal trainers.

Child care centers have difficulty attracting and retaining experienced professionals and are sometimes forced to hire people with virtually no training. Turnover is high. Children lose the caregivers they have become attached to, and centers must bear administrative burdens caused by staff shortages and continually hiring and training new workers. Longtime child care teachers make a tremendous financial sacrifice to stay in the profession.

Because of parents' inability to pay more, improving the quality of child care jobs and the quality of care is highly dependent on greater public investment. Public subsidies should be linked to higher wages and benefits, and to providing access to training and education for child care workers. The Center for the Child Care Workforce advocates public and private financial support for training and increased pay or bonuses for workers who meet training standards and agree to remain in the industry.[61]

Unionization has long been the best route to improved wages and benefits for workers. Labor unions have been increasingly successful at organizing service workers, particularly in sectors that are funded by the government. Local chapters of the American Federation of State, County and Municipal Unions (AFSCME) and the Service Employees International Union (SEIU) are organizing child care workers in Seattle, Philadelphia, New York and Boston. One union strategy to raise quality is to negotiate with employers to establish "career ladders" and pay workers more who have met training and education standards. But it will be difficult to significantly increase wages and benefits without simultaneously increasing government funding and targeting some of those funds to training and education.[62]

Linking publicly subsidized pay increases entirely to training and education, however, would leave many child care workers out, including many relatives, nannies, and family-day-care providers. All child care providers should get a decent wage and have access to training and education, with scholarships for low-income providers.[63]

To assure fair pay for child care workers, we recommend a wage pass-through of at least one dollar above our recommended $8 federal minimum wage. Pay increases and bonuses tied to training and education standards should be over and above that, and any such requirements must address the question of access to the courses necessary to meet the standards.

"A Decent Home"

More than half a century ago, Congress passed the National Housing Act with the goal of assuring a decent home and suitable living environment for every American family. Congress reaffirmed this policy in 1968, declaring, "The highest priority and emphasis should be given to meeting the housing needs of those families for which the national goal has not become a reality."[64]

Instead of making housing a priority, the Reagan and Bush I administrations slashed the funding. Federal funding for low-income housing was cut by a devastating 80 percent from 1978 to 1991, adjusting for inflation. While there has been some recovery since then, the housing budget is still about 60 percent (adjusting for inflation) lower than it was in 1977.[65] President George W. Bush's FY2002 housing budget, "has modest increases in a few areas, flat funding in a few more, and cuts to some others, including public housing and homeless assistance, two of HUD's programs that serve the poorest people."[66]

The goal of assuring a decent home for every American family has grown more distant. As the Center on Budget and Policy Priorities reported, "In 1970, the number of low-cost rental units exceeded the number of low-income renters by 300,000. By 1995, there were only 6.1 million low-rent units for the nation's 10.5 million low-income renter households, a shortage of 4.4 million units."[67]

The Department of Housing and Urban Development reports that 4.9 million very low-income households (with 10.9 million people, including 3.6 million children) had "worst case needs" in 1999. These are households without housing assistance with incomes below 50 percent of the local area median income who pay more than half of their income for housing (rent and utilities) or live in severely substandard housing. The nearly 5 million households with worst case needs do not

> **M**ost sewing machine workers live together. We either share an apartment or a house. That is the only way that we can make ends meet.
>
> *Silvestre Cristobal, sewing machine operator, quoted in Los Angeles Alliance for a New Economy,* **The Other Los Angeles.**

> **H**ere in Silicon Valley, you can visit houses where every room plus the garage houses a family—not a worker, a family.
>
> *Amy Dean, director of Working Partnerships USA, quoted in* **Mother Jones,** *September/October 2000.*

include people who are homeless or living in shelters. Eight out of ten "nonelderly, nondisabled" households with worst case needs have earnings as their primary source of income.[68]

The generally accepted standard of housing affordability established by Congress and HUD is that housing should cost no more than 30 percent of income. Yet, three out of four working poor renters spend more.[69] The latest survey of cities by the U.S. Conference of Mayors found that "low-income households spend an average of 51 percent of their income on housing."[70] Even at a wage of $8 per hour, 30 percent of annual income would equal $4,992, or $416 a month—considerably less than the annual rent of even a one-bedroom apartment at the HUD Fair Market Rent.

The National Low Income Housing Coalition reports that almost half of all renter households and one-fourth of all owner households have either moderate or severe housing problems; 40 percent of renters faced cost/affordability problems compared to 20 percent of owners.[71] The affordable housing crisis has been driven by rents increasing at 1.5 times the general inflation rate and home purchase prices rising at twice the inflation rate coupled with low-wage jobs and severely inadequate government housing programs.[72]

By 1999, for every 100 renter households with incomes below 50 percent of the local area median income there were only 70 units that were affordable and available (either vacant for rent or already occupied by very low-income renters). There were only 40 affordable and available units for every 100 extremely low-income renter households with incomes below 30 percent of the local median (that's approximately where the official poverty line lies).[73]

The affordable housing crisis has taken a big toll. On any given night, some 750,000 people are homeless; many more are the "hidden homeless," missed in varied counts. Over the course of a year, some 2 to 3.5 million people experience homelessness for some period of time. More than one-third of the homeless are families with children.[74]

In its 2000 survey of 25 major cities, the U.S. Conference of Mayors found that requests for emergency shelter by homeless families had risen 17 percent during the past year; 27 percent of the requests went unmet. In half the cities, "families may have to break up in order to be sheltered." The Mayors also found that more than a fourth of the homeless were employed.

The Mayors' report observes, "Lack of affordable housing leads the list of causes of homelessness identified by the city officials. Other causes cited, in order of frequency, include low paying jobs, substance abuse and the lack of needed services, mental illness and the lack of needed services, domestic violence, poverty, and changes and cuts in public assistance."[75]

There is a boom market in homelessness... They are children, hundreds of thousands of them, twice as likely to repeat a grade or be hospitalized and four times as likely to go hungry as the kids with a roof over their heads... Not since the Great Depression have this many babies, toddlers and kids had no place like home...

Twenty years ago, when the story of the homeless in America became a staple of news reporting, the solution was presented as a simple one: affordable housing. That's still true, now more than ever...

"Give me your tired, your poor," it says on the base of the Statue of Liberty... Oh, but they are already here, the small refugees from the American dream, even if you cannot see them.

Anna Quindlen, Newsweek, March 12, 2001.

HOUSING ASSISTANCE NOW MOSTLY FOR THE HAVES

The biggest government support for housing comes in the form of the tax deduction for mortgage interest on owner-occupied first and second homes. Much of the tax write-off goes to higher-income families. Incredibly, the more you can already afford to spend—up to a cap of $1 million (previously $5 million)—the more the government subsidizes you.

Tax-paying low-income renters actually subsidize the vacation homes of high-income homeowners. As the *New York Times* reported in 1999, for each dollar in tax savings from the mortgage-interest deduction "going to the average taxpayer making $200,000 or more, the average taxpayer in all lower income groups combined saves just 6 cents."[76]

Most low-wage workers cannot afford to purchase homes and take advantage of the mortgage interest and property tax deductions that significantly reduce net housing costs for homeowners, nor do they benefit as homeowners do from the capital gains exclusion on home sales. Taking all housing benefits (including tax expenditures as well as rental and other assistance) into account, 63 percent go to households in the top fifth of the income distribution compared to 18 percent for the bottom fifth. Less than 20 percent of households in the bottom fifth receive housing assistance.[77]

For the fiscal year ending September 30, 2001, the mortgage deduction adds up to about $61 billion. That's double the total spending by the Department of Housing and Urban Development; more than 4 times the Section 8 rental assistance budget; and 19 times as much as the Low-Income Housing Tax Credits provided to develop-ers of affordable housing.[78]

"Fewer than one out of four families eligible for all forms of federal rental assistance [including public housing, Section 8 vouchers, etc.] actually receives it," HUD reports."[79] Unlike the mortgage interest deduction, federal rental assistance is means-tested and subject to appropriations so inadequate that most eligible people don't receive help. Waiting lists for housing assistance are often years long.

Section 8 housing vouchers address affordability by providing a subsidy for eligible renters equal to the difference between 30 percent of a household's income and the payment standard established by the local public housing authority, according to HUD guidelines (the range is 90-110 percent of the fair market rent, but exceptions are allowed). However, numerous barriers exist. Currently, there are far fewer vouchers in circulation than the number of households with worst case housing needs.

Even with a voucher in hand, a family may not be able to use it. If an available apartment exceeds the payment standard, a tenant must pay the additional rent, up to 40 percent of her or his income—despite the government's own affordability standard of 30 percent of income. In tight housing markets there may be no apartments available that meet even the 40 percent requirement, thus making the voucher unus-able. In addition, landlords often illegally discriminate against voucher holders.[80]

To make matters worse, HUD has adopted a new "Mark to Market" policy to mainstream the more than 1 million subsidized pri-vate rental units with Section 8 contracts (expiring in the next ten years) into the conventional real estate market without subsidies or use restrictions. This policy "is the antithesis of preservation of exist-ing affordable housing."[81]

It is essential we strengthen the Section 8 voucher program by increasing voucher numbers and payment amounts to reduce the cost of housing for low-income families and also facilitate the transition of families off welfare. There also needs to be greater encouragement of landlords to participate in the program, and enforcement of prohibi-tions against housing discrimination. The National Housing Institute estimates that housing vouchers for all eligible low-income households would cost about $50 billion dollars a year—much less than the cost of the very popular mortgage interest deduction and small potatoes com-pared to recent tax cuts.[82]

However, a concerted program to increase the affordability of hous-ing for low-income families is insufficient if little is done to increase the availability of affordable housing. In the words of former HUD

> **I**t did not escape my attention, as a temporarily low-income person, that the housing subsidy I normally receive in my real life—over $20,000 a year in the form of a mortgage-interest deduction—would have allowed a truly low-income family to live in relative splendor. Had this amount been available to me in monthly installments in Minneapolis, I could have moved into one of those "executive" condos with sauna, health club, and pool.
>
> *Barbara Ehrenreich,* Nickel and Dimed.

Secretary Andrew Cuomo, "Housing vouchers alone are not a housing program for the nation. We also need to produce units... We need a production program that works."[83]

NATIONAL AFFORDABLE HOUSING TRUST FUND

The National Low Income Housing Coalition (NLIHC) is calling for the establishment of a National Affordable Housing Trust Fund for the production of new housing and preservation or rehabilitation of existing housing that is affordable for low-income people. The initial goal of the Fund is to produce, rehabilitate and preserve 1.5 million units of housing by 2010. Related legislation has been introduced in Congress.[84]

The Trust Fund would be capitalized in part with excess revenues generated by the Federal Housing Administration (FHA)—above what the FHA needs to maintain 3 percent capital in reserves—and Ginnie Mae, the Government National Mortgage Association.[85] NLIHC recommends that other sources of revenue be identified from other federal housing programs and additional appropriations be made, if necessary, to meet the goal.

The Trust Fund would be used primarily for rental housing, with 15 to 25 percent of the funds used for homeownership assistance serving low-income people. Households would pay no more than 30 percent of their incomes toward rent, and the housing funded through the Trust Fund would be required to remain affordable for the useful life of the property. States, localities or nonprofit organizations receiving Trust Fund assistance would be required to match the federal funds. New housing production and financing would be done in such a way as to prevent segregation by income groups.

The Trust Fund is intended to expand the supply of housing, not supplant existing programs, and the NLIHC recommends substantial increases in the HOME Investment Partnership Program (intended to support local affordable housing strategies), Community Development Block Grant and Rural Housing Programs (under the U.S. Department of Agriculture), as well as examination of ways to reform the Low Income Housing Tax Credit program to improve access by a wider range of nonprofit, community-based housing developers. In recent decades, community-based groups have made important progress in developing affordable housing and revitalizing neighborhoods, using a range of housing funding and models, including subsidized mortgages and downpayment assistance funds, community land trusts, limited-equity cooperatives, mutual housing associations, sweat equity, resident management, nonprofit rentals and so on.[86]

RACE, EQUITY AND HOMEOWNERSHIP

"Homeownership has long been a central part of the American dream," the Children's Defense Fund observes. "It is also a major source of financial security and stability for young families, and an essential means of accumulating the equity that has enabled countless families later to borrow money in order to stave off a crisis, send a child to college, or help start a family business."[87]

The homeownership rate reached 67.4 percent of households in 2000. But, only half the households with income less than the median income owned homes while more than three quarters of those above the median did. The homeownership rates for households headed by someone less than 55 years old were lower in 2000 than in 1982.[88]

Because of employment, housing, insurance and other discrimination, black and Latino families are far less likely than whites to own the homes in which they live. The 2000 homeownership rate was 73.8 percent for non-Hispanic white households, 47.2 percent for blacks and 46.3 percent for Hispanic households.[89]

In the words of *Shifting Fortunes*, "Back when the government was heavily involved in the housing business, the beneficiaries were mostly white Americans, giving them an unfair advantage in buying homes—an advantage that has reinforced the asset gap between whites and people of color to this day. Whites benefited directly by having higher rates of ownership and, indirectly, through the college educations, businesses and inheritances that home equity helped pay for."[90]

The Federal Housing Administration was created in 1934 to provide guaranteed mortgages for new construction. The GI Bill of 1944 provided Veterans Administration (VA) loan guarantees to subsidize home mortgages for returning veterans, almost all in heavily segregated suburbia. The FHA and VA programs insured about one-third of all homes purchased in the 1950s.[91]

"All through the 1930s and 1940s," explains political scientist Dennis Judd, "FHA administrators advised and sometimes required developers of residential projects to draw up restrictive covenants against nonwhites as a condition of obtaining FHA-insured financing." The U.S. Supreme Court ruled in 1948 that racial covenants could not be enforced, but de facto segregation continued. "Between 1946 and 1959, less than 2 percent of all the housing financed with the assistance of federal mortgage insurance was made available to blacks," writes Judd.[92]

While blacks and other people of color were kept out of suburbia, they were "redlined" in the cities. A 1968 National Commission on Urban Problems deplored the "tacit agreement among all groups—lending institutions, fire insurance companies, and FHA"—to redline inner city neighborhoods, denying them credit and insurance.[93]

Housing discrimination has remained a problem through the present, as numerous reports by HUD, the Federal Reserve Board, regional Federal Reserve Banks, the Urban Institute, ACORN and other governmental and nonprofit organizations and investigative reports have shown. In 1999, for example, the *Kansas City Star* analyzed mortgage applications taken by more than 500 area banks and mortgage companies from 1992 to 1997. As reported by Ted Sickinger, a former commercial loan officer, "lenders still reject minority mortgage applicants far more frequently than they do whites. Even high-income minorities are rejected more frequently than whites with lower incomes."

Moreover, "most loans made in minority neighborhoods refinance existing debt and are made by companies that often charge higher interest rates and fees. In white neighborhoods, by contrast, most loans are made at market rates and go to buy homes—the kind of lending that helps borrowers build wealth." Unlike the overt redlining of the past, the *Kansas City Star* found "discrimination with a smile."[94]

As the HUD report, *Unequal Burden*, found, "predatory lending is making homeownership far more costly for blacks and poor families than for whites and middle-class families."[95] Unfortunately, predatory lending and home equity loan scams, where homeowners are swindled and foreclosed, are among many ways low-income communities end up paying literally or proportionately more than higher-income communities for banking, credit, housing, insurance, transportation, food, health care and other goods and services.[96]

We need much better enforcement of fair housing laws and the Community Reinvestment Act—which requires fair banking practices in low-income neighborhoods—and significantly increased support for community-based initiatives to revitalize neighborhoods.

Unions and Labor Laws

Union jobs typically provide much better wages and benefits than nonunion ones. The median weekly wage of a full-time worker who belonged to a union in 2000 was $696, compared with $542 for those who did not.[97] That's an annual wage differential of $8,008, not including significantly better health, pension and other benefits paid to union members.

For women and people of color the union "premium" is even more significant, as seen in the table below. For women, the median annual union differential is $7,488 while for men it is $6,188. For black workers, the union difference is $8,320. For Latinos, it is $10,764, which is more than the total pay of a minimum wage worker.

Unions are good for worker livelihoods and also good for business productivity. As *Business Week* reported, in the 1970s "many executives believed that unions inflated prices by lifting wages above some presumed market level. Since then, however, more than 50 quantitative studies have concluded that the higher productivity of unionized companies offsets most of their higher costs."[98]

It is no coincidence that union membership has fallen, and no coincidence that wages and benefits dropped along with union membership. Union jobs disappeared under waves of downsizing, outsourcing, globalization and union busting. With weaker unions, conservative business and political groups were more successful in their efforts to roll back government social services.

President Reagan—who purposely let the minimum wage shrivel without a raise—green lighted union busting when, in 1981, he fired striking air traffic controllers. According to an analysis of National Labor Relations Board (NLRB) figures cited in *Business Week*, "employers illegally fired 1 of every 36 union supporters during organizing drives in the late 1980s, vs. 1 in 110 in the late '70s and 1 in 209 in the late '60s... Unlawful firings occurred in one-third of all representation elections in the late '80s, vs. 8% in the late '60s... 'Even more significant

> **F**ew American managers have ever accepted the right of unions to exist, even though that's guaranteed by the 1935 Wagner Act. Over the past dozen years, in fact, U.S. industry has conducted one of the most successful antiunion wars ever, illegally firing thousands of workers for exercising their rights to organize.
>
> Business Week, *May 23, 1994.*

TABLE 6-4
Median Weekly Pay for Full-Time Workers by Union Affiliation, 2000

	UNION MEMBERS	NON-UNION	52 WEEK UNION DIFFERENCE
All workers	$696	$542	$8,008
Men	739	620	6,188
Women	616	472	7,488
White	716	565	7,852
Men	757	641	6,032
Women	631	482	7,748
Black	596	436	8,320
Men	619	479	7,280
Women	564	408	8,112
Hispanic	584	377	10,764
Men	631	394	12,324
Women	489	346	7,436

Source: U.S. Bureau of Labor Statistics, *Employment and Earnings 2000*, January 2001.

than the numbers is the perception of risk among workers, who think they'll be fired in an organizing campaign,' says Harvard law professor Paul C. Weiler. Indeed, when managements obey the law, they don't defeat unions nearly as often."[99]

Business Week highlighted the link between declining union membership, on the one hand, and lower wages and benefits and widening income disparities on the other: "The resulting drag on pay for millions of people accounts for at least 20% of the widening gap between rich and poor." Weakening unions are "a key reason for the six-percentage-point slide in the 1980s in the share of employees with company pension plans, for the seven-point decline in those with employer health plans, and for a 125-fold explosion in unlawful-discharge suits now that fewer employees have a union to stick up for them."[100]

Only 13.5 percent of workers are union members now, down from 16.1 percent in 1990, 21.9 percent in 1980, 27.3 percent in 1970, 31.4 percent in 1960 and 35.5 percent in 1945.[101]

It is essential that government support the right of workers to organize. The National Labor Relations Act, passed by Congress in 1935, gives workers the right to form and join labor unions and to bargain collectively with their employers. It is illegal for employers to "interfere with, restrain, or coerce" workers who are trying to organize or join a

> **W**ith the possible exception of Hong Kong and South Korea, the U.S. provides workers with less legal protection than any other industrialized country... [It] has the smallest proportion of workers covered by collective bargaining agreements.
> The U.S. has become a cheap labor haven for global capital looking for low wage and benefit costs, high productivity, and a nonunion environment... For example, German firms such as BMW, Adidas, Siemens, and Mercedes are moving into the Carolinas, where huge tax breaks are available and the unionization rate is below 5%.
> *Labor Research Association*, American Labor Yearbook 1993.

union, but in reality, says Human Rights Watch, many such workers are "spied on, harassed, pressured, threatened, suspended, fired, deported or otherwise victimized in reprisal for their exercise of the right to freedom of association."[102]

Employers illegally fire workers who are trying to form unions in about a third of organizing campaigns. Half of all employers threaten to shut down if employees vote for a union. Enforcement of existing labor law is weak. Fired workers who believe their rights have been violated can file unfair labor practice charges with the National Labor Relations Board. However litigation can drag on for years, complaints are issued in fewer than 15 percent of cases, and remedies are frequently as inadequate as posting a notice promising not to repeat unlawful conduct and paying back pay to the worker fired for organizing. Back pay amounts are often small since the worker's earnings from another job in the interim period are subtracted from the award.[103]

There must be tougher consequences for employers who fire workers illegally. When an NLRB investigation finds merit and a complaint is issued, the worker should be reinstated while the case goes through the hearing and appeal process. Back pay awards should be paid in full without subtracting interim earnings. Substantial fines and punitive damages should be added when employers willfully break the law.

In most cases voting on whether to form a union is conducted under the supervision of the NLRB after workers file a petition seeking an election. Too often these NLRB elections are rampant with employer actions to discourage workers from voting for a union. Eighty percent of employers hire consultants to run anti-union campaigns. Employers frequently use "captive audience" meetings to actively discourage workers from joining unions, including group meetings and one-on-

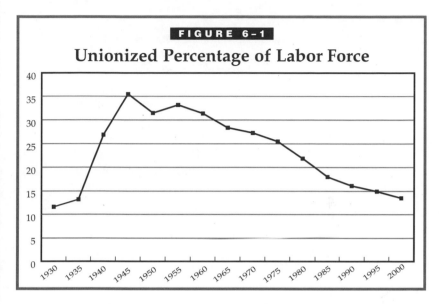

FIGURE 6-1

Unionized Percentage of Labor Force

one meetings between supervisors and employees. Government should encourage use of the nonconfrontational card-check system in which a union is recognized if a majority of workers sign cards showing that they support the union as their bargaining agent. This system is already used on a voluntary basis when employers agree to it. When sufficient safeguards are in place to ensure that the cards are signed voluntarily, it is an effective way to avoid worker intimidation that often accompanies NLRB-supervised elections.[104]

Even after workers succeed in winning a union, employers may use delaying tactics to avoid negotiating a contract. Refusing to bargain in good faith is prohibited by existing labor law, but is common. One-third of the time that workers win an NLRB election, their employer never negotiates a contract with them. Going through the motions of negotiating without any real intention of reaching an agreement is called "surface bargaining," but can be very difficult to prove. This problem is particularly extreme in workplaces that are newly organized and where employers put up fierce opposition during the election process. There should be stronger penalties, including punitive damages, for employers' willful refusal to bargain in good faith. In those instances where workers have formed a new union in a previously unorganized workplace and the employer is found to bargain in bad faith, third-party arbitration should be used to produce a contract.[105]

Undocumented immigrant workers, fearing deportation, are particularly vulnerable to various forms of retaliation for labor organizing. While current immigration law contains employer sanctions for hiring

> [In 1999] unions posted their largest absolute membership gain in 20 years, adding 265,000 new members and pushing the total number of unionized workers in the U.S. to 16.5 million...
>
> Los Angeles has emerged as the unlikely national epicenter of labor organizing, adding 90,000 new union members in 1999. Most prominent was the unionization of 74,000 home health care workers with the Service Employees International Union (SEIU), the largest single union victory since Ford's River Rouge plant was organized in 1941. But organizing successes have included a dizzying range of industries and occupations. Physicians at County-USC Hospital, casino staffers at local card clubs, non-studio workers in the film industry, teaching assistants at UCLA, and over 85 percent of the workers at the new Staples Center all became unionized in 1999. And in the spring of 2000, an earthquake called "Justice for Janitors" rumbled through the office towers of Los Angeles, winning the largely immigrant members of SEIU Local 1877 a greatly improved contract, national recognition and the admiration of Angelenos.
>
> *Los Angeles Alliance for a New Economy,*
> *The Other Los Angeles.*

undocumented workers, the law is selectively enforced. Employers who profit by exploiting undocumented workers with the lowest pay and unpaid overtime, turn around and threaten to call the Immigration and Naturalization Service (INS) to have workers deported for trying to form or join a union. Immigrant workers are often afraid to bring unfair labor practice charges or testify in NRLB proceedings because they fear their status will be questioned.[106] The INS has a discretionary policy not to conduct raids while an NLRB election is pending. This should be a mandatory policy. NLRB rules should prohibit the questioning of an immigrant worker's status during NLRB investigations or proceedings.

Wage and hour laws require workers to be paid a minimum wage and to be paid overtime (time and a half) for work in excess of 40 hours per week. Wage and hour law violations are rampant in certain industries such as agriculture, janitorial services and low-wage manufacturing. According to the Office of the California Labor Commissioner, garment contractors have a history of 80 percent noncompliance with labor laws, and the problem is apparently getting worse.[107] Adequate enforcement is essential to protect workers as well as a law-abiding employers who are being undercut by unfair competition.

"Contingent workers" in nonstandard jobs such as temps, contract workers, leased workers, on-call workers, day laborers and part-time workers typically receive lower pay and benefits than regular full-time workers who do the same job. Indeed, many workers have found themselves suddenly reclassified from regular to contingent employees by companies reorganizing and outsourcing to save money. Contingent workers are excluded from coverage by many employment and labor laws, and lack an effective right to organize a union and bargain collectively. Laws should be reformed to prevent discrimination on the basis of employment status, work schedules or site of work.[108]

Workplace injuries kill over 6,000 U.S. workers every year. An additional 6 million people experience nonfatal workplace injuries. In the words of the Occupational Safety & Health Administration (OSHA), "Many workplace injuries and illnesses are predictable and preventable. Workplaces must be encouraged to make breakthrough improvements in injury and illness rates."[109]

Repetitive stress injuries are widely considered the biggest work-

A century ago, the workers who were victimized in [New York City's] sweatshops were primarily Jewish and Italian immigrants. Today, they are primarily Chinese immigrants. That's about all that has changed in a sub-economy based on subjugation...

But aren't there laws to protect these people? Yes, and those laws are consistently broken. The minimum wage is not paid. There is no extra money for overtime... They must toil seven days a week. And some of them are mere children...

As for safety regulations, The News found that fire doors are routinely blocked or locked. Just as they were back in 1911 when the Triangle Shirtwaist fire in Manhattan killed 146 young women. My, how far we have come...

The solution to all this? Enforcement, enforcement, enforcement... Each must receive the minimum wage. Overtime must be paid for work beyond 40 hours a week. There must be no children working... If a fire door is chained, take the owner out in handcuffs.

Editorial, New York Daily News, *July 9, 2001.*

There are currently hundreds of community residents, mostly women of color, working as "substitute" teachers assistants and substitute school bus monitors—many of whom have been in these positions for three, four, and even five years. The School Department classifies these workers as "substitute," but in reality, most of them are in the same classroom or the same school bus route working with the same students day after day, month after month. The workers now make $7.65 an hour and receive no benefits, while those who are in permanent positions doing the same work make over $10 an hour, receive health insurance, a pension and professional development.

[Prompted by DARE], the School Department made an agreement with Laborers Local 1033 to give a small pay raise to substitutes in September, and to fill all vacant teacher assistant positions by October 15, by making current "substitutes" permanent.

Direct Action for Rights & Equality (DARE),
press release, Providence, RI, October 23, 2000.

place safety problem in the country. Some 1.8 million such injuries occur each year, including neck aches, back sprains, tendonitis, and carpal tunnel syndrome, costing about $50 billion in medical bills and sick days. These painful injuries account for one-third of all serious injuries and many can be prevented through reducing ergonomic hazards such as adjusting keyboard heights and revamping assembly lines.[110] Women are 64 percent of those injured each year, although they make up only 46 percent of the workforce.[111]

In 1990, the first President Bush's Labor Secretary Elizabeth Dole called for developing rules to reduce repetitive stress injuries. After a decade of study and debate, President Clinton put OSHA ergonomics rules in place in January 2001. According to OSHA, the rules would cost $4.5 billion to carry out and save health and money by preventing nearly 500,000 injuries a year.[112] At the urging of the second President Bush, Congress voted to repeal these rules in March 2001. The repeal must be reversed.

UNEMPLOYMENT INSURANCE

Obviously, you can't earn wages if you can't find a job. Government policies should promote full employment—the long ignored other mandate of the Federal Reserve Board. Full employment means a job for everyone who needs one, not 6 or 4 percent unemployment. But to make matters worse for the unemployed, unemployment insurance is not ensured. In recent years only about a third of all officially unemployed workers received any unemployment insurance (UI) benefits, and they received less than half of their former weekly wages in benefits. In most states, UI benefits are limited to 26 weeks, whether the person has found work or not.[113]

According to a General Accounting Office (GAO) report, "In the past 5 decades, many states have tightened their UI regulations, increasing limitations on eligibility... For instance, when the UI program was first established, people who quit their jobs for compelling personal reasons, such as pressing family obligations like lack of child care, were not disqualified from receiving UI benefits... [Now] most states disqualify a claimant for UI if he or she quit a job because of a temporary lack of child care." Many states do not allow workers to receive UI if they leave their jobs because of sexual harassment or domestic violence.

Low-wage workers and contingent workers are less likely than others to qualify for unemployment benefits. The GAO reports, "From 1992 to 1995, low-wage workers were twice as likely to be out of work as higher-wage workers but only half as likely to receive UI benefits."

States have made it harder to collect UI by raising minimum earnings and work time requirements and disqualifying those looking for part-time work. According to the GAO, "In eight states, working 20 hours a week for 6 months at the minimum wage would be insufficient to qualify an unemployed worker for benefits." As is often the case with government policy, UI provides less help to those who need it most. "For example, a worker in Florida earning the minimum

> **I**t's so hard to get out of bed. How I battle in the morning to open my hands. Tell me, who will hire me with hands like these?
>
> *Gloria Palomino, searching for a job after being laid off from a chicken processing plant, quoted in*
> **Los Angeles Times, March 7, 2001.**

> **T**his has been an all-out effort that involves virtually the entire Washington business community.
>
> *Michael Baroody, chief lobbyist for the National Association of Manufacturers, on the successful GOP effort to kill ergonomic workplace protections, quoted in*
> **Congress Daily, March 7, 2001.**

wage of $5.15 per hour must work 660 hours to qualify for UI, while a worker earning $10.00 per hour would need to work a little over one-half as long to qualify."[114]

Women leaving welfare suffer greatly under these restrictions. According to the GAO, "While many welfare recipients joined the labor force and became employed during the latter half of the 1990s, many in low-wage jobs, it appears that they experienced higher than average unemployment rates. According to Department of Health and Human Services Data, about 30 percent of those with jobs during the late summer 1998 were no longer employed by January 1999. Unemployment rates for former welfare recipients entering the labor force in 1996 and 1997 have been estimated as high as 35 percent and 33 percent, respectively."[115]

Unemployment benefits should be increased substantially and UI should cover workers seeking part-time work and workers quitting jobs for "good cause" like family care responsibilities and domestic violence. Low-wage and contingent workers should not face discrimination in the form of overly restrictive minimum earnings and work time requirements.[116]

Pay Equity

E mployment discrimination is a form of theft. Laws prohibiting discrimination on the basis of race, gender, age and disability should be strongly enforced. Further, Congress should pass legislation prohibiting employment discrimination on the basis of sexual orientation as proposed in the Civil Rights Amendments Act of 2001.

A significant gap persists between men and women's earnings—despite the fact that equal pay has been the law for nearly four decades. The Equal Pay Act of 1963 prohibits unequal pay for equal or "substantially equal" work. Title VII of the Civil Rights Act of 1964 prohibits wage discrimination on the basis of race, color, sex, religion or national origin. This applies to situations even when the jobs are not identical, as the Supreme Court made clear in 1981.[117] As we saw in Chapter Five, full-time women workers make only 72 percent of what men earn. Working families lose $200 billion annually because of unequal pay—an average of more than $4,000 per family.[118]

One reason the pay gap still exists is because many women and people of color work in traditionally female occupations such as sales, clerical and service jobs, including jobs women historically performed without pay in the home such as child care and cleaning. These jobs pay less than traditionally male occupations that require similar levels of education, skill level and responsibility. Men who work in female-dominated jobs also experience direct pay losses.

Numerous states have enacted pay equity legislation. Pay equity means eliminating gender and race discrimination and setting wages based on legitimate job requirements. "A study of 16 state government pay equity programs, conducted by the Institute for Women's Policy Research, found that in most of the states most of the workers who benefited were women, but in two states, Connecticut and Oregon, 51 percent of those who received pay equity increases were men."[119] Federal legislation such as the Fair Pay Act, introduced in the House and Senate but not passed, would "expand the Equal Pay Act's protections against wage discrimination to workers in equivalent jobs with similar skills and responsibilities, even if the jobs are not identical."[120]

Education and Training

I deally, everyone should have access to lifelong, high quality learning opportunities, from early childhood on. Free, universal public education is one of the bedrocks of a nation's ability to provide equal opportunity to its citizens and to provide a well-educated workforce to support a strong, innovative economy.

Education is often portrayed as the great ladder out of poverty, and sometimes it is. But the school system is rigged in favor of the already privileged. The so-called public school system is heavily weighted against low-income students because of reliance on property taxes for funding—and increasingly on a school's ability to collect activity fees and fundraise, and its willingness to treat its students as captive audiences for corporate advertising and product sales linked to school dollars.

"Typically," writes Jonathan Kozol, "very poor communities place high priority on education, and they often tax themselves at higher rates than do the very affluent communities," but the higher rates cannot offset the income gaps.[121] And, like the mortgage interest deduction, the property tax deduction subsidizes higher income people the most.

Children of color and low-income whites are tracked by race and income into the most deficient and demoralizing schools and classrooms. While in high-income school districts, kids take well-stocked libraries, laboratories and state-of-the-art computers for granted, many poor schools are rationing ludicrously out-of-date textbooks in overcrowded, crumbling facilities.

Two fundamental principles should guide an expanded state and federal role in education policy: assuring equity across race and class lines, and providing public schools with the resources to make needed improvements and sustain effective programs. As with child care and early childhood education, salaries are an important factor in attracting and retaining high quality teachers, which in turn has a big impact on the quality of education.

Education and training play a critical role in improving incomes. For example, while women full-time workers who did not graduate from high school earned a median income of $17,015 in 1999, high school graduates made $23,061. Women with an associate degree made $30,919 while women with a bachelor's degree made $37,993; women with a masters made $48,097 and women with a doctorate or professional degree earned about $60,000. For men working full time, the comparable figures are $25,035, $33,184, $41,638, $52,985, $66,243, $81,687 for a doctorate and much more for a professional degree.[122]

A college degree is becoming as important for decent wages as a high school degree once was, but economic barriers stand in the way. "Even as a good education has become the litmus test in the job market," said *Business Week* in 1994, "the widening wage chasm has made it harder for lower-income people to get to college. Kids from the top quarter have had no problem: 76% earn bachelor's degrees today, vs. 31% in 1980. But less than 4% of those in bottom-quarter families now finish college, vs. 6% then."[123]

During the 1980s and 1990s, as tuition costs skyrocketed, student financial aid came increasingly in the form of loans, not grants, making it even harder for low-income students to go to college. Between 1990 and mid-1997, students borrowed at least $140 billion—more than total student borrowing over the prior three decades combined.[124] The Nellie Mae National Student Loan Survey (Nellie Mae, a subsidiary of the nonprofit Nellie Mae Foundation, is one of the nation's largest student loan providers), found that large numbers of respondents said that because of their student loan payments they had dropped out of undergraduate school, decided against graduate school, changed career plans, or delayed buying a house, purchasing a car or having children. Students of color who did not complete a degree were more likely than white students to say that loans had prevented them from staying in school. About 70 percent of people of color gave this response compared to 43 percent of white borrowers. Forty percent of the overall undergraduate population said that their undergraduate debt had prevented them from attending graduate school.[125]

The 1944 GI Bill of Rights gave millions of Americans the chance to go to college—many the first in their family. Individuals, families and society all gained. Today, the federal government should greatly expand needs-based grants and refundable tuition tax credits so that college is affordable to everyone. That's good for our democracy and our economy.

> [The GI Bill of Rights] benefited millions of returning G.I.s in their effort to readjust to civilian life by making available temporary unemployment relief, guaranteeing insured loans for homes, farms, and businesses, and paying for education. The educational benefits in the bill probably had the widest effect: more than half the nation's World War II veterans, or 7,800,000 availed themselves of its opportunities during the twelve years it was in operation. The program cost upwards of $14 billion, but few if any have ever doubted that this vast sum was an excellent investment.
>
> *The Annals of America: 16, 1940-1949,*
> *Encyclopedia Britannica, 1968.*

WELFARE REFORM UNDERMINES EDUCATION— AND LABOR RIGHTS

Studies that have tracked welfare recipients who completed two- or four-year degrees have found that 90 percent of these graduates leave welfare and earn far more than other recipients.[126] But the 1996 welfare reform Personal Responsibility and Work Opportunity Reconciliation Act (PRWORA) places a strong emphasis on quickly finding a job—any job—at the expense of training and education. Never mind that training and education are key to achieving long-term financial independence.

PRWORA allows only limited vocational training of less than 12 months for a small portion of recipients to count under work participation rules. A shift in focus in welfare-to-work programs from building people's education and job skills toward "work first" strategies promoting quick job placement has sharply curtailed access to postsecondary education and training for welfare recipients. A recent GAO report on welfare reform in seven states found that the percentage of adult welfare-to-work participants involved in education and training dropped by 31 to 83 percent in the states studied.[127] Colleges have seen dramatic impacts on their student bodies. At the City University of New York, for example, the number of enrolled students receiving public assistance has declined from 28,000 (10 percent of the student body) to only 10,000.[128]

Instead of education, the welfare act encourages workfare, assigning recipients to "work off their benefits" by doing jobs such as sweeping city streets, cleaning public agency bathrooms or clerical work at private agencies. Less than 4 percent of workfare participants end up employed in regular jobs, and those that do find jobs tend to find only short-term minimum wage jobs.[129]

To make matters worse, workfare is being used to displace higher paid unionized public workers from their jobs. New York City is a prime case in point. By 1998, four years after Rudolph Giuliani was elected mayor, city payroll had been reduced by 20,000 employees, who were replaced by 34,100 poorly paid, poorly treated so-called Work Experience Program workers.[130]

Workfare is not an updated Depression-era Works Progress Administration (WPA) or a substitute for full employment. By creating a large category of sub-minimum wage workers and displacing higher-paid workers, workfare undermines unions and puts downward pressure on wages generally. Welfare reform should be reformed to encourage education and regular employment with decent wages and benefits and full labor rights. At the same time, a public benefits system must provide adequate support for those who can't work or can't find a job, including those whose employment history makes them ineligible for disability or unemployment benefits.

JOB TRAINING

The welfare "work first" strategy implies that people will receive ongoing training once employed that will allow them to increase their skills and earn better wages and benefits. Employers provide training on the job to less than one-third of full-time workers, and most of this training is aimed at higher-level managerial and technical employees. With the understanding that continuous learning increases productivity, some employers are creating job ladders that enable low-wage workers to advance to higher paying jobs requiring stronger skills.[131] Government-funded job training programs should support on-the-job training that helps low-wage workers advance, and ensure that all students, including welfare recipients, can participate in vocational training programs of sufficient scope to prepare them for higher-paying jobs.

Women in particular benefit from programs that provide training and support for higher wage nontraditional occupations (occupations in which women—or men—hold 25 percent or less of the jobs). Nontraditional jobs typically pay 20 to 30 percent more than jobs traditionally held by women.[132] Programs aimed at displaced homemakers and single parents are also important for overcoming barriers to employment.[133] Job training programs aimed at nontraditional jobs, displaced homemakers and single parents must be adequately funded and promoted.

By filling a spectrum of jobs—from feeding hospital patients to painting park benches to translating at welfare centers—workfare participants have quietly become an important, but unofficial part of New York City's municipal work force...

"We're doing the same job as regular workers, but we're not getting paid for it," said Ms. Mathis, the Health Department cleaner, who works 24 hours a week and receives not wages but a $124 welfare check every two weeks and Medicaid coverage...

Workfare participants typically receive $5,000 to $12,000 a year in benefits, depending on their rent and the number of children they have. In contrast, a civil service janitor or clerk earns about $20,000 a year, and a civil service painter, $40,000.

Steven Greenhouse, New York Times, *April 13, 1998.*

The federal government has sued the Giuliani administration, charging it with doing too little to protect women in workfare jobs from sexual and racial harassment by their supervisors...

In the past, the Giuliani administration has said that welfare recipients in the city's workfare program were not employees and had no legal rights to protection from sexual discrimination or sexual harassment in the workplace.

Steven Greenhouse, New York Times, *July 15, 2001.*

Savings and Investment

Our minimum needs budgets do not include savings or investment for college education, retirement or other purposes. They are minimal budgets, not desirable budgets. Yet building assets is essential to long-term economic security. As *Shifting Fortunes* observes, "Asset-building policies have been an integral part of U.S. history, from the Homestead Act in the 19th century to the mid-20th century GI Bill that allowed millions of Americans to have debt-free college educations to current homeownership and retirement subsidies through the tax code."[134]

We have talked about the importance of expanding government support for education and housing, two traditional pillars of asset building. We have talked about the importance of higher wages. Government should also strengthen Individual Retirement Account (IRA) programs, for example, so that they are more helpful to low- and middle-income families and expand support for Individual Development Account (IDA) programs.

IDAs have broader uses than IRAs and are targeted to low- and moderate-income households to assist them in asset building. Participants in IDAs may have their contributions matched by public or private dollars. Participants can withdraw funds from IDAs in order to purchase a home, invest in education or job-training, or finance a small business. A number of private charities have financed pilot IDA programs through community-based organizations.

Through the Assets for Independence Act (AFIA) of 1998, the federal government authorized the Department of Health and Human Services to conduct a five-year IDA demonstration, through which grants are made to nonprofit organizations. Nonprofit organizations administer the program and raise their own matching funds, up to $1 million, in order to receive federal money. While the AFIA received strong bipartisan support, Congress only recently funded the program at $25 million.[135] That's a drop in the bucket compared to programs disproportionately benefiting higher-income Americans such as the mortgage interest deduction, property tax deduction and capital gains exclusion on home sales.[136] The future success of IDA programs depends upon greater government contributions and additional tax policy changes that promote investment on the part of financial institutions and individuals alike.

7

■ ■ ■ ■ ■

Turning Point

We will go backward unless we go forward...

We have had great changes, but they have been the changes which had to come if our people were to have a chance for full development. To be sure some of the things were very new; now they seem very old. I can remember when we started old-age pensions. Now the idea is not very shocking to us—a mutual contribution towards this security in old age...

We believe that together we should strive to give every individual a chance for a decent and secure existence; and in evolving our social patterns we are trying to give both hope for better things in the future and security from want, as far as possible, in the present.

Eleanor Roosevelt, 1955.[1]

We are at a turning point in our nation's history. Will we build on the legacy of the New Deal—or undo it? Will we widen the road to equal opportunity—or narrow it? Will we take the high road to progress?

Public opinion is clear. Poll after poll shows strong support for raising the minimum wage, taking poverty out of full-time work and implementing effective policies to assure adequate housing, child care, nutrition, education, job training and public works, even if this requires higher taxes. Americans want a strong government role in reducing poverty. Americans support the right to universal health care.[2]

Yet our government has gone backward, not forward. The minimum wage is a poverty wage. Millions of Americans are deprived of

> ### We Cannot Afford Not To Invest In Our Children
>
> A dollar invested in good early childhood programs for low-income children saves $7.00.
>
> A dollar spent in the Women, Infants and Children (WIC) nutritional program saves $3.07 during a baby's first year.
>
> Every year we allow a child to grow up in poverty costs $9,000 in lost future productivity over his or her working life.
>
> *Children's Defense Fund*, The State of America's Children Yearbook 2001.

adequate health care, child care, housing and education. School buildings and bridges are falling apart. Measured as a share of the Gross Domestic Product, federal spending is at the lowest level since 1966 and projected by 2011 to fall to the lowest level since 1951.[3]

The obstacle to decent, forward-thinking policies has not been public opinion, but rather political will. Too often politicians who didn't pull themselves up by their own bootstraps pretend that everyone can and should. Take conservative Texas Senator Phil Gramm: "Born in Georgia in 1942, to a father who was living on a veterans disability pension, Gramm attended a publicly funded university on a grant paid for by the federal War Orphans Act. His graduate work was financed by a National Defense Education Act fellowship, and his first job was at Texas A&M University, a federal land-grant institution."[4]

Many of the same politicians responsible for cutting millions of women and children off welfare defend an 1872 law that allows giant mining companies to turn public lands into wastelands—strip the minerals, reap the profits, pay next to nothing in return and leave behind toxic waste. Politicians who say government shouldn't interfere with "the free market" by raising the minimum wage, wouldn't dream of stopping the flood of subsidies to giant agribusinesses who don't need them.

Let's not fool ourselves. If we have the will to make sure no American is working poor, we have the wallet. If we have the will to raise the floor for everyone, we have the wallet.

We are, after all, the richest nation on earth. There is no reason we must remain number 1 in wealth and economic output, but number 16 in living standards among our poorest children, number 32 in under-five child mortality and number 37 in overall health.

We all benefit when government spends our money wisely on preventive policies and a strong safety net. We benefit when everyone is healthier and more educated—reaching their full potential of talents, skills, contributions and creativity.

Mortgaging Our Future

There are things we can't afford. We cannot afford to give the wealthiest Americans a giant tax break—the real point of the Economic Growth and Tax Relief Reconciliation Act of 2001— while shortchanging the most impoverished Americans. The top 1 percent of Americans has an average yearly income of over $1 million and 38 percent of the nation's wealth. They pay about 24 percent of all federal taxes, but will reap 38 percent of the tax cut benefits. According to Citizens for Tax Justice, the top 1 percent of taxpayers—with incomes of $373,000 or more—will get an average tax cut of $53,123 per year. That tax cut is nearly the amount two full-time average workers make in a year, or five workers make at minimum wage.

Middle-income households—with incomes ranging from $27,000 to $44,000—get an average tax cut of $600, maybe enough for a month's rent. The bottom 20 percent—with incomes less than $15,000—will get a tax cut of just $66.[5] The average taxpayer in the top 1 percent is getting more than 800 taxpayers combined in the bottom 20 percent.

The wealthiest 1 percent already has nearly as much wealth as the

A $26,000-a-year couple, with two kids, would have their income tax liability eliminated. The savings: $20. They still would pay $2,689 in payroll taxes. Thus this widely billed 100% tax cut amounts to less than 1% of their federal tax liability...

The Bush plan raises the level at which the [child tax] credit starts to phase out to $200,000, from $110,000. But the credit wouldn't be refundable, so families that don't pay any income taxes—but may pay payroll levies—wouldn't get it.

Thus a middle-management couple, with two kids, making $180,000 a year would get a...tax break. But the $18,000-a-year busboy and his spouse with two kids wouldn't get anything. Is that pro-family or good tax or social policy?

Albert R. Hunt, Wall Street Journal, *February 8, 2001.*

When President Bush launched his public-relations campaign to sell his [tax cut]...he gathered a group of middle-class families at the White House and talked of how much they would gain from his plan— $1,100 a year for one couple he introduced, Paul and Debbie Peterson. Asked who was there to represent those in the top tax bracket, Mr. Bush replied to laughter: "Well, I beg your pardon. I'm representing [them]..."

Here is what the president didn't say: If his full income-tax cut had been in place in 1999...he and Laura Bush could have gotten a break 20 to 60 times that of the Petersons. Vice President Cheney and his wife, Lynne, meanwhile, could have gotten a break in 1999 of more than a quarter of a million dollars...

Financial-disclosure forms [Bush] filed during the campaign suggest that, if his estate remains at least at its current value when he dies, his heirs could save between $6 million and $12 million from the proposed repeal [of the estate tax]. Mr. Cheney's forms suggest a savings to his heirs of between $10 million to $45 million.

Only about 2% of all estates in the country face the estate tax and thus would benefit from repeal. But financial-disclosure forms suggest that, in addition to Messrs. Bush and Cheney, as many as 14 of their 17 cabinet members may be wealthy enough to gain from eliminating the tax [including Treasury Secretary Paul O'Neill, with assets ranging from $63-$103 million, and Defense Secretary Donald Rumsfeld, with assets ranging from $61-$243 million].

Jacob M. Schlesinger and Laura Heinauer,
Wall Street Journal, February 7, 2001.

bottom 95 percent of Americans combined. The tax cuts will widen our vast income and wealth disparities and make the tax system more regressive, putting more of the burden on payroll taxes and families struggling to make ends meet. Three out of four families already pay more in regressive payroll taxes—which consume a larger share of the income of low- and middle-income families than of high-income families—than they pay in income taxes.

According to a Center on Budget and Policy Priorities report on the latest comprehensive Congressional Budget Office data on income

> **I**t makes me so angry. I work hard. I get taxes taken out of my paycheck every week. I opened the letter thinking I'd get a rebate—and find out I'm not. The government is giving rebates to plenty of people who don't need the money, and not giving rebates to plenty of people who do. It's just not right. Who is this tax cut really for?
>
> *Nicole Flynt, environmental organizer and mother of two, Dorchester, MA, author interview, July 24, 2001.*

IRS

Department of the Treasury
Internal Revenue Service

Notice 1276 (June 2001)
Catalog Number 31990X
www.irs.gov

Dear Taxpayer:

We are pleased to inform you that the United States Congress passed and President George W. Bush signed into the law the Economic Growth and Tax Relief Reconciliation Act of 2001, which provides long-term tax relief for all Americans who pay income taxes.

In general, individuals who had taxable income and paid federal income taxes in 2000, and who could not be claimed as a dependent on someone else's tax return, are eligible to receive immediate tax relief in the form of a check. According to the information on your 2000 federal tax return, you either did not pay any federal income taxes in 2000, did not have taxable income, or were claimed as a dependent on someone else's return.[1] Therefore, you will not be receiving a check at this time.

However, if you pay income taxes in 2001, and are otherwise eligible, you will be able to claim a credit on your 2001 tax return. Instructions on how to determine if you qualify for the credit will be provided with your 2001 federal income tax return. In addition, you may be eligible for tax relief in future years as federal taxes are scheduled to be reduced further.

trends and federal taxes, the average after-tax income of the top 1 percent of households skyrocketed 157 percent during 1979-1997, adjusting for inflation. Income in the bottom 20 percent of households, by contrast, fell about 1 percent.

The top 1 percent gained $414,200, after adjusting for inflation, reaching $677,900 in after-tax income. The bottom 20 percent lost $100 from their already inadequate incomes, bringing their 1997 after-tax income to $10,800. "In 1997, the 2.6 million people who made up the top one percent of the population had as much after-tax income as the 100 million Americans with the lowest incomes."[6]

The tax cuts, especially the rebates, are like a home equity loan scam. Here, the con artist says, you have surplus equity in your house—use it to renovate, pay off your credit cards. They hide the real, unconscionable fees and interest rates. Too late, you find you've mortgaged your future to loan sharks.

"Like the rest of the Bush tax plan, the rebates have been carefully designed to give as little as possible to those who need the money, and as much as possible to those who don't," says Robert McIntyre, director of Citizens for Tax Justice. In reality, 34 million taxpayers—26

My family is in that top 2 percent of wealthy Americans who [will gain] a windfall if the estate tax [is] eliminated...

Estate tax repeal would...undercut the very things that help Americans from all walks of life to get ahead and create new businesses and wealth. For even when wealth is a product of hard work, it's not "self-made." It often results from a strong economy and a lot of support from public programs paid for, in part, by the estate tax.

In my own case, I received a good public school education and used free libraries and museums paid for by others. I went to college under the GI Bill. I went to graduate school to study computers and language on a complete government scholarship, paid for by others. While teaching at Syracuse University for 25 years, my research was supported by numerous government grants—again, paid for by others.

My university research provided the basis for a language technology company I formed in 1991 with some graduate students and my son, Larry. Our company thrived in the technology-driven economic expansion—a boom fueled by continual public and private investment. Five years later, Syracuse Language Systems sold for $30 million, a sizeable part of which went to my family and me.

I've never once heard my family complain about the prospect of part of their inheritance going toward an estate tax. That's because we all believe that paying estate tax does not mean choosing between taking care of your children and grandchildren, or giving back to society. You can do both. I was able to provide well for my family and, upon my death, I hope taxes on my estate will help fund the kind of programs that benefited me and others from humble backgrounds—a good education, money for research, and targeted investment in poor communities, to help bring opportunity to all Americans.

Martin Rothenberg, member of Responsible Wealth,
Philadelphia Inquirer, September 7, 2000.

percent—get no tax rebate checks at all and another 17 million—13 percent—get only partial rebates. Among taxpayers making less than $44,000 a year, 62 percent get no rebates.[7] The rebates can't be more than what you paid in income tax in 2000—payroll taxes don't count—and can't exceed 5 percent of taxable income reported on your 2000 return. The more you need the rebate, the less you get.

The IRS is adding insult to injury by using tax dollars to send millions of Americans a reject letter telling them they are NOT getting a rebate check. In the words of *USA Today*, the tax rebates "have a hidden price: $116 million picked from the public's pockets. That's how much it costs to notify taxpayers that the checks are coming and to process the payments." There was a cheaper way: notify employers to reduce withholding, giving taxpayers more in their paychecks.[8]

What's $116 million? The total annual pay of 10,829 full-time workers making the minimum wage. It's more than five times as much as the government is spending this year on the Individual Development Accounts pilot program. It's a computer for about 170,000 classrooms.

Choices

The Bush plan robs Peter to pay Paul. It pays for the giant tax breaks for the wealthy by undermining Social Security and Medicare, shortchanging children's programs, and cutting the budgets of the Departments of Labor, Justice, Agriculture, Energy and Interior, the Environmental Protection Agency, the Small Business Administration and the Equal Opportunity Commission.

That so-called budget surplus being squandered on the tax cuts is the necessary buildup in the Medicare and Social Security trust funds for the large baby boom generation and the product of years of government shortchanging of budgets for affordable housing, health care, environmental programs, education, public works and so on.

If your family saved money by neglecting your kids and going without health care and home repairs would you say you had a budget surplus? Would you celebrate your "surplus" by cashing out your retirement savings and giving most of it away to the wealthiest people in town?

If your town saved money by letting schools fall apart, ignoring decaying bridges and roads, cutting mass transit, cutting housing assistance and laying off health inspectors, building inspectors and other city workers, would you say it had a budget "surplus"?

We have real surpluses to reduce:

The surplus of Americans whose lives and livelihoods are jeopardized by their lack of health insurance.

The surplus of parents who can't afford to take leave when their children are born or adopted.

The surplus of kids on waiting lists for Head Start.

The surplus of kids going to school in crumbling, overcrowded buildings.

The surplus of women denied unemployment insurance if they leave their job because of domestic violence.

The surplus of homeless families.

The surplus of seniors who can't retire because of inadequate pensions and Social Security.

The surplus of environmental projects we supposedly can't afford.

We've been down this road before. Twenty years ago Ronald Reagan gave us big tax cuts for the wealthy and big budget deficits—paid off with payroll tax hikes and painful cutbacks in housing, education, health care and other crucial programs.

In the famous words of Reagan Budget Director David Stockman, "Greed came to the forefront. The hogs were really feeding."[9]

Looking back on his interviews with David Stockman from the perspective of history repeating today, reporter William Greider warns:

> After Reagan cut taxes for the wealthy and business in 1981, he turned around two years later and raised Social Security payroll taxes dramatically on workers (earnings above $76,000 are exempted from Social Security taxes). Ever since, workers have been paying in extra money toward their future retirement—trillions more than needed now by Social Security—and the government simply borrows the surplus revenue to spend on other things...
>
> When FICA taxes were raised in 1983, Reagan at first objected and reminded aides that he was opposed to raising taxes—of any kind. David Stockman reassured him. If the rising payroll-tax burden was imposed on young working people, they would eventually revolt and Social Security would self-destruct of its own weight. The Gipper liked that and gave his OK. The same objective, now called privatization, shows up again this year on George W. Bush's agenda. He proposes to "save" Social Security by destroying it.[10]

We're getting swindled again. When you see you are getting swindled you blow the whistle and stop it. That's what we need to do.

As Citizens for Tax Justice points out, most of the tax cuts for the top 1 percent take effect after 2001. "For most Americans," says Robert McIntyre, "the post-2001 Bush tax cuts offer little gain, but lots of pain.

That's because most people will get little more in tax reductions after the first year, while losing large amounts in public services as the remaining upper-income tax cuts are phased in."[11]

The ink was barely dry on the tax cut bill before Bush administration officials began warning the "surplus" was shrinking and deeper budget cuts would be needed. Congress must reverse the costly tax cuts for the wealthy scheduled to take effect over the next decade.

We have other choices to make. We can shift some money out of the still-bloated military budget and put it to work in defense of our people's security at home. As the Children's Defense Fund recommends, instead of spending the $4 billion appropriated in Fiscal Year 2001 to build new F-22s, we could:

- provide all eligible 3- and 4-year olds a Head Start, or

- provide 1.2 million children in working families quality child care, or

- provide 2.8 million uninsured children health coverage.

Instead of eliminating the estate tax, benefiting the very wealthiest top 2 percent of Americans, at a cost of more than $266 billion over the next ten years, we could:

- fully fund Head Start for 3- and 4-year olds for the next ten years and fully fund Early Head Start for the last five of those years, or

- provide health insurance for every uninsured child for ten years.[12]

In this book we've advocated a higher minimum wage and common sense policies in health care, housing, child care and other crucial areas. What will be our legacy for America?

Will we go backward or forward? We're at a turning point. Let's take the high road to progress.

Afterword

■ ■ ■ ■ ■

By Marie C. Wilson

PRESIDENT, MS. FOUNDATION FOR WOMEN

My parents were great believers in hard work. Despite growing up in the Depression and growing up poor, they maintained the belief that if they just worked hard enough, all would go well. If I called my mother this very day and asked, "Mom, how did you and Dad get out of public housing back in 1947?" I know she would say, "We worked hard."

And she would be partly right. But she would not be completely right, because my mother and father got their family out of public housing because of good social policy. My father was a veteran of World War II. They got a subsidized Veterans Administration loan—that's how they were able to buy their first small home. That's how many Americans were able to buy their homes.

The VA loan program is a good social policy. It's a popular policy, seen as benefiting people who are "deserving." No one questions whether veterans deserve this help—they served their country, they fought for their country. But many people fight every day to earn money for their families.

People work year round, often holding down more than one job, and yet their families go without. They take care of our children and our seniors. They take care of us in hospitals. They make our clothes and harvest our food. Our country depends upon their hard work. Yet, with the low wages they make, they can't buy housing and health insurance, clothing and adequate food. They are in a constant no-win fight to make ends meet.

We at the Ms. Foundation believe that these women and men are also deserving, and that good social policy should ensure that people can meet their family's basic needs. Our country deserves no less. Our country needs the kinds of policies recommended in this book: strengthening the Earned Income Tax Credit, expanding housing and child care programs, providing health insurance for all low-income

Eleanor Roosevelt was a New Deal and human rights visionary. The Ms. Foundation for Women's Raise the Floor Campaign advocates an $8 minimum wage and other policies to assure that everyone can make ends meet.

families, and raising the federal minimum wage to $8 an hour so at the very least it supports the needs of a single adult worker.

A woman making today's minimum wage of $5.15 an hour cannot support herself, let alone a family—two out of three minimum wage workers are women. Couples with children, working hard at full-time jobs paying the minimum wage, cannot support their families.

Who can forget the speech where President Clinton talked about all the new jobs his administration had created, and the response offered, "I know you did, I've got three of them."

This is exactly the problem. No one should have to work three jobs to make ends meet.

The Ms. Foundation has long supported organizations that are organizing low-wage workers to improve wages, benefits and working conditions for working people and their families. This includes organizations waging living wage campaigns, fighting for more equitable economic development policies, organizing current and former welfare recipients, and organizing garment workers, contingent workers and child care workers.

We want all of our daughters and sons to grow up in an America in which they have the resources to support themselves, control their lives and influence the world around them. We think that work should pay. We hope you will join us in working to make that true for everyone.

APPENDIX A

BACKGROUND TABLES

■ ■ ■ ■ ■

TABLE A-1

Expenditures As Percent of Minimum Needs Budget Without Employment Health Benefits

EXPENDITURE	SINGLE ADULT	TWO ADULT	SINGLE PARENT, ONE CHILD	SINGLE PARENT, TWO CHILDREN	TWO ADULTS, ONE CHILD	TWO ADULTS, TWO CHILDREN
Housing	37.9	26.7	26.9	23.4	24.7	21.7
Health Care	18.5	27.1	22.1	19.3	20.4	17.9
Food	10.6	15.1	9.7	12.9	14.9	17.1
Child Care	0.0	0.0	15.9	13.9	14.7	12.9
School-Age Care	0.0	0.0	0.0	9.0	0.0	8.3
Transportation	7.8	8.0	6.0	5.2	6.6	5.8
Clothing and Personal	3.7	4.9	3.1	2.9	3.7	3.8
Household Expenses	3.0	2.1	1.7	1.5	1.6	1.4
Telephone	3.3	2.3	1.9	1.7	1.8	1.5
Payroll Tax	6.5	6.6	6.7	6.9	6.8	6.9
Federal Tax (incl. credits)	7.3	5.8	4.4	1.9	3.7	1.4
State Tax (incl. credits)	1.4	1.4	1.5	1.4	1.3	1.3
TOTAL	100.0	100.0	100.0	100.0	100.0	100.0

Expenditures As Percent of Minimum Needs Budget With Employment Health Benefits

EXPENDITURE	SINGLE ADULT	TWO ADULT	SINGLE PARENT, ONE CHILD	SINGLE PARENT, TWO CHILDREN	TWO ADULTS, ONE CHILD	TWO ADULTS, TWO CHILDREN
Housing	44.2	33.7	33.4	28.2	29.7	25.1
Health Care	8.8	13.5	10.9	9.2	9.7	8.2
Food	12.4	19.1	12.1	15.5	17.8	19.8
Child Care	0.0	0.0	19.8	16.7	17.6	14.9
School-Age Care	0.0	0.0	0.0	10.8	0.0	9.6
Transportation	9.1	10.1	7.4	6.3	7.9	6.7
Clothing and Personal	4.3	6.2	3.9	3.5	4.4	4.4
Household Expenses	3.4	2.6	2.1	1.8	1.9	1.6
Telephone	3.9	3.0	2.4	2.0	2.1	1.8
Payroll Tax	6.5	6.7	7.0	7.2	7.0	7.0
Federal Tax (incl. credits)	6.3	4.0	-0.1	-2.2	1.0	0.0
State Tax (incl. credits)	1.2	1.0	1.2	1.1	1.1	1.0
TOTAL	100.0	100.0	100.0	100.0	100.0	100.0

TABLE A-3

Minimum Wage, Unemployment Rate and Poverty Rate, 1938-2000

Year	Minimum Wage _in 2000 dollars_	Official Unemployment Rate	Official Poverty Rate	Year	Minimum Wage _in 2000 dollars_	Official Unemployment Rate	Official Poverty Rate
1938	$3.05	19.0		1970	$7.10	4.9	12.6
1939	3.72	17.2		1971	6.80	5.9	12.5
1940	3.69	14.6		1972	6.59	5.6	11.9
1941	3.51	9.9		1973	6.21	4.9	11.1
1942	3.17	4.7		1974	6.99	5.6	11.2
1943	2.99	1.9		1975	6.72	8.5	12.3
1944	2.94	1.2		1976	6.96	7.7	11.8
1945	3.83	1.9		1977	6.54	7.1	11.6
1946	3.53	3.9		1978	7.00	6.1	11.4
1947	3.09	3.9		1979	6.88	5.8	11.7
1948	2.86	3.8		1980	6.48	7.1	13.0
1949	2.89	5.9		1981	6.35	7.6	14.0
1950	5.36	5.3		1982	5.98	9.7	15.0
1951	4.97	3.3		1983	5.79	9.6	15.2
1952	4.87	3.0		1984	5.55	7.5	14.4
1953	4.84	2.9		1985	5.36	7.2	13.6
1954	4.80	5.5		1986	5.26	7.0	14.0
1955	4.82	4.4		1987	5.08	6.2	13.4
1956	6.33	4.1		1988	4.88	5.5	13.0
1957	6.13	4.3		1989	4.65	5.3	12.8
1958	5.96	6.8		1990	5.01	5.6	13.5
1959	5.92	5.5	22.4	1991	5.37	6.8	14.2
1960	5.82	5.5	22.2	1992	5.22	7.5	14.8
1961	6.62	6.7	21.9	1993	5.06	6.9	15.1
1962	6.56	5.5	21.0	1994	4.94	6.1	14.5
1963	7.03	5.7	19.5	1995	4.80	5.6	13.8
1964	6.94	5.2	19.0	1996	5.21	5.4	13.7
1965	6.83	4.5	17.3	1997	5.53	4.9	13.3
1966	6.64	3.8	14.7	1998	5.44	4.5	12.7
1967	7.22	3.8	14.2	1999	5.32	4.2	11.8
1968	7.92	3.6	12.8	2000	5.15	4.0	not available
1969	7.51	3.5	12.1				

Note: Minimum wage adjusted for inflation using CPI-U.

Sources: U.S. Department of Labor, Employment Standards Administration, U.S. Bureau of Labor Statistics, U.S. Census Bureau

TABLE A-4

Minimum Wage, Average Wage and Productivity, 1973-2000

YEAR	MINIMUM WAGE 2000 dollars	AVERAGE HOURLY EARNINGS 2000 dollars	OUTPUT PER HOUR 1973=100
1973	$6.21	$15.28	100
1974	6.99	14.81	98.4
1975	6.72	14.50	101.0
1976	6.96	14.71	104.8
1977	6.54	14.92	106.4
1978	7.00	15.03	107.8
1979	6.88	14.61	107.4
1980	6.48	13.92	107.0
1981	6.35	13.73	108.4
1982	5.98	13.70	107.7
1983	5.79	13.87	112.7
1984	5.55	13.79	115.0
1985	5.36	13.72	116.6
1986	5.26	13.76	120.1
1987	5.08	13.61	120.5
1988	4.88	13.51	122.1
1989	4.65	13.41	123.0
1990	5.01	13.19	124.4
1991	5.37	13.05	125.8
1992	5.22	12.97	130.5
1993	5.06	12.91	131.2
1994	4.94	12.92	132.9
1995	4.80	12.92	134.2
1996	5.21	12.97	137.6
1997	5.53	13.18	140.1
1998	5.44	13.50	143.9
1999	5.32	13.69	148.0
2000	5.15	13.74	154.2

Note: Hourly wages for production and nonsupervisory workers on private nonfarm payrolls, accounting for about 80 percent of the civilian workforce. Wages adjusted for inflation with CPI-U. Between 1973 and 2000, productivity grew 54.2 percent.

Sources: U.S. Department of Labor Employment Standards Administration, U.S. Bureau of Labor Statistics, *Economic Report of the President, 2001.*

TABLE A-5

Median Income By Race, Ethnicity, Household Type and Work Experience, 1999

	ALL	WHITE NON-HISPANIC	BLACK	LATINO
Male	27,275	30,594	20,579	18,234
Female	15,311	15,922	14,771	11,314
Male full-time worker	37,574	41,406	30,297	23,342
Female full-time worker	27,370	29,369	25,142	20,052
Households	40,816	44,366	27,910	30,735
Families	48,950	54,121	31,778	31,663
Female householder	23,732	28,627	18,244	18,701
Male householder	37,396	41,656	33,796	30,425

Source: U.S. Census Bureau, *Money Income in the United States 1999*, September 2000.

TABLE A-6

Cost of Minimum Wage Increase as Percent of Net Receipts by Industry

INDUSTRY	COST OF MINIMUM WAGE INCREASE TO $8	NET RECEIPTS*	COST AS PERCENT OF WAGE INCREASE TO NET RECEIPTS
Agriculture	3,729,997,444		n.a.
Mining	306,890,047	141,121,333,783	0.2
Construction	3,384,293,258	635,774,728,954	0.5
Manufacturing	11,402,875,140	3,186,869,869,067	0.4
Transportation	3,458,059,293	331,285,180,750	1.0
Communications	578,837,065	269,256,154,179	0.2
Utilities/Sanitary Services	487,449,462	403,330,323,377	0.1
Wholesale Trade	3,074,615,473	4,039,784,160,575	0.1
Retail Trade	27,432,295,634	2,272,057,313,994	1.2
FIRE	4,073,622,827	2,129,623,956,782	0.2
Private Households	2,725,555,600		n.a.
Business, Auto & Repair	5,589,265,607	371,103,578,789	1.5
Personal Services	4,364,246,992	99,789,385,382	4.4
Entertainment/Recreation	2,079,274,132	119,513,495,805	1.7
Hospitals	2,520,249,443	182,914,125,178	1.4
Medical Services, excl. Hosp.	4,774,319,635	195,884,300,101	2.4
Educational Services	7,017,709,370	78,770,649,395	8.9
Social Services	4,204,366,368	53,014,225,620	7.9
Other Professional Services	2,609,778,248	322,856,292,564	0.8
Forestry and Fisheries	88,700,003	3,251,194,934	2.7
Public Administration	2,569,187,693		n.a.
TOTAL	$96,471,588,732	$14,891,940,181,002	0.6%

* Total receipts minus total payroll and benefits.

n.a.: Company statistics data were not available for these sectors.

Sources: Solutions for Progress, analysis of Current Population Survey Outgoing Rotation Group files, July 1999–June 2000 and Current Population Survey Annual Demographic Supplement, March 2000; U.S. Census Bureau, *Statistics of U.S. Businesses, 1997*; U.S. Bureau of Labor Statistics, *Employer Costs For Employee Compensation*, March 2000. Receipts data adjusted to 1999 dollars using CPI-U; payroll data adjusted to 1999 dollars using Employment Cost Index.

TABLE A-7

Cost of Minimum Wage Increase as Percent of Total Cost of Goods Sold by Industry

INDUSTRY	COST OF MINIMUM WAGE INCREASE TO $8	COST OF GOODS SOLD*	COST AS PERCENT OF WAGE INCREASE TO COST OF GOODS SOLD
Agriculture, Forestry and Fishing	3,812,416,237	84,198,893,596	4.5
Mining	306,834,514	96,166,237,261	0.3
Construction	3,384,959,389	672,907,657,513	0.5
Manufacturing	11,402,750,019	3,456,302,247,588	0.3
Transportation	2,689,865,975	186,347,164,278	1.4
Communication and Utilities	1,057,327,932	343,227,747,788	0.3
Wholesale Trade	3,074,778,865	1,911,405,910,228	0.2
Retail Trade	27,431,582,067	1,880,467,395,117	1.5
FIRE	4,072,871,082	754,113,367,553	0.5
Personal Services (incl. hotels)	7,214,399,539	61,969,831,781	11.6
Business, Auto, Repair Services	5,592,604,454	276,676,247,276	2.0
Entertainment and Recreation Services	2,080,935,191	59,969,912,445	3.5
Other Services	21,033,588,721	163,488,619,847	12.9
TOTAL	$97,671,806,705	$10,476,816,144,335	0.9%

* As defined by the IRS, the cost of goods sold consists of "the direct costs incurred...in producing goods and providing services. Included were costs of materials used in manufacturing; costs of goods purchased for resale; direct labor; and certain overhead expenses, such as rent, utilities, supplies, maintenance and repairs."

Sources: Solutions for Progress, analysis of Current Population Survey Outgoing Rotation Group files, July 1999–June 2000; Current Population Survey Annual Demographic Supplement, March 2000; U.S. Internal Revenue Service, *Statistics of Income. Corporation Returns 1996, Partnership Returns 1996* and *Sole Proprietorship Returns 1996*; U.S. Bureau of Labor Statistics, *Employer Costs for Employee Compensation*, March 2000. Cost of Goods data adjusted to 1999 dollars using the CPI-U.

TABLE A-8

Workers In Industries by Wage Category

INDUSTRY	EMPLOYMENT	WAGE <$5.15*	WAGE <$6.15	WAGE <$6.65	WAGE <$8.00
Agriculture	1,769,623	139,285	488,809	624,375	923,984
Mining	526,232	7,396	16,809	24,891	43,750
Construction	6,869,113	82,136	312,146	447,826	900,465
Manufacturing – Durable	11,758,075	80,905	461,757	658,720	1,391,698
Manufacturing – Nondurable	7,524,397	102,175	555,687	778,148	1,394,425
Transportation	5,706,469	106,930	268,130	362,836	743,223
Communications	1,867,969	9,147	48,128	67,712	139,321
Utilities/Sanitary Services	1,522,206	5,797	37,320	46,075	100,132
Wholesale Trade	4,661,886	60,117	269,036	401,338	793,097
Retail Trade	20,115,539	883,224	4,976,638	6,524,839	9,677,149
FIRE**	7,666,247	133,261	344,833	473,029	980,938
Private Households	940,044	267,777	401,487	451,091	594,916
Business, Auto and Repair Services	7,501,674	161,713	699,214	919,081	1,605,873
Personal Services	2,762,989	163,392	582,050	781,218	1,196,582
Entertainment & Recreation Services	2,197,442	84,748	461,475	580,234	847,333
Hospitals	5,030,321	50,780	206,776	290,451	649,030
Medical Services	5,803,431	97,815	526,416	712,928	1,347,052
Educational Services	10,837,605	303,103	975,138	1,218,671	1,953,938
Social Services	2,889,308	151,856	539,846	687,034	1,063,495
Other Professional Services	5,189,227	124,551	275,645	366,246	656,870
Forestry and Fisheries	93,128	3,698	10,039	12,211	19,741
Public Administration	5,958,354	70,334	200,696	267,615	514,205
TOTAL	119,191,280	3,090,142	12,658,076	16,696,572	27,537,214

For example, 9,677,149 workers in retail trade earn less than $8.

* Workers paid less than $5.15. Workers paid exactly $5.15 are included in the next wage category. With these wage categories we can see who will be affected by proposed minimum wage increases because we show the workers who earn less than a given wage rather than equal to or less than a given wage.

** Fire, Insurance and Real Estate

Source: Solutions for Progress, analysis of Current Population Survey Outgoing Rotation Group files, July 1999–June 2000.

TABLE A-9

Female Workers Within Industries by Wage Category

INDUSTRY	TOTAL EMPLOYMENT	WAGE <$5.15	WAGE <$6.15	WAGE <$6.65	WAGE <$8.00
Agriculture	460,141	18,992	101,838	140,146	209,192
Mining	59,017	734	1,860	2,667	3,758
Construction	668,922	18,727	50,707	65,521	124,035
Manufacturing – Durable	3,324,825	29,173	214,655	300,921	638,080
Manufacturing – Nondurable	3,000,137	62,608	338,663	468,036	806,554
Transportation	1,572,541	32,900	91,668	126,008	257,169
Communications	756,331	2,245	24,379	38,308	80,654
Utilities/Sanitary Services	327,614	197	7,874	9,272	22,355
Wholesale Trade	1,503,508	21,117	122,900	185,892	313,458
Retail Trade	10,411,962	516,548	2,915,549	3,871,195	5,706,986
FIRE	4,715,283	83,196	230,494	326,019	709,915
Private Households	862,981	242,037	363,032	409,438	543,047
Business, Auto and Repair Services	2,837,453	62,764	295,053	405,608	702,492
Personal Services	1,772,014	120,625	432,775	591,790	880,763
Entertainment & Recreation Services	926,816	43,727	222,610	282,993	401,289
Hospitals	3,843,648	38,472	148,818	214,084	509,466
Medical Services	4,886,487	80,682	451,383	612,619	1,179,100
Educational Services	7,533,098	233,009	700,989	892,835	1,445,938
Social Services	2,327,633	116,837	441,950	576,842	897,216
Other Professional Services	2,666,057	63,135	165,699	226,413	425,407
Forestry and Fisheries	22,128	2,163	5,124	5,812	7,789
Public Administration	2,638,359	37,775	112,213	155,421	290,926
TOTAL	57,116,957	1,827,664	7,440,233	9,907,841	16,155,589

For example, 5,706,986 female employees in retail trade are paid less than $8.

Source: Solutions for Progress, analysis of Current Population Survey Outgoing Rotation Group files, July 1999-June 2000.

TABLE A-10

Selected Federal Social Expenditures

Expenditure Area	Program	Source	Total Cost	Persons Served	Per Capita Cost
Health Care	Federal Employee Health Benefits	Budget of the United States FY 2001	$18 billion	9 million beneficiaries	$2,000 per person
Health Care	Medicaid	Budget of the United States FY 2001	$125 billion	34 million people	$3,676 per person
Health Care	Medicare-partial*	Budget of the United States FY 2001	$109 billion	20 million people	$5,450 per person
Health Care	State Children's Health Insurance Fund	Budget of the United States FY 2001	$4.2 billion	2.5 million children	$1,680 per child
Child Care	Head Start	Budget of the United States FY 2001	$6.3 billion	950,000 children	$6,632 per child
Child Care	Early Head Start	Department of Health and Human Services FY 2001 Budget	$.57 billion	54,000 children	$10,556 per child
Child Care	Child Care and Development Fund	Budget of the United States FY 2001	$3.5 billion	2.2 million children	$1,591 per child
Child Care	Child and Dependent Care Tax Credit	Budget of the United States FY 2001	$2.4 billion	6 million families	$400 per family
Child Care	Child Care and Development Block Grant	Department of Health and Human Services FY 2001 Budget	$2 billion	150,000 children	$13,333 per child
Income Support	Temporary Assistance to Needy Families	Budget of the United States FY 2001	$16.7 billion	2.4 million families	$6,958 per family
Income Support	Supplementary Security Income	Budget of the United States FY 2001	$30.5 billion	6.4 million people	$4,755 per person
Income Support	Earned Income Tax Credit	Budget of the United States FY 2001	$31.9 billion	19 million families	$1,680 per family
Food and Nutrition	Food Stamps	Department of Agriculture FY 2001 Budget Summary	$21 billion	18.9 million people	$1,111 per person

Expenditure Area	Program	Source	Total Cost	Persons Served	Per Capita Cost
Food and Nutrition	Women, Infants & Children	Budget of the United States FY 2001	$4.1 billion	7.5 million people	$547 per person
Food and Nutrition	Child Nutrition Programs	Department of Agriculture FY 2001 Budget Summary	$10.4 billion	27.8 million meals per day	$374
Social Security	Social Security—partial*	Budget of the United States FY 2001	$211.1 billion	22.7 million people	$9,320 per person
Education	Title I	Budget of the United States FY 2001	$9.1 billion	12.2 million students	$746 per student
Education	Class Size Reduction	Budget of the United States FY 2000	$1.4 billion to states and school districts		
Education	Special Education	Budget of the United States FY 2001	$6.4 billion		
Education	Pell Grants	Budget of the United States FY 2001	$8.5 billion	3.9 million students	$2,179 per student
Education	Work-Study	Budget of the United States FY 2001	$1 billion	1 million students	$1,000 per student
Education	Hope Scholarships	Budget of the United States FY 2001	$5.1 billion	5.6 million students	$911 per student
Education	Lifetime Learning Tax Credits	Budget of the United States FY 2001	$2.4 billion	7.2 million students	$333 per student
Education	Federal Student Loans	Budget of the United States FY 2001	$43 billion	6.3 million students	$6,825 per student
Education	After School Programs	Budget of the United States FY 2001	$1 billion	10,000 schools 2.5 million students	$400 per student
Housing	Public Housing Operating Fund	Budget of the United States FY 2001	$3.2 billion	1.2 million housing units	$2,667 per unit
Housing	Public Housing Capital Fund	Budget of the United States FY 2001	$2.95 billion		
Housing	HOME Investment Partnership Program	Department of Housing and Urban Development FY 2001 Budget	$1.3 billion	103,000 households	$12,621 per household
Housing	Low-Income Housing Tax Credit	Department of Housing and Urban Development FY 2001 Budget	$3.2 billion	75,000 to 90,000 units per year	$35,556 per unit
Housing	Homeless Assistance Grants	Budget of the United States FY 2001	$1.2 billion		
Housing	Section 8	Department of Housing and Urban Development FY 2001 Budget	$13 billion	3 million families	$4,333 per family

Expenditure Area	Program	Source	Total Cost	Persons Served	Per Capita Cost
Housing	Welfare-to-Work Housing vouchers	Budget of the United States FY 2001	$.47 billion	82,000 vouchers	$5,732 per family
Housing	Low Income Home Energy Assistance Program	Health and Human Services Budget FY 2001	$1.1 billion	4 million households	$275 per household
Job Training	Adult Grants	Department of Labor, ETA FY 2001 Budget	$.95 billion	380,000 people	$2,500 per person
Job Training	Native Americans	Department of Labor, ETA FY 2000 Budget	$.054 billion	20,000 people	$2,690 per person
Job Training	Migrant and Seasonal Farm Workers	Department of Labor, ETA FY 2000 Budget	$.071 billion	37,900 people	$1,873 per person
Job Training	Youth Activities Grants	Department of Labor, ETA FY 2001 Budget	$1 billion	612,000 participants	$1,634 per person
Job Training	Dislocated Worker Employment and Training	Department of Labor, ETA FY 2001 Budget	$1.8 billion	984,000 dislocated workers	$1,829 per person
Job Training	Job Corps	Department of Labor, ETA FY 2001 Budget	$1.4 billion	73,000 people	$19,134 per person
Job Training	Welfare-to-Work	Department of Labor, ETA FY 2000 Budget; Status of the Welfare-to-Work (WtW) Grants Program After One Year, the Urban Institute, September 1999	$1 billion		$2,500 per person
OTHER SOCIAL EXPENDITURES					
Federal Pensions	Federal Retirement and Insurance Programs	Budget of the United States FY 2001	$44 billion	2.3 million federal civilian retirees and survivors	$19,130 per person
Health Care	Medicare	Budget of the United States FY 2001	$109 billion	20 million people	$5,450 per person
Social Security		Budget of the United States FY 2001	$211.1 billion	27.7 million people	$9,320 per person

* The data above was adjusted to reflect that an estimated 50 percent of the elderly population would be poor without the benefits of government programs. Kathryn Porter, Wendell E. Primus, Lynette Rawlings and Esther Rosenbaum, *Strengths of the Safety Net: How the EITC, Social Security and Other Government Programs Affect Poverty*, Center on Budget and Policy Priorities, March 1998, p.29.

APPENDIX B

MINIMUM NEEDS BUDGET METHODOLOGY

■ ■ ■ ■ ■

Housing

To calculate housing costs, we assumed that no more than two persons share one bedroom and that children do not share a bedroom with their parents. Under these assumptions, a one-bedroom apartment would be sufficient for households without children. Households with children would require at least a two-bedroom apartment. Because we do not decompose family composition by gender, we assume that two children share a bedroom.

Housing costs for households without children are determined by calculating the average of HUD Fair Market Rents for one-bedroom apartments weighted by the proportion of the U.S. population residing in the county or MSA. Housing costs for other household compositions reported here are determined by computing the average of HUD Fair Market Rents for two bedroom apartments weighted by the proportion of the U.S. population residing in the county or MSA. HUD Fair Market Rents represent rent costs at the 40th percentile of area rents and include the cost of all utilities except telephone.[1]

Health Care

To calculate health care costs, we assumed that health care expenditures include premium payments and out-of-pocket payments. For single individuals, we used average out-of-pocket costs for single individuals. For other family configurations, we used average out-of-pocket costs for households earning between $30,000 and $39,999. Because this income bracket includes median household income, we assumed that out-of-pocket costs would not be misleadingly high due to a lack of insurance or discretionary health care spending or spuriously low because of income constraints. We assumed that out-of-pocket spending for the median income household reflects expenditures by a household with adequate health insurance and therefore reflects a conservative estimate of out-of-pocket costs. Indeed, this income bracket has the lowest out-of-pocket costs with the exception of those earning below $15,000.

Premium costs for single individuals were taken from average total single premium for employer coverage and average employee contribution to total single premium in private sector establishments. Premium costs for families were taken from average total family premium for employer coverage and average employee contributions in private sector establishments.

Calculations for the minimum needs budget without employment-based health insurance coverage include total premium cost for single persons and families in addition to out-of-pocket costs. Calculations for the minimum needs budget with employment-based health coverage include the average total employee premium contribution for single persons and families as well as out-of-pocket costs as described above. The figures are adjusted using the medical care services component of the CPI-U.

We used data from a 1998 Consumers Union report to provide a measure of out-of-pocket payments for health care.[2] The data in this report updates health care expenditures from the 1987 National Medical Expenditure Survey to 1996. We used data from the 1996 Medical Expenditure Panel Survey to calculate premium costs.[3]

Food

For our estimates of the cost of food, we use the December 1999 U.S. average cost for the USDA Low-Cost Food Plan rather than the USDA Thrifty Food Plan used in the calculation of the Census poverty threshold.[4] Most needs budget studies we reviewed also used the USDA Low-Cost Food Plan.

The USDA developed four food plans—Thrifty, Low Cost, Moderate Cost and Liberal—based on 1977-78 Nationwide Food Consumption Survey Data and updated using the CPI. The plans are based on the consumption patterns of families at different food spending levels. The Thrifty Plan is based on the consumption patterns of families eligible for food stamps, while the Low-Cost Food Plan is based on the consumption patterns of families in the second quartile of consumers.[5]

A drawback of the Low-Cost Food Plan is that it does not incorporate the cost of food consumed away from home. Although the USDA food plans are regularly updated using the CPI for selected food items, the plans are based on 1977-78 food consumption survey data. The 1998 Consumption Expenditure Survey shows that food away from home accounts for approximately two-fifths of all spending on food for households and more than one-third of all spending on food for households in the lowest quintile of income.[6] We made the conservative assumption that all meals are prepared in the home since minimum nutritional needs can be met without consuming food away from home.

We assumed that adults in a household are between 20 and 50 years old, that households with one child have a preschool-age child between 3 and 5 years old, and that households with two children have a preschool-age child and a young school age child between 6 and 8 years old. We assumed this specific family structure for families with children to ensure that both child care and school-age care costs would be part of the minimum needs budget. The cost of food is calculated by adding the cost of the Low-Cost Food Plan for individuals in the relevant age/gender categories for each household composition.

For single adult and single parent households, the cost of food for the adult member was calculated by weighting the cost of the Low-Cost Food Plan for individuals 20-50 years of age by the proportion of female and male single person and single parent households.[7]

Child Care For a Preschool Child

To calculate the average cost of child care services we assumed that families with children have one child 3 or 4 years old in full-time child care provided by a non-relative to reflect the most common age of children in child care and to provide conservative cost estimates. Although many young children cared for by relatives receive free care, we did not weight the cost calculation to reflect the proportion of children cared for by relatives. Rather, we sought to determine what child care would cost, on average, for a family that purchases these services in the market.

We calculated the costs of child care for preschoolers (children 3 and 4 years old). To calculate average child care costs, we used cost figures for children 4 years of age reported in the Children's Defense Fund 1998 report, *Child Care Challenges*.[8] We used data from a 2000 Urban Institute report based on the 1997 National Survey of American Families to determine the proportion of children 3 and 4 years of age cared for in child care centers or by non-relatives in family-provider child care.[9] We also used U.S. Census Bureau Population Estimates for the U.S. and states by age to determine the proportion of the population 3 and 4 years of age residing in each state.

We calculated the costs of child care for preschoolers (children 3 and 4 years old). We use cost figures reported in *Child Care Challenges* for 4-year-olds and the proportion of children cared for in child care centers and in family-provider child care homes in each state as reported in a 2000 Urban Institute report. For states for which the Urban Institute did not have representative data, their national average estimates for child care arrangements were used in calculating average child care costs. The Urban Institute found substantial variability in child care arrangements across states. Using their 1997 National Survey of America's Families, they found that nationally 32 percent of children of working mothers were in center-based care while 16 percent were in family child care by non-relatives. Yet, while nearly 39 percent of children in Alabama are in center-based care, only 19 percent of children in California are in center-based care. Similarly, 20 percent of children are in family-provider child care in Wisconsin compared to 10 percent in Massachusetts.

We calculate a weighted average of child care costs in each state based on these proportions. Next, we compute a national average of child care costs for children 3 and 4 years old weighted by the child care population in each state in these age categories to the national child care population in these age categories. As used herein, child care population refers to the number of children 5 years of age and under in non-relative care (i.e., at center-based child care or in family-provider child care). Child care costs are converted to 1999 dollars using the CPI-U.

Average child care costs for children 3 and 4 years of age are estimated at $4,582, and this is the cost used in our minimum needs budget. Employing the same methodology with data for children under three years of age, we estimated average child care costs for children under three years of age to be considerably higher, at $5,297. Average child care costs for the total child care population (all children under 5 years of age) are estimated at $4,828.

Care For a School-Age Child

We also included the cost of school-age care in the minimum needs budget. We assume that all adult members of households work and that school-age children 12 years old and under will require some form of paid care. To calculate average child care costs, we used cost data derived from the 1995 National Household Education Survey.[10]

To calculate costs for care for a school-age child, we assumed that families with two children have one child in before- or after-school care, and that the school-age child requires care during the summer months. We multiplied the weighted average weekly cost by 40 weeks to determine the cost of school-age care during the school year. To calculate the cost of care for school-age children during the summer months, we multiplied the cost per hour of care, the average number of hours spent in before-and after-school care plus six (representing the length of the school day) and 60 (representing the number of days summer care is required).[11] School-age care costs are adjusted using the CPI-U.

We calculate the average weekly cost for before- and after-school care provided by a non-relative or at a center weighted by the proportion of the child care population receiving care at these sites, respectively. Next, we adjust the average weekly cost to reflect the cost of care during the school year and the cost of care during the summer months. The average cost of before- and after-school care using this methodology was estimated at $2,968.

Although the National Household Education Survey data and the data provided by the Children's Defense Fund reflect the cost of care for children who are roughly 8 or 9 years old, we assume those costs also apply to children 12 years old and younger.

Transportation

Transportation expenses are a standard element in all minimum needs budgets. We used the 1998 Consumer Expenditure Survey to calculate transportation costs and Bureau of Labor Statistics "Expenditures on Public Transportation" to derive the proportion of public transportation spending on mass transit and local taxi fares. We used data on the percentage of person miles traveled by trip purpose from the 1995 National Personal Transportation Survey.[12] We also used data on person miles traveled by mode of transportation to estimate public transit and private vehicle usage.[13]

To calculate transportation costs, we assumed that households own a used car, as explained in Chapter One. We include the purchase cost of a car as well as financing charges. Although the purchase cost of a car typically is a one-time cost, many low-income families, particularly in urban areas, do not own a car. Rental, lease and license charges are excluded from the calculation of transportation costs. We use average annual expenditures on transportation reported by consumer units in the first quintile of income for the purchase cost of a car, gasoline and motor oil, vehicle finance charges and public transportation and by consumer units in the second quintile of income for maintenance and repairs and vehicle insurance in the BLS Consumer Expenditure Survey.

Average expenditures by units in the second quintile of income for insurance and maintenance and repairs are used to ensure that families are adequately insured and are capable of meeting transportation needs safely. For our estimates of transportation costs for two-adult families, we calculate the ratio of spending in the appropriate quintile as described above to spending in the third quintile (which includes median income) for each cost category. We apply this ratio to average annual expenditures on transportation for single person households and two-adult families and to average annual expenditures on transportation for consumer units with two or more persons and one earner (for single parent households) or two earners (for two parent households).

Almost one-third (31.7 percent) of public transportation costs by consumer units in the first quintile of income are attributable to spending on local mass transit and taxi fare. We only include this portion of public transportation costs in our calculations. We also exclude 31.1 percent of the calculated transportation costs for each household composition representing the proportion of miles traveled by persons for social and recreational purposes. Finally, we weight public and private transportation costs based on actual average usage of these modes of transportation.[14] Transportation costs are adjusted to 1999 dollars using the transportation component of the CPI-U.

Clothing And Personal Expenses

The needs budgets reviewed included cost of clothing and other personal expenses, either as a separate category or in the more inclusive category of miscellaneous expenses. We assume that average annual expenditures for clothing and personal expenses by consumers in the first quintile of income are sufficient to meet a household's minimum needs in these categories. For our estimates of the cost of clothing and personal services, we use average annual expenditures on apparel and services and personal care products and services reported by consumer units in the first quintile of income by the Bureau of Labor Statistics Consumer Expenditure Survey.[15]

For single person households, we compute a weighted average of clothing expenses based on the relative proportion of male and female single person households. For all other households, clothing expenses are calculated by adding the cost of apparel for individuals in the relevant age/gender categories.[16] We adjust clothing expenditures by the apparel component of the CPI-U and personal care products by the CPI-U.

Household Expenses

Most of the needs budget studies we reviewed also included household expenses, although the studies varied as to which expenses were included. We assume that average annual expenditures on household expenses and household operations by consumers in the first quintile of income are sufficient to meet a household's minimum needs in these categories. We exclude expenditures on household textiles, furniture, floor coverings, large appliances, small appliances and miscellaneous household equipment from the calculation of household expenses because these items typically represent one-time costs.[17] We adjust these expenditures by the CPI-U.

Telephone Services

To estimate the costs of telephone services, we assumed that average annual expenditures on telephone services by households in the first quintile of income are sufficient to meet a household's minimum needs in these categories. For our estimates of the cost of telephone services, we use the average annual household expenditures for households in the first quintile of income in 1997 reported in the Federal Communications Commission Reference Book of Rates, July 1998.[18] This figure is adjusted using the CPI-U.

Taxes

To estimate average taxes for the minimum needs budget, we first assumed that families earn an income sufficient to meet their minimum needs. While the earned income tax credit and other federal and state programs reduce the tax liability of low-income families, the minimum needs budget is not designed to reflect what poor people actually spend, but rather the income necessary to meet minimum needs. Therefore, the tax calculation must reflect the actual average tax liability of families with an income just sufficient to meet their minimum needs, not the average tax liability of low-income families.

In the tax calculation, we included federal payroll taxes, federal income tax, state income taxes, and any tax credits for which a household with an income sufficient to meet its basic needs would be eligible. Sales taxes are not included in this calculation since they are included in the annual expenditures for specific cost categories reported in the Consumer Expenditure Survey. For the purpose of tax calculations, we assume all adults are under the age of 65 years and work in the labor force. We also assumed that single parent households file as heads of household and two-adult families (with and without children) file as married couples filing a joint return. (We realize that couples who are not legally married in the eyes of the state cannot presently reap the tax advantages of filing jointly, but since most two-adult families are married couples by the IRS definition we made that tax assumption.)

We took 7.65 percent of the pre-tax minimum needs budget to represent the employee's share of FICA and other payroll taxes (Social Security and Medicare). We used the federal personal income tax form 1040 to calculate federal income taxes and credits, based on the pre-tax minimum needs budget for households in each of our composition categories. Because we calculated tax liability on the basis of the minimum income necessary to meet basic needs, only families with children and employer-provided health insurance would be eligible for the Earned Income Tax Credit under the 1999 eligibility standard.

We used actual state tax forms for the 1999 tax year to separately calculate state personal income taxes and any credits for which a household earning an income sufficient to meet their minimum needs might be eligible for all six household configurations for all states except for Alaska, Florida, Nevada, New Hampshire, South Dakota, Tennessee, Texas, Washington and Wyoming (either those states do not levy personal income taxes or households with incomes just sufficient to meet the respective pre-tax minimum needs budgets are not required to file personal income tax returns in these states). We weighted state taxes by the proportions of households in each composition category and filing status to calculate average state taxes. To determine the proportion of families in each household composition category and filing status, we used data from the March 1999 Annual Demographic Supplement to the Current Population Survey.

APPENDIX C

REGIONAL VARIATIONS IN MINIMUM NEEDS BUDGETS: NEW YORK, NY; LOS ANGELES, CA; DES MOINES, IA; KANSAS CITY, MO; AND GADSDEN, AL

■ ■ ■ ■ ■

The minimum needs budgets presented earlier reflect nationally average minimum costs. However, there are wide variations in the cost of living across the country. For example, the Wider Opportunities for Women Self-Sufficiency Standard found that a single adult in Rapid City, Iowa would need $1,067 to meet their monthly needs compared to $1,308 in Philadelphia, PA; $1,610 in the New York City borough of Queens; and $1,897 in San Francisco, CA (2000 dollars).[1] In its new report detailing basic budgets for communities nationwide, the Economic Policy Institute finds that yearly costs for a two-adult, two-child family range from a high of $52,114 in Nassau and Suffolk counties in New York to a low of $27,005 in Hattiesburg, Mississippi (1999 dollars). Hattiesburg is followed by rural Mississippi at $27,456 and Jonesboro, Arkansas at $28,097. The second-highest cost city is Boston, at $49,795; New York City is eighth highest at $46,567 for a two-adult, two-child family.[2]

For illustrative purposes, we calculated minimum needs budgets for New York, NY; Los Angeles, CA; Des Moines, IA; Kansas City, MO; and Gadsden, AL, using the same methodology as our national minimum needs budget. We selected these relatively high-cost, moderate-cost and low-cost areas based largely on differences in their housing costs. As shown in the tables below, we found that the cost of supporting a household varies substantially across these five metropolitan areas. Housing and, to a lesser extent, child care and food expenditures are responsible for most of the variation. As seen in Table C-3, annual housing costs in New York City exceed the national average by more than $3,000 and exceed housing costs in Gadsden by about $6,000.

Metropolitan Areas Methodology

In order to calculate the minimum needs budgets for the selected metropolitan areas, we made the same assumptions, employed the same methodology and used the same data sources as the national minimum needs budget. Remember, our goal here is to provide a sense of the broad range of expenditures around the country from which the national budget average is derived, so methodological consistency is important. If specific metropolitan area data were available (such as HUD Fair Market Rents), those estimates were utilized. If data regarding the specific metropolitan area were not available, state data or regional data were used, depending on availability. Data was available at the Metropolitan Statistical Area level for housing costs, food, transportation, clothing and personal expenses, and household expenses for New York City, Los Angeles and Kansas City.[3]

Housing costs for households with no children are determined by the HUD Fair Market Rents for one-bedroom apartments in the MSA. Housing costs for households with children are determined by the HUD Fair Market Rents for two-bedroom apartments in the MSA.

To calculate food costs, we use the USDA Low-Cost Food Plan for individuals in the relevant age/gender categories for each household composition. We then use the Consumer Expenditure Survey to derive average food costs for each MSA by computing food expenditures in the MSA (or region) as a percentage of the national average. We multiply these percentages with the average cost of food in the national minimum needs budget to estimate the cost of food in each MSA.

We use state child care cost figures reported in *Child Care Challenges* for 4 year olds (to estimate the cost of care for children 3 and 4 years old). We use data from the Urban Institute's 1997 *National Survey of American Families* to estimate the proportion of children in this age category cared for in child care centers and in family-provider child care in Alabama, Iowa, Missouri, California and New York. From these data, we calculate a weighted average of child care costs in each of these states and use these estimates to represent child care costs in each of the selected metropolitan areas. Child care costs are converted to 1999 dollars using the CPI-U.

To remain consistent with the methodology we used for our national minimum needs budget, we use the *Child Care Challenges* as the basis for metropolitan area child care costs. However, the data reported therein is largely based on state averages, and does not illuminate cost variation within states. For example, child care costs are generally significantly higher in New York City than in upstate New York. It may be more appropriate to use state human service agency market surveys of child care costs, where possible, to obtain better data at the MSA level.[4] Indeed, the 2000 *Self-Sufficiency Standard for the City of New York* estimated the annual cost of child care for a preschooler at $8,832 ($736 a month). The WOW study used the Market Rate Survey conducted by the New York State Office of Children and Family Services as the basis for their estimation of child care costs.[5]

We use state child care cost figures reported in *Child Care Challenges* for 8 year olds to estimate the cost of before- and after-school as well as vacation care for school-age children. We used data from the 1995 National Household Education Survey to estimate the total proportion of children receiving nonparental care in centers or in family-provider home settings. From these data, we calculated a weighted average of school-age care costs in each state and used these estimates to represent child care costs in each of the selected metropolitan areas. Once again, the lack of local data on school-age care costs may underestimate the cost of care, particularly in New York City.[6] Estimated costs for school-age care are adjusted to 1999 dollars using the CPI-U.

To calculate transportation costs, we use the Consumer Expenditure Survey to derive average transportation costs for each MSA by computing average transportation expenditures in the MSA (or region for Des Moines and Gadsden) as a percentage of the national average expenditures on transportation. We multiply these percentages with the average cost of transportation in the national minimum needs budget for our six household compositions to estimate the cost of transportation in each MSA. Transportation costs are adjusted to 1999 dollars using the transportation component of the CPI-U.

To calculate health care costs, we assume that health care expenditures include premium payments and out-of-pocket payments. For single individuals, we use average out-of-pocket costs for single individuals. For our other family categories, we use average out-of-pocket costs for households earning between $30,000 and $39,999, as explained in the national minimum needs budget methodology appendix. Premium costs for single individuals are taken from the average total single premium for employer coverage and average employee contribution to total single premium in private sector establishments in New York, California, Iowa, Missouri and Alabama. Premium costs for families are taken from average total family premium for employer coverage and average employee contribution in private sector establishments in New York, California, Iowa, Missouri and Alabama.[7] Calculations for the minimum needs budget without employment-based health insurance coverage include total premium cost for single persons and families in addition to out-of-pocket costs. Calculations for the minimum needs budget with employment-based health insurance coverage include the average total employee premium contribution for single persons and families as well as out-of-pocket costs as described above. The figures are adjusted using the medical care services component of the CPI-U.

For our estimates of the cost of clothing and personal services, we use the Consumer Expenditure Survey to derive average costs for apparel and services and personal care products and services in each MSA by computing the ratio of these expenditures in the MSA (or region) to the national average. We multiply these ratios to the average cost of apparel and services and personal care products and services in the minimum needs budget for each household composition to estimate the cost of clothing and personal expenses in each MSA. Clothing expenses are adjusted to 1999 dollars using the apparel component of the CPI-U and personal care products are adjusted using the CPI-U.

To calculate annual household expenses, we use the Consumer Expenditure Survey to derive average household expenses for each MSA by computing expenditures in the MSA (or region) as a percentage of the national average. We multiply these percentages by the average cost of household expenditures in the national minimum needs budget for each household composition to estimate the cost of household items in each MSA. Household expenses are adjusted to 1999 dollars using the CPI-U.

To calculate the cost of telephone services in each metropolitan area, we use the FCC Reference Book of Rates to derive a ratio of costs in the MSA to the national average. We then apply this ratio to the average cost of telephone services in the national minimum needs budget to estimate the cost of telephone services in each MSA. These figures were adjusted to 1999 dollars using the CPI-U.

Our estimates of taxes include federal and state personal income taxes, credits and the employee share of federal payroll taxes. We assume that individuals and families earn an income sufficient to meet their minimum needs budgets for the purpose of the tax calculation. The minimum needs budget is designed to reflect the income required to meet minimum needs, not what

low-income individuals and families actually spend. Therefore, the tax calculation must reflect the average tax liability of families with an income just sufficient to meet minimum needs, not the average tax liability of low-income
families. We include FICA, federal personal income tax, state personal income
tax and any tax credits (federal and state) for which a family with an income
sufficient to meet its basic needs would be eligible.

We apply 7.65 percent of the minimum needs budget net of taxes for each
MSA to represent the employee's share of FICA and other payroll taxes
(Social Security and Medicare). We used Federal Tax Form 1040 to calculate
federal income taxes and credits for households in each family composition
category. We used state personal income tax forms for Alabama, New York,
California, Iowa and Missouri to calculate state income taxes and credits.[8] We
also estimated New York City tax liability (not applicable to other cities).

TABLE C-1

Annual Minimum Income Needed Without Employment Health Benefits In Selected Metropolitan Areas

HOUSEHOLD COMPOSITION	NATIONAL MINIMUM NEEDS BUDGET	GADSDEN, ALABAMA	DES MOINES, IOWA	KANSAS CITY, MISSOURI	LOS ANGELES, CALIFORNIA	NEW YORK, NEW YORK
Single Adult, No Children	$16,549	$13,268	$15,169	$16,210	$18,300	$22,422
Two Adults, No Children	23,522	19,939	21,757	23,196	25,126	30,586
Single Parent, One Child	28,796	22,221	26,563	28,656	32,755	37.140
Single Parent, Two Children	32,999	25,484	30,115	33,787	38,648	42,768
Two Adults, One Child	31,255	24,865	29,395	31,524	35,397	40,247
Two Adults, Two Children	35,637	28,762	33,170	36,943	41,633	46,450

Source: Solutions for Progress.

TABLE C-2

Annual Minimum Income Needed With Employment Health Benefits in Selected Metropolitan Areas

HOUSEHOLD COMPOSITION	NATIONAL MINIMUM NEEDS BUDGET	GADSDEN, ALABAMA	DES MOINES, IOWA	KANSAS CITY, MISSOURI	LOS ANGELES, CALIFORNIA	NEW YORK, NEW YORK
Single Adult, No Children	$14,196	$11,298	$13,277	$13,859	$15,867	$19,738
Two Adults, No Children	18,614	16,024	17,646	18,435	20,590	24,634
Single Parent, One Child	23,179	17,799	21,683	23,148	28,136	31,042
Single Parent, Two Children	27,439	21,322	25,370	28,460	34,045	36,431
Two Adults, One Child	26,076	20,582	24,697	26,464	30,777	34,152
Two Adults, Two Children	30,812	24,596	29,038	32,152	36,993	40,112

Source: Solutions for Progress.

TABLE C-3

National and Metropolitan Minimum Needs Budgets Without Employment Health: Single Adult, No Children

EXPENDITURE	NATIONAL	GADSDEN, ALABAMA	DES MOINES, IOWA	KANSAS CITY, MISSOURI	LOS ANGELES, CALIFORNIA	NEW YORK, NEW YORK
Housing	$6,272	$3,804	$5,424	$5,724	$7,260	$9,720
Health Care	3,066	2,906	2,897	3,013	3,090	3,270
Food	1,759	1,633	1,725	2,106	1,859	2,237
Child Care	0	0	0	0	0	0
School Age Care	0	0	0	0	0	0
Transportation	1,285	1,312	1,269	1,340	1,542	1,261
Clothing and Personal	610	539	537	511	554	695
Household Expenses	489	459	441	496	625	459
Telephone	550	574	532	532	559	537
Payroll Tax	1,073	859	981	1,050	1,185	1,391
Federal Taxes	1,211	754	1,016	1,159	1,444	1,879
State Taxes	234	428	347	279	182	973
TOTAL	16,549	13,268	15,169	16,210	18,300	22,422

TABLE C-4

National and Metropolitan Minimum Needs Budgets With Employment Health: Single Adult, No Children

EXPENDITURE	NATIONAL	GADSDEN, ALABAMA	DES MOINES, IOWA	KANSAS CITY, MISSOURI	LOS ANGELES, CALIFORNIA	NEW YORK, NEW YORK
Housing	$6,272	$3,804	$5,424	$5,724	$7,260	$9,720
Health Care	1,244	1,387	1,361	1,189	1,201	1,288
Food	1,759	1,633	1,725	2,106	1,859	2,237
Child Care	0	0	0	0	0	0
School Age Care	0	0	0	0	0	0
Transportation	1,285	1,312	1,269	1,340	1,542	1,261
Clothing and Personal	610	539	537	511	554	695
Household Expenses	489	459	441	496	625	459
Telephone	550	574	532	532	559	537
Payroll Tax	923	743	864	910	1,040	1,239
Federal Taxes	889	514	769	866	1,136	1,556
State Taxes	175	333	356	185	90	746
TOTAL	14,196	11,298	13,277	13,859	15,867	19,738

TABLE C-5

National and Metropolitan Minimum Needs Budgets Without Employment Health: Two Adults, No Children

EXPENDITURE	NATIONAL	GADSDEN, ALABAMA	DES MOINES, IOWA	KANSAS CITY, MISSOURI	LOS ANGELES, CALIFORNIA	NEW YORK, NEW YORK
Housing	$6,272	$3,804	$5,424	$5,724	$7,260	$9,720
Health Care	6,376	6,016	5,928	6,107	6,188	6,823
Food	3,557	3,302	3,488	4,078	3,758	4,523
Child Care	0	0	0	0	0	0
School Age Care	0	0	0	0	0	0
Transportation	1,881	1,921	1,857	1,961	2,258	1,846
Clothing and Personal	1,152	1,125	1,124	1,073	1,168	1,449
Household Expenses	489	459	441	496	625	459
Telephone	550	574	532	532	559	537
Payroll Tax	1,551	1,316	1,438	1,528	1,669	1,940
Federal Taxes	1,369	874	1,129	1,316	1,616	2,186
State Taxes	325	548	396	381	25	1,103
TOTAL	23,522	19,939	21,757	23,196	25,126	30,586

TABLE C-6

National and Metropolitan Minimum Needs Budgets With Employment Health: Two Adults, No Children

EXPENDITURE	NATIONAL	GADSDEN, ALABAMA	DES MOINES, IOWA	KANSAS CITY, MISSOURI	LOS ANGELES, CALIFORNIA	NEW YORK, NEW YORK
Housing	$6,272	$3,804	$5,424	$5,724	$7,260	$9,720
Health Care	2,517	2,977	2,563	2,428	2,541	2,357
Food	3,557	3,302	3,488	4,078	3,758	4,523
Child Care	0	0	0	0	0	0
School Age Care	0	0	0	0	0	0
Transportation	1,881	1,921	1,857	1,961	2,258	1,846
Clothing and Personal	1,152	1,125	1,124	1,073	1,168	· 1,449
Household Expenses	489	459	441	496	625	459
Telephone	550	574	532	532	559	537
Payroll Tax	1,256	1,083	1,180	1,246	1,390	1,598
Federal Taxes	746	381	589	724	1,031	1,466
State Taxes	194	398	448	172	0	679
TOTAL	18,614	16,024	17,646	18,435	20,590	24,634

TABLE C-7

National and Metropolitan Minimum Needs Budgets Without Employment Health: Single Parent, One Child

EXPENDITURE	NATIONAL	GADSDEN, ALABAMA	DES MOINES, IOWA	KANSAS CITY, MISSOURI	LOS ANGELES, CALIFORNIA	NEW YORK, NEW YORK
Housing	$7,733	$4,392	$6,696	$6,888	$9,192	$11,040
Health Care	6,376	6,016	5,928	6,107	6,188	6,823
Food	2,801	2,600	2,747	3,211	2,960	3,562
Child Care	4,582	3,560	4,644	4,931	6,080	5,742
School Age Care	0	0	0	0	0	0
Transportation	1,726	1,762	1,704	1,800	2,258	1,694
Clothing and Personal	904	932	923	881	954	1,199
Household Expenses	489	459	441	496	625	459
Telephone	550	574	532	532	559	537
Payroll Tax	1,925	1,553	1,807	1,901	2,190	2,376
Federal Taxes	1,280	-395	768	1,195	1,866	2,256
State Taxes	430	768	374	715	69	1,452
TOTAL	28,796	22,221	26,563	28,656	32,755	37,140

TABLE C-8

National and Metropolitan Minimum Needs Budgets With Employment Health: Single Parent, One Child

EXPENDITURE	NATIONAL	GADSDEN, ALABAMA	DES MOINES, IOWA	KANSAS CITY, MISSOURI	LOS ANGELES, CALIFORNIA	NEW YORK, NEW YORK
Housing	$7,733	$4,392	$6,696	$6,888	$9,192	$11,040
Health Care	2,517	2,977	2,563	2,428	2,541	2,357
Food	2,801	2,600	2,747	3,211	2,960	3,562
Child Care	4,582	3,560	4,644	4,931	6,080	5,742
School Age Care	0	0	0	0	0	0
Transportation	1,726	1,762	1,704	1,800	2,258	1,694
Clothing and Personal	904	932	923	881	954	1,199
Household Expenses	489	459	441	496	625	459
Telephone	550	574	532	532	559	537
Payroll Tax	1,630	1,320	1,549	1,619	1,911	2,034
Federal Taxes	-31	-1,335	-410	-77	1,242	1,536
State Taxes	278	558	294	439	0	882
TOTAL	23,179	17,799	21,683	23,148	28,136	31,040

TABLE C-9

National and Metropolitan Minimum Needs Budgets Without Employment Health: Single Parent, Two Children

EXPENDITURE	NATIONAL	GADSDEN, ALABAMA	DES MOINES, IOWA	KANSAS CITY, MISSOURI	LOS ANGELES, CALIFORNIA	NEW YORK, NEW YORK
Housing	$7,733	$4,392	$6,696	$6,888	$9,192	$11,040
Health Care	6,376	6,016	5,928	6,107	6,188	6,823
Food	4,243	3,939	4,161	3,211	4,483	5,396
Child Care	4,582	3,560	4,644	4,931	6,080	5,742
School Age Care	2,968	2,110	2,462	3,312	4,290	3,506
Transportation	1,726	1,762	1,704	1,800	2,258	1,694
Clothing and Personal	959	986	978	935	1,009	1,271
Household Expenses	489	459	441	496	625	459
Telephone	550	574	532	532	559	537
Payroll Tax	2,266	1,821	2,107	2,285	2,639	2,790
Federal Taxes	631	-1,043	110	669	1,419	1,741
State Taxes	476	908	352	969	92	1,769
TOTAL	32,999	25,484	30,115	33,787	38,648	42,768

TABLE C-10

National and Metropolitan Minimum Needs Budgets With Employment Health: Single Parent, Two Children

EXPENDITURE	NATIONAL	GADSDEN, ALABAMA	DES MOINES, IOWA	KANSAS CITY, MISSOURI	LOS ANGELES, CALIFORNIA	NEW YORK, NEW YORK
Housing	$7,733	$4,392	$6,696	$6,888	$9,192	$11,040
Health Care	2,517	2,977	2,563	2,428	2,541	2,357
Food	4,243	3,939	4,161	3,211	4,483	5,396
Child Care	4,582	3,560	4,644	4,931	6,080	5,742
School Age Care	2,968	2,110	2,462	3,312	4,290	3,506
Transportation	1,726	1,762	1,704	1,800	2,258	1,694
Clothing and Personal	959	986	978	935	1,009	1,271
Household Expenses	489	459	441	496	625	459
Telephone	550	574	532	532	559	537
Payroll Tax	1,971	1,588	1,850	2,003	2,360	2,448
Federal Taxes	-601	-1,738	-959	-430	834	1,021
State Taxes	302	713	298	701	0	960
TOTAL	27,439	21,322	25,370	28,460	34,045	36,431

TABLE C-11

National and Metropolitan Minimum
Needs Budgets Without Employment Health:
Two Adults, One Child

EXPENDITURE	NATIONAL	GADSDEN, ALABAMA	DES MOINES, IOWA	KANSAS CITY, MISSOURI	LOS ANGELES, CALIFORNIA	NEW YORK, NEW YORK
Housing	$7,733	$4,392	$6,696	$6,888	$9,192	$11,040
Health Care	6,376	6,016	5,928	6,107	6,188	6,823
Food	4,649	4,316	4,559	5,330	4,912	5,912
Child Care	4,582	3,560	4,644	4,931	6,080	5,742
School Age Care	0	0	0	0	0	0
Transportation	2,056	2,099	2,030	2,144	2,468	2,018
Clothing and Personal	1,142	1,107	1,107	1,060	1,149	1,430
Household Expenses	489	459	441	496	625	459
Telephone	550	574	532	532	559	537
Payroll Tax	2,110	1,723	1,984	2,103	2,385	2,598
Federal Taxes	1,154	-144	891	1,139	1,739	2,189
State Taxes	414	763	583	794	101	1,499
TOTAL	31,255	24,865	29,395	31,524	35,297	40,247

TABLE C-12

National and Metropolitan Minimum
Needs Budgets With Employment Health:
Two Adults, One Child

EXPENDITURE	NATIONAL	GADSDEN, ALABAMA	DES MOINES, IOWA	KANSAS CITY, MISSOURI	LOS ANGELES, CALIFORNIA	NEW YORK, NEW YORK
Housing	$7,733	$4,392	$6,696	$6,888	$9,192	$11,040
Health Care	2,517	2,977	2,563	2,428	2,541	2,357
Food	4,649	4,316	4,559	5,330	4,912	5,912
Child Care	4,582	3,560	4,644	4,931	6,080	5,742
School Age Care	0	0	0	0	0	0
Transportation	2,056	2,099	2,030	2,144	2,468	2,018
Clothing and Personal	1,142	1,107	1,107	1,060	1,149	1,430
Household Expenses	489	459	441	496	625	459
Telephone	550	574	532	532	559	537
Payroll Tax	1,814	1,491	1,727	1,821	2,106	2,256
Federal Taxes	259	-951	-128	290	1,146	1,469
State Taxes	285	558	527	544	0	932
TOTAL	26,076	20,582	24,697	26,464	30,777	34,152

TABLE C-13

National and Metropolitan Minimum Needs Budgets Without Employment Health: Two Adults, Two Children

EXPENDITURE	NATIONAL	GADSDEN, ALABAMA	DES MOINES, IOWA	KANSAS CITY, MISSOURI	LOS ANGELES, CALIFORNIA	NEW YORK, NEW YORK
Housing	$7,733	$4,392	$6,696	$6,888	$9,192	$11,040
Health Care	6,376	6,016	5,928	6,107	6,188	6,823
Food	6,104	5,667	5,985	6,997	6,449	7.762
Child Care	4,582	3,560	4,644	4,931	6,080	5,742
School Age Care	2,968	2,110	2,462	3,312	4,290	3,506
Transportation	2,056	2,099	2,030	2,144	2,468	2,018
Clothing and Personal	1,343	1,416	1,421	1,364	1,469	1,840
Household Expenses	489	459	441	496	625	459
Telephone	550	574	532	532	559	537
Payroll Tax	2,463	2,011	2,306	2,507	2,855	3,039
Federal Taxes	511	-475	174	601	1,336	1,726
State Taxes	462	933	552	1,064	122	1,958
TOTAL	35,637	28,762	33,170	36,943	41,633	46,450

TABLE C-14

National and Metropolitan Minimum Needs Budgets With Employment Health: Two Adults, Two Children

EXPENDITURE	NATIONAL	GADSDEN, ALABAMA	DES MOINES, IOWA	KANSAS CITY, MISSOURI	LOS ANGELES, CALIFORNIA	NEW YORK, NEW YORK
Housing	$7,733	$4,392	$6,696	$6,888	$9,192	$11,040
Health Care	2,517	2,977	2,563	2,428	2,541	2,357
Food	6,104	5,667	5,985	6,997	6,449	7.762
Child Care	4,582	3,560	4,644	4,931	6,080	5,742
School Age Care	2,968	2,110	2,462	3,312	4,290	3,506
Transportation	2,056	2,099	2,030	2,144	2,468	2,018
Clothing and Personal	1,343	1,416	1,421	1,364	1,469	1,840
Household Expenses	489	459	441	496	625	459
Telephone	550	574	532	532	559	537
Payroll Tax	2,168	1,779	2,048	2,226	2,576	2,697
Federal Taxes	-12	-1,170	-370	9	744	1,006
State Taxes	314	733	586	826	0	1,148
TOTAL	30,812	24,596	29,038	32,152	36,993	40,112

APPENDIX D

SUMMARY OF SUCCESSFUL LIVING WAGE CAMPAIGNS

■ ■ ■ ■ ■

* indicates a living wage that is indexed and adjusted annually

PLACE	DATE	WAGE WITH HEALTH INSURANCE	WAGE WITHOUT HEALTH INSURANCE
Harvard University, Cambridge, MA	**May 2001**	**$10.25 for some workers**	
After student protests calling for a living wage for all Harvard employees, Harvard University negotiated a wage increase for Local 26 of the Hotel Employees and Restaurant Employees International Union. Under the new contract, all dining service workers employed for more than one year will make at least $10.25. Harvard also agreed to a 10% cap on the number of hours worked by "casuals" (temporary employees who do not receive fringe benefits) and agreed to form a committee to assess Harvard's employment policies.			
Pittsburgh, PA	**May 2001**	**$9.12***	**$10.62***
Covers the city and certain service contractors, recipients of city subsidies and certain employers who lease property through the city. Covers for-profit employers with more than 10 employees and nonprofits with more than 25. Nonprofit employers will be phased in over three years.			
Santa Monica, CA	**May 2001**	**$10.50**	**$12.25; $13.00 in 2002**
Covers employers operating within the city's Coastal Zone tourist district with revenues of more than $5 million a year. The ordinance is the first to cover employers who have no direct financial relationship with the city.			
Ventura County, CA	**May 2001**	**$8.00**	**$10.00**
Covers county contractors and subcontractors. Exempts in-home support workers, board and care services, and printing or copying services.			
Miami Beach, FL	**April 2001**	**$8.56***	**$9.81***
Covers the city itself and certain service contractors with contracts over $100,000 pay employees.			
Pittsfield Township, MI	**April 2001**	**$8.70***	**$10.20***
Covers service contractors and recipients of financial assistance such as tax breaks, loans and grants worth more than $10,000. Covers for-profit employers with at least 5 employees and nonprofits with at least 10 employees.			
Eastpointe, MI	**March 2001**	**$8.23***	**$10.00***
Covers companies receiving service contracts or tax incentives of at least $5,000 from Eastpointe. The wage is defined as 125% of the poverty level for a family of 4 if health benefits are not provided, or 100% if they are.			
Richmond, VA	**March 2001**	**$8.50**	**$10.13**
Covers workers employed by the School Board.			

PLACE	DATE	WAGE WITH HEALTH INSURANCE	WAGE WITHOUT HEALTH INSURANCE
Missoula, MT	**March 2001**	**$7.95***	
Requires recipients of city economic development assistance to at least match the pay of the lowest-paid full-time employees of the City of Missoula and provide health benefits.			
Ann Arbor, MI	**March 2001**	**$8.70***	**$10.20***
Covers recipients of grants, loans, tax abatement and other subsidies or city service contracts that exceed $10,000.			
Ferndale, MI	**February 2001**	**$8.50***	**$9.75***
Covers firms who receive service contracts worth at least $25,000 from the city.			
Rochester, NY	**January 2001**	**$8.52***	**$9.52***
Requires all employers who enter into city service contracts worth at least $50,000 to pay employees on those contracts a living wage.			
Santa Cruz, CA	**October 2000**	**$11.00**	**$12.00**
Highest living wage in the country at this writing. Covers city employees and employees of nonprofit and for-profit city service contractors.			
Berkeley & Berkeley Marina, CA	**June 2000, October 2000**	**$9.75**	**$11.37**
Covers direct city employees, businesses with city contracts, financial assistance recipients and businesses that lease land from the city after the ordinance goes into effect. In October, the ordinance was amended to provide an immediate living wage to all employees at the Berkeley Marina, which is city-owned public land, creating the first area-based living wage policy in the nation. As of July 1, 2001, child care workers employed by agencies under contract with the city are eligible.			
Eau Claire County, WI	**September 2000**	**$6.67**	**$7.40**
Covers companies that contract with the county in an amount over $100,000.			
San Francisco, CA	**August 2000**		**$10.00 in 2001; then 2.5% raise for the next 3 years.**
Applies to city service contractors, including nonprofit agencies and leaseholders at San Francisco International Airport. Employers are also required to give workers 12 paid days off and 10 unpaid days for family emergencies. Companion legislation requires covered employers to provide workers health insurance, join a city-run health insurance pool or pay into the city's public health system fund at the rate of $1.25 an hour per employee.			
St. Louis, MO	**August 2000**	**$8.84***	**$10.23***
Covers city service contractors with contracts worth at least $50,000 and any business that receives economic development subsidies from the city worth at least $100,000. Living wage defined as a wage sufficient to lift a family of 3 above the eligibility level for food stamps.			

Place	Date	Wage with Health Insurance	Wage without Health Insurance
Cleveland, OH	**June 2000**		**$8.20 since Jan. 2001; $9.20 in October 2002***

Requires recipients of city assistance, in the form of contracts and subsidies with aggregate value at least $75,000 to pay workers who work at least 30 hours per week a living wage. The ordinance covers for-profit employers with at least 2 employees and nonprofit employees with at least 50 employees and a wage ratio greater than 5:1, as well as subcontractors and leaseholders or tenants of recipients of assistance. At least 40% of new hires must be residents of Cleveland, and additional incentives will be provided to employers by the city to encourage provision of health benefits.

Place	Date	Wage with Health Insurance	Wage without Health Insurance
Alexandria, VA	**June 2000**		**$9.84***

Covers city service contractors.

Place	Date	Wage with Health Insurance	Wage without Health Insurance
Toledo, OH	**June 2000**	**$8.58***	**$10.14***

Covers employees working on city contracts over $10,000 (and more than 25 employees) and employees working for recipients of subsidies from the city of more that $100,000 (with more than 50 employees). When health insurance is provided, wages will be indexed at 110% of the federal poverty level for a family of 4, and when employers do not provide health insurance, wages will be indexed at 130% of the poverty level. Employees of tenants in properties that have benefited from financial assistance from the city are covered.

Place	Date	Wage with Health Insurance	Wage without Health Insurance
Wesleyan University, CT	**April 2000**	**Up to $9.40**	

Students at Wesleyan University helped 29 janitors form a union and negotiate a better contract. Workers are entitled to health care benefits and paid vacation, greater job security and a one-year pay increase period, after which they are eligible to receive a maximum wage of up to $9.40.

Place	Date	Wage with Health Insurance	Wage without Health Insurance
Omaha, NE	**April 2000**	**100% federal poverty threshold for family of 4***	**110% federal poverty threshold for family of 4***

Covers direct city employees, as well as employees of city service contractors, subcontractors and other firms who benefit from at least $75,000 from the city.

Place	Date	Wage with Health Insurance	Wage without Health Insurance
San Fernando, CA	**April 2000**	**$7.25**	**$8.50**

Covers firms holding city service contracts or receiving city grants of more than $25,000, including employees of temporary employment agencies. (The health benefits provision does not apply to temporary workers.) The ordinance also requires at least 6 compensated and 6 uncompensated days off annually for sick leave, vacation or personal leave.

Place	Date	Wage with Health Insurance	Wage without Health Insurance
Denver, CO	**February 2000**		**$8.50***

Covers city contractor or subcontractor with a contract of $2,000 or more engaged in the work of a parking lot attendant, security guard, clerical support worker, or child care worker on city owned or leased property.

Place	Date	Wage with Health Insurance	Wage without Health Insurance
Warren, MI	**January 2000**	**$8.83***	**$11.04***

Requires firms that receive city contracts or tax breaks worth at least $50,000 to pay workers a wage at least equivalent to the federal poverty line for a family of 4. Firms that do not provide health benefits must pay at least 125% of the poverty line.

Place	Date	Wage with Health Insurance	Wage without Health Insurance
Corvallis, OR	**November 1999**		**$9.00***

Voters in Corvallis passed an initiative prohibiting the city from entering into a contract worth $5,000 or more with any company that fails to provide its employees a living wage and benefit package.

Place	Date	Wage with Health Insurance	Wage without Health Insurance
Hartford, CT	**September 1999**	**110% of federal poverty threshold for family of 4***	**110% of federal poverty threshold for a family of 4, plus payments in lieu of benefits***

Covers employees on certain city service contracts as well as employees on development projects receiving over $100,000 in city assistance. The living wage is defined as 110% of the federal poverty level for a family of 4, with a health benefit plan that requires employees to pay no more than 3% of their annual wages. Without such benefits, employers must make payments to employees in lieu of benefits to be calculated annually by the director of human relations, based on the average cost of comprehensive health insurance in the state. Covers service contracts over $50,000 in the following categories: food service, security services, custodial/maintenance, clerical/office, transportation, parking services. The ordinance also includes a provision requiring development projects to allow workers to be represented by a union in exchange for guaranteed "labor peace" (no-strike clause).

Place	Date	Wage with Health Insurance	Wage without Health Insurance
Kankakee County, IL	**September 1999**	**$11.42***	

Covers labor practices, benefits and wages paid by companies benefiting from local Enterprise Zone tax breaks. Companies required to pay wages of at least $11.42 per hour or 130% of the federal poverty level, whichever is higher, provide at least 80% of health and dental for full-time employees at any new development, and offer pension or profit sharing plans. Requires businesses receiving subsidies to repay all funds if they relocate within 5 years or fail to create and maintain at least 50 new jobs. Applicants for abatements must provide detailed information on other public subsidies they've received and their record of hiring and wages. Prohibits use of public money for anti-union campaigns, requires prevailing wages on construction projects involving tax abated property, and participation in approved apprenticeship training programs.

Place	Date	Wage with Health Insurance	Wage without Health Insurance
Tucson, AZ	**September 1999**	**$8.00***	**$9.00***

Covers contractors providing the following services to the city: facility and building maintenance, refuse collection and recycling, temporary employee services, janitorial and custodial, landscape maintenance and weed control, pest control, security and moving services. The ordinance also requires that covered contractors maintain a workforce of at least 60% city residents on all such city contracts.

PLACE	DATE	WAGE WITH HEALTH INSURANCE	WAGE WITHOUT HEALTH INSURANCE
Buffalo, NY	**August 1999**	**$6.22 in 2000; $7.15 in 2001; $8.08 in 2002.**	**$7.22 in 2000; $8.15 in 2001; $9.08 in 2002.**

Covers service contractors and subcontractors working on contracts greater than $50,000. Covers workfare workers. Requires that applicants for contracts submit information on projected hiring and wage goals prior to award, and submit quarterly reports on hiring and wages after securing a contract.

PLACE	DATE	WAGE WITH HEALTH INSURANCE	WAGE WITHOUT HEALTH INSURANCE
Los Angeles County, CA	**June 1999**	**$8.32**	**$9.46**

Los Angeles County Board of Supervisors is the largest governmental entity in the nation to adopt a living wage law. Requires that a living wage be paid to full-time employees of firms contracting with the county (and their subcontractors) for over $25,000 worth of services. The ordinance prohibits the use of part-time employees on county contracts without justifiable cause and prohibits the use of county funds to inhibit employee organization. Stipulates that a collective bargaining agreement may supersede the requirements.

PLACE	DATE	WAGE WITH HEALTH INSURANCE	WAGE WITHOUT HEALTH INSURANCE
Ypsilanti, MI	**June 1999**	**$8.50**	**$10.00**

Covers companies receiving city service contracts or financial assistance valued at over $20,000 in a given year. Requires tax abated firms to make good faith efforts to hire local residents for jobs created by the assistance and provides that the city give preference, when possible, to local contractors.

PLACE	DATE	WAGE WITH HEALTH INSURANCE	WAGE WITHOUT HEALTH INSURANCE
Ypsilanti Township, MI	**June 1999**	**$8.50**	**$10.00**

Requires companies with city service contracts or financial assistance valued at over $10,000 ($20,000 for nonprofits) in a given year to pay employees on that contract or project (and employees of their subcontractors or leaseholders) a living wage.

PLACE	DATE	WAGE WITH HEALTH INSURANCE	WAGE WITHOUT HEALTH INSURANCE
Somerville, MA	**May 1999**		**$8.83***

Covers full- and part-time direct employees of the City of Somerville, as well as employees of firms carrying out service contracts with the city for at least $50,000 (this threshold decreases to $30,000 in 2 years and $10,000 or more two years after that). The living wage is set at the poverty line for a family of 4.

PLACE	DATE	WAGE WITH HEALTH INSURANCE	WAGE WITHOUT HEALTH INSURANCE
Miami-Dade County, FL	**May 1999**	**$8.56**	**$9.81**

Covers some service contractors and airport licensees (for ground service personnel) with county service contracts worth at least $100,000. Establishes a Living Wage Commission to enhance compliance and review the effectiveness of the law.

PLACE	DATE	WAGE WITH HEALTH INSURANCE	WAGE WITHOUT HEALTH INSURANCE
Cambridge, MA	**May 1999**		**$10.68***

Covers the City of Cambridge, as well as companies or nonprofits with service contracts or subcontracts with the city worth at least $10,000 and firms that benefit from at least $10,000 in city subsidies in a year (as well as their tenants and leaseholders). Directs the city agencies to report annually on subsidies and establishes a Community Advisory Board to review and recommend action on waiver requests.

Place	Date	Wage with Health Insurance	Wage without Health Insurance
Hayward, CA	**April 1999**	**$8.00***	**$9.25***
Madison, WI	**March 1999**		**110% federal poverty threshold for family of 4***
Dane County, WI	**March 1999**		**$8.03***
Hudson County, NJ	**January 1999**	**$7.73***	
San Jose, CA	**November 1998**	**$10.10**	**$11.35**
Detroit, MI	**November 1998**	**$8.83***	**$11.03***
Multnomah County, OR	**October 1998**	**$9.00***	

Hayward, CA
Covers direct employees of the city, as well as employees of certain firms contracting with the city for at least $25,000. Requires a minimum of 12 paid days off and 5 uncompensated days off per year. Stipulates that a collective bargaining agreement may supersede the requirements.

Madison, WI
Covers city employees and firms with city service contracts (and their subcontractors) worth at least $5,000 and firms receiving $100,000 or more in financial assistance (and their contractors) from the city. Stipulates that a collective bargaining agreement may supersede the requirements.

Dane County, WI
Covers county employees, employees of county service contractors, subcontractors and beneficiaries of economic development assistance of $5,000 or more from the county.

Hudson County, NJ
Covers county service contractors employing security, food service and janitorial workers (all working at least 20 hours per week on county contracts. Pays 150% of the federal minimum wage. Contractors must also provide health benefits and one week paid vacation to these employees.

San Jose, CA
Covers companies with city service contracts worth at least $20,000. Requires companies seeking service contracts to provide assurances of good labor relations and requires successor contractors to offer jobs to employees of predecessor contractors who performed those services. Employees of companies receiving direct financial grants from the city valued at $100,000 or more in a year are also covered. The contracted service categories covered under the policy are: automotive repair and maintenance, food service, janitorial, landscaping, laundry, office/clerical, parking lot management, pest control, property maintenance, recreation, security shuttle services, street sweeping and towing.

Detroit, MI
Covers city service contractors or recipients of city financial assistance worth $50,000 or more. Requires companies to attempt to hire Detroit residents to fill any new jobs created as a result of the contract or assistance granted by the city.

Multnomah County, OR
Covers county janitorial, security services and food service contractors. The resolution includes a retention provision requiring new janitorial contractors to first interview employees of the previous contractor before hiring new workers.

Place	Date	Wage with Health Insurance	Wage without Health Insurance
Boston, MA	**September 1998**		**$9.14***
Amended version of earlier, more comprehensive living wage ordinance. Covers city service contracts worth at least $100,000 (or subcontracts of at least $25,000), indexed annually on July 1 to whichever is higher—the adjusted poverty guidelines or 110% of the state minimum wage. The measure also includes community hiring provisions for both contractors and recipients of subsidies or other financial assistance, requires covered companies to report on jobs created and wages paid, and creates a Living Wage Advisory Committee to oversee the implementation of the ordinance.			
Pasadena, CA	**September 1998**	**$7.25**	**$8.50**
Covers city service contractors (with contracts worth at least $25,000) and city employees.			
Cook County, IL	**September 1998**		**$7.60**
Covers county contractors of any size.			
Chicago, IL	**July 1998**		**$7.60**
Covers some for-profit city contractors and subcontractors: home and health care workers, security guards, parking attendants, day laborers, cashiers, elevator operators, custodial workers and clerical workers.			
San Antonio, TX	**July 1998**		**$9.27 (non-durable goods manufacturing and service companies); $10.13 (durable goods manufacturing)**
Guidelines and criteria pertaining to tax abatements includes a requirement for beneficiaries to pay at least 70% of employees in new jobs a living wage. The guidelines deem retail industry facilities ineligible for tax abatements. In addition, businesses may be eligible for more tax abatement if they fill 25% of new jobs created with economically disadvantaged individuals.			
Oakland, CA	**March 1998**	**$8.00; Currently $9.13***	**$10.50***
Covers companies or nonprofits with city service contracts worth at least $25,000 or firms that benefit from at least $100,000 in city subsidies in a year (as well as their tenants and leaseholders). Requires 12 paid days off per year. Stipulates that a collective bargaining agreement may supersede the requirements.			
Durham, NC	**January 1998**		**$7.55***
Requires city service contractors to pay their employees working on city projects an hourly wage at least equal to the minimum hourly wage rate paid to Durham City employees.			

Place	Date	Wage with Health Insurance	Wage without Health Insurance
Portland, OR	**1996, 1998**	**$6.75 on July 1, 1996; $7.00 in 1997; $7.50 on July 1, 1998; $8.00 in July 1999 through 2000**	

Covers city contractors employing janitors, parking lot attendants, temporary clerical services and security workers. Requires basic medical benefits for employees performing work for the city.

Place	Date	Wage with Health Insurance	Wage without Health Insurance
West Hollywood, CA	**October 1997**	**$7.25**	**$8.50**

Covers city service contracts worth at least $25,000 and city grant recipients. Requires temporary employment agencies to pay at least $9.00 an hour.

Place	Date	Wage with Health Insurance	Wage without Health Insurance
Duluth, MN	**July 1997**	**$6.50**	**$7.25**

Requires recipients of city economic development assistance of $25,000 or more to pay at least 90% of employees on the assisted project a living wage.

Place	Date	Wage with Health Insurance	Wage without Health Insurance
Milwaukee, WI	**1995, 1996, May 1997**		**$6.67* for city service contractors; $7.70 for MPS employees; $6.25 for certain service jobs***

A November 1995 City Council ordinance required certain city service contractors to pay employees a living wage adjusted annually to the poverty level for a family of 3. In 1996, school board measures required all Milwaukee Public School system employees and employees of MPS contractors to be paid $7.70 per hour. The county Board of Supervisors voted in May 1997 to require county contractors to pay at least $6.25 per hour in the areas of janitorial, security and parking lot attendant, indexed to increased wages of county employees.

Place	Date	Wage with Health Insurance	Wage without Health Insurance
New Haven, CT	**April 1997**		**$9.14***

Covers city service contractors. Requires contractors to give first consideration to referrals from community based hiring halls to fill vacant service positions.

Place	Date	Wage with Health Insurance	Wage without Health Insurance
Los Angeles, CA	**March 1997**	**$7.25 in 1997; $7.72***	**$8.97***

Covers public service contracts worth $25,000 or more as well as any business benefiting from a subsidy of at least $1,000,000 in one year or $100,000 on a continuing annual basis. Affected workers are entitled to 12 paid days off a year. Stipulates that a collective bargaining agreement may supersede the requirements.

Place	Date	Wage with Health Insurance	Wage without Health Insurance
Minneapolis, MN	**March 1997**		**$8.83***

Covers businesses benefiting from $100,000 or more in city assistance in one year. Defined and indexed as 110% of the federal poverty level for a family of 4. Employers receiving city assistance must also set a goal that 60% of new jobs created will be held by city residents. Prohibits privatization of services currently performed by city employees that would result in lower wages, and preferences for assistance to union-friendly businesses (defined as neutrality on union organizing, providing complete list of names and addresses of employees, access to facilities during non-work hours, card-check recognition, etc.)

Place	Date	Wage with Health Insurance	Wage without Health Insurance
St. Paul, MN	**January 1997**	8.03*	$8.83*
Covers recipients of $100,000 or more of city economic development assistance in one year. At least 60% of new jobs created as a result of such assistance must go to St. Paul residents.			
New York City, NY	**September 1996***		
Requires that employees of city contractors for security, temporary, cleaning and food services be paid the applicable prevailing wage for the industry to be determined by the city comptroller.			
Jersey City, NJ	**June 1996**	$7.50	
Covers city contractors employing clerical, food service, janitorial workers, or security guards.			
Des Moines, IA	**1988, 1996**	$9.00 in 1996	$7.00 in 1988
Covers city-funded urban renewal and loan projects.			
Santa Clara County, CA	**1995**	$10.00	
Covers manufacturing firms applying for tax abatements to disclose jobs, wage and benefit information, and additional subsidies they are seeking. Tax-abated firms must pay a living wage and provide health insurance or a suitable alternative to permanent employees. The measure gives the county money-back guarantee protection if goals are not met.			
Baltimore, MD	**December 1994**	$6.10 in 1994, currently $7.70	
Covers companies that have city service contracts. *This bill is commonly referred to as the first living wage ordinance in the country, and has been credited with starting the current living wage movement.*			
Gary, IN	**1991**	**prevailing wage***	
Ordinance requires recipients of any tax abatement to pay a prevailing wage and provide complete health benefits package to employees working over 25 hours a week. Includes public disclosure provisions.			

Main Source: Jennifer Kern, "Living Wage Successes: A Compilation of Living Wage Policies on the Books" (June 2001), "Living Wage Successes (Short Wins List)" (April 2001), ACORN Living Wage Resource Center, Association of Community Organizations for Reform Now (ACORN). www.livingwagecampaign.org.

Supplemental Sources: A. Larrison Campbell, "USLAC prevails after sit-in at admission office," *Wesleyan Argus Online*, Middletown, CT, April 7, 2000; Daniela J. Lamas "University Makes Sense of Living Wage Figure," *Harvard Crimson Online*, June 7, 2001; Amit R. Paley, "Dining Workers Ratify Contract with Wage Hike," *Harvard Crimson Online*, May 18, 2001; Ross A. Macdonald, "PSLM Gathers to Commemorate Sit-In," *Harvard Crimson Online*, May 14, 2001; "Council Boosts Wages of Child-Care Workers," *Los Angeles Times*, June 29, 2001; Janine DeFao and Pia Sarkar, "Living Wage Costs Easily Absorbed; Impact of Increasingly Popular Measure Seems Mostly to be Felt Where Intended—in Workers' Wallets," *San Francisco Chronicle*, June 3, 2001.

APPENDIX E

METHODOLOGY FOR COMPUTING MINIMUM WAGE INCREASE

■ ■ ■ ■ ■

The recommended $8 federal minimum wage was defined by an iterative process. We used the U.S. Census Bureau Current Population Survey Outgoing Rotation Group files for July 1999 through June 2000 to calculate hourly wages. If workers reported an hourly wage, we used this reported value in our estimations.

For workers who did not report an hourly wage but reported weekly earnings and usual hours worked per week, we calculated hourly wages by dividing weekly earnings by usual hours for workers who were not self-employed.[1] For workers who did not report an hourly wage and usual hours worked, we calculated hourly wages by dividing weekly earnings by actual hours worked. We adjusted for overtime for individuals who reported that they had earnings from overtime and who worked more than forty hours. Some workers did not report an hourly wage and reported that their hours varied. To calculate hourly wages for these workers, we divided weekly earnings by 40 if the individuals indicated that they worked full-time and weekly earnings by 20 if the individuals indicated that they worked part-time. Alternatively, hourly wages for these individuals could have been calculated by using regression analysis to impute usual hours based on the usual hours of workers with similar characteristics.

The reported hourly wage figure does not include tips or commissions. Therefore, the hourly wage is likely to underestimate wages earned by tipped workers. In order to estimate the wages of tipped workers, we adjusted hourly wages for workers in specific occupations.[2] For workers in "tipped" occupations, we calculated hourly wages by dividing weekly earnings by usual hours worked (or actual hours worked if usual hours were not reported). We used the adjusted hourly wage for "tipped" workers in our analysis even if an hourly wage was reported.

Calculating an hourly wage for all workers in the sample enabled us to examine the wage distribution of workers by industry. Analyzing the wage distribution by industry provided information on the estimated number and proportion of workers in each industry that earn wages below each wage level analyzed. Low-wage workers tend to be concentrated in specific industries, such as agriculture, retail trade, private household services and personal services. As the wage level increases, a larger proportion of each industry's workers earns less than the given wage and would be affected by a wage increase.

For each wage level, we calculated the cost of increasing the current minimum wage to that wage level. This methodology is similar to that used in prospective studies of municipal living wage ordinances.[3] The direct cost of the wage increase was estimated as the product of the number of workers earning less than the specified wage, the difference between the specified wage and the average wage earned by those workers, the average weekly hours worked by those workers and average weeks worked.[4]

Direct cost of wage increase (DC) = $N_{W0<W*}$ * (W*—W_{AVG}) * (H_{AVG}) * (wks$_{AVG}$).

Where $N_{W0<W*}$ is the number of workers earning less than the specified hourly wage, $W*$ is the specified hourly wage, W_{AVG} is the average hourly wage for workers earning less than $W*$, H_{AVG} is the average hours worked per week by workers earning less than $W*$, and wks_{AVG} is the average weeks worked per year by workers earning less than $W*$. We use average hours to control for the concentration of part-time employment in low-wage industries. We use average weeks worked to control for seasonal variations in employment across industries and also to reflect the differences in weeks worked among low-wage workers and other workers as well as among different demographic groups.

We also measured the indirect costs of an increase in the recommended federal minimum wage to the specified level. In addition to the increase in wages for workers earning below a specified level, it is likely that this wage increase will have a "ripple" effect as firms adjust their wage hierarchy.[5] Therefore, we estimated the cost of increasing the wages of workers earning slightly more than the specified wage level.

There is uncertainty in the empirical literature concerning the extent of the ripple effect. However, research on minimum wage increases has revealed that the effect diminishes rapidly as pay rates increase. That is, the wage distribution within firms becomes more equal as wages increase. We estimated the size of the ripple effect for workers earning wages between $W*$ and $W*+\$1$ by assuming that workers earning slightly above $W*$ will receive wage increases, but that these increases will not be as large proportionally as that received by workers initially earning less than $W*$.

The ripple effect is calculated as follows:

1) the wages of those workers earning between $W*$ and $W*+\$.50$ will increase by 1/2 of the percentage increase in wages for those earning less than $W*$;

2) the wages of workers earning between $W*+\$.51$ and $W*+\$1$ will increase by 1/4 of the percentage increase in wages for those earning less than $W*$.

The cost of the ripple effect was estimated as the product of the number of workers earning between $W*$ and $W*+\$1$, the average wage of workers in this wage tier, the average hours worked by workers in this wage tier, the average weeks worked and the percentage increase described above.

We also calculated the additional payroll costs to be paid by employers as a result of a wage increase. These included employee benefits and employer contributions to federal and state taxes.

We estimated the additional cost of employee benefits and employer taxes resulting from the wage increase (B). Only benefits that are tied to wage or salary levels would be affected by the wage increase. Health insurance would not be affected. The Bureau of Labor Statistics calculates employer costs per hour for employee compensation for industry groups. The benefit costs reported in the BLS data include paid leave, supplemental pay, insurance (life, health and disability), retirement and savings, legally required benefits and other benefits. Legally required benefits include Social Security and Medicare, federal and state unemployment insurance and workers compensation. We used the proportion of legally required benefits to wages and salaries to estimate the increase in taxes resulting from the wage increase.[6] This data permitted us to calculate the proportion that wages and specific benefits contribute to employee cost. For the purpose of this report, we subtract the cost of insurance from the total cost of benefits, since these benefits are not typically tied to income.

We estimated the increase in total employee compensation by applying the proportion of cost due to wages and salaries as reported in the BLS data to the increase in wages $(DC + R)$. Then we estimated the increase in cost of specific benefits (for example, paid leave, retirement and savings and taxes) by applying the proportion of the cost of those benefits to total employee compensation cost, as reported in the BLS data (B).

The total costs of an increase in the recommended federal minimum wage to a specific level were calculated by adding direct costs and indirect costs.

Total costs = $DC + R + B$.

Our estimate of the cost of the wage increase is conservative in that it does not include an analysis of the benefits accruing to firms from increased wages. In some cases, paying higher wages may reduce turnover and training costs for the firm. Higher wages may improve employee morale and enhance productivity whether or not the firm consciously pursues a policy to increase productivity. Therefore, the net cost of the wage increase may actually be lower that the total cost from our calculations.

In our discussion of the capacity of business to absorb the wage increase we looked at overall productivity, profits and other variables. We also analyzed the impact at the industry level. We gauged the impact of a wage increase on sectors and firms by comparing the total cost of the increase (as described above) to other relevant costs of business operations, including total receipts minus payroll and benefits and the total costs of goods sold in the sector.[7] This allowed us to identify sectors most affected by a minimum wage increase.

Data on total industry payroll and total industry receipts (1997) for industries were provided by the U.S. Census Bureau. These data include all non-governmental employer businesses with at least one paid employee at some point during the year. We adjusted the data for industry payroll to 1999 dollars using the wage and salary component of the Employer Cost Index and industry receipts were adjusted to 1999 dollars using the CPI-U. Receipts minus payroll and benefits were calculated by subtracting total payroll and estimated benefit costs (where benefit costs were estimated using proportions of total benefits to wages and salaries derived from the BLS Employer Costs for Employee Compensation, March 1999). Data for 1996 on the cost of goods sold were computed from the Internal Revenue Service Statistics of Income for Corporations, Partnerships and Sole Proprietorships. The cost of goods sold consists of "the direct costs incurred…in producing goods and providing services. Included were costs of materials used in manufacturing; costs of goods purchased for resale; direct labor; and certain overhead expenses, such as rent, utilities, supplies, maintenance and repairs." Figures for 1996 for the cost of goods sold were adjusted to 1999 dollars using the CPI.

We also isolated the impact of the wage increase by firm size using Statistics of U.S. Businesses provided by the U.S. Census Bureau. Using this data, we calculated the proportion of industry establishments, employment, payroll, total receipts and receipts minus payroll and benefits in firms of various size categories. We applied the proportion of industry payroll by firm size to the total cost of the wage increase to determine the cost to firms in each size category. Next, we compared the cost of the increase borne by firms in each industry and size category to receipts minus payroll and benefits for those firms. We found that sector, not size, was the key variable.

NOTES

■ ■ ■ ■ ■

OVERVIEW

1 For example, in a 2000 poll, 94 percent agreed with the statement, "As a country, we should make sure that people who work full time should be able to earn enough to keep their families out of poverty." Support for this exists across all demographic groups. *A National Survey of American Attitudes Towards Low-Wage Workers and Welfare Reform*, summary of poll conducted by Lake Snell Perry & Associates for Jobs for the Future, a Boston-based employment research organization, April 27-30, 2000.

2 United Nations Childrens Fund, Innocenti Research Centre, *A League Table of Child Poverty in Rich Nations*.

3 Arthur B. Kennickell, et al., "Recent Changes in U.S. Family Finances: Results from the 1998 Survey of Consumer Finances," *Federal Reserve Bulletin*, January 2000.

4 Lawrence Mishel, Jared Bernstein and John Schmitt, *The State of Working America, 2000-2001* (Washington, D.C.: Economic Policy Institute), p. 8.

5 Edward N. Wolff, "Recent Trends in Wealth Ownership, 1983-1998," April 2000, Table 1.

6 U.S. Conference of Mayors, *A Status Report on Hunger and Homelessness in America's Cities 2000* (December 2000), p. i. Also see America's Second Harvest, *Hunger 1997: The Faces and Facts* (March 1998), www.secondharvest.org.

7 United Nations Childrens Fund, *The State of the World's Children 2001*, "Under-five mortality rankings," p. 77.

8 "Executive Summary," *No Health Insurance? It's Enough to Make You Sick*, Decision 2000 Campaign, www.acponline.org; John Z. Ayanian, et al., "Unmet Health Needs of Uninsured Adults in the United States," *JAMA* (Journal of the American Medical Association), October 25, 2000.

9 Linda J. Blumberg and David W. Liska, *The Uninsured in the United States: A Status Report* (Washington, D.C.: Urban Institute, April 1996); *Los Angeles Times*, "42 million lack health insurance," April 27, 1996, citing report by the American College of Physicians; Spencer Rich, "For Those with Modest Incomes, Health Insurance Bill is Little Help," *Washington Post*, May 3, 1996. Also see Dennis P. Andrulis, "Access to Care is the Centerpiece in the Elimination of Socioeconomic Disparities in Health," Annals of Internal Medicine, September 1, 1998 and Roni Rabin, "Queens Health: Taking a Risk Living Without a Safety Net: Insurance a Key to Healthy Lives, but Many Have None," *Newsday*, November 15, 1998.

10 "Second Class," *Consumer Reports* special report, September 2000, citing the *New England Journal of Medicine*. Also see FamiliesUSA, *Getting Less Care: The Uninsured with Chronic Health Conditions*, February 2001.

11 Ichiro Kawachi, Richard G. Wilkinson and Bruce P. Kennedy, "Introduction," in Kawachi, Kennedy and Wilkinson, eds., *The Society and Population Reader: Income Inequality and Health* (New York: The New Press, 1999), p. xiii; UNCIEF, *The State of the World's Children 2001*, Table 1, "Basic Indicators." Also see Norman Daniels, Bruce Kennedy and Ichiro Kawachi, *Is Inequality Bad for Your Health* (Boston: Beacon Press, 2000) and Alvrin R. Tarlov and Robert F. St. Peter, eds., *The Society and Population Reader: A State and Community Perspective* (New York: The New Press, 2000).

12 John W. Lynch, George A. Kaplan, Elsie R. Pamuk, et al., "Income Inequality and Mortality in Metropolitan Areas of the United States," *American Journal of Public Health*, July 1998; "A Modern Tale of 282 Cities...Exposes America's Hidden Virus," *Too Much* (United for a Fair Economy), October 1998.

13 In most cases, we do not duplicate footnotes here for material discussed in depth in later chapters.

14 Eric Schlosser, *Fast Food Nation* (New York: Houghton Mifflin, 2001), pp. 259-260; Greg Hernandez, *Los Angeles Times*, May 26, 2000; Carey Sweet, *Phoenix New Times*, December 28, 2000.

15 Mark Weisbrot and Michelle Sforza-Roderick, *Baltimore's Living Wage Law: An Analysis of the Fiscal and Economic Costs of Baltimore City Ordinance 442* (Washington, D.C.: Preamble Center, October 1996).

16 Tim Styer, Judy Wicks and Hal Taussig, *Philadelphia Inquirer*, June 21, 2000.

17 U.S. Small Business Administration, "State Winner! Mo's Enterprises, Inc.," and SBA News Release, "Alabama Entrepreneur is National Small Business Person of the Year: Oregon, Pennsylvania and Florida Winners are Runners-Up," May 8, 2001, www.sba.gov.

18 "The 2001 ICIC-Inc Magazine *Inner City 100* Fast Facts," www.innercity100.org. Also see Initiative for a Competitive Inner City, press release, "Leaders of the New Economy: 2nd Annual ICIC-Inc. Magazine Inner City 100," 2000, www.icic.org.

19 Internal Revenue Service, *1996 Corporation Returns*, "Explanation of Terms," p. 169.

20 Economic Policy Institute, "Medicare at the crossroads: Vouchers take us in the wrong direction," *Paycheck Economics*, January 2001.

21 Barbara Bergmann, "Decent Child Care at Decent Wages," *The American Prospect*, January 1-15, 2001, p.9.

22 National Committee on Pay Equity, *Questions and Answers on Pay Equity*, http://www.feminist.com/fairpay/f_qape.html.

CHAPTER 1

1 U.S. Census Bureau, press release, July 9, 1999, on release of *Extended Measures of Well-Being: Meeting Basic Needs, 1995*.

2 Margaret Andrews, et al., U.S. Department of Agriculture, Economic Research Service, *Household Food Security in the United States, 1999* (Fall 2000).

3 Heather Boushey, Chauna Brocht, Bethney Gundersen and Jared Bernstein, Economic Policy Institute, *Hardships In America: The Real Story of Working Families*, July 2001; Sheila Rafferty Zedlewski, Urban Institute, "Family Economic Well-Being," *Findings from the National Survey of America's Families* (Washington D.C.: 2000), www.urban.org. Also see, NPR/Kaiser/Kennedy School poll, "Poverty in America," NPR Online, 2001.

4 Lydia Saad, "One-Third of Americans worry about paying 'normal monthly bills,'" Gallup News Service, survey conducted April 6-8, 2001. Also see the Gallup Social Audit of "Haves and Have Nots," survey conducted April-May 1998. www.gallup.com.

5 U.S. Census Bureau, "Poverty Thresholds in 2000, by Size of Family and Number of Related Children Under 18 Years," January 26, 2001.

6 The "poverty thresholds" calculated by the Census Bureau are used mainly for statistical purposes such as measuring the number of Americans in poverty. The Department of Health and Human Services publishes "poverty guidelines." "The guidelines are a simplification of the poverty thresholds for use for administrative purposes—for instance, determining eligibility for certain federal programs" such as food stamps and Head Start. The HHS guidelines are designated by the year they are issued even though they reflect price changes from the prior year. The 2001 HHS guidelines are approximately equal to the Census Bureau thresholds for 2000 (which are issued in 2001). The 2001 HHS Poverty Guidelines for the 48 contiguous states and D.C. (Alaska and Hawaii are calculated separately under the guidelines, but not the thresholds) are $8,590 for one person, $11,610 for a family of two, $14,630 for a family of three and $17,650 for a family of four. The Census Bureau 2000 poverty thresholds for those respective family sizes are $8,787, $11,234, $13,737 and $17,601. See "The 2001 HHS Poverty Guidelines," http://aspe.hhs.gov/poverty/01poverty.htm. Also see, "Preliminary Estimate of Weighted Average Poverty Thresholds for 2000," January 24, 2001. www.census.gov.

7 Craig Gundersen, et al., *A Safety Net for Farm Households*, USDA Economic Research Service, October 2000, pp. 2-3.

8 U.S. Department of Health and Human Services, *HHS Fact Sheet*, "The State Children's Health Insurance Program (SCHIP)," February 2, 2001.

9 U.S. Department of Agriculture, Consumer Nutrition Division, Human Nutrition Information Service, "USDA Family Food Plans, 1983: Low Cost, Moderate and Liberal," November 1982 (slightly revised March 1983).

10 Arloc Sherman, *Wasting America's Future: The Children's Defense Fund Report on the Costs of Child Poverty* (Boston: Beacon Press, 1994), pp. 6, 8.

11 Orshansky, et al. "Measuring Poverty: A Debate," *Public Welfare* 36(2), pp. 46-55 (1978), cited in Trudi J. Renwick and Barbara R. Bergmann, "A Budget-Based

Definition of Poverty: With an Application to Single-Parent Families," *Journal of Human Resources*, Vol. XXVIII, No. 1, (1993), p.6.

12 Sherman, *Wasting America's Future*, pp. 6, 8.

13 May 27, 1964 memo from Mollie Orshansky to Herman Miller at the U.S. Bureau of the Census; Gordon M. Fisher, "The Development of the Orshansky Poverty Thresholds and Their Subsequent History as the Official U.S. Poverty Measure," (May 1992, partially revised September 1997),http://www.census.gov/hhes/poverty/povmeas/papers/orshansky.html. Also see Mollie Orshansky, "Technical Paper #1" in U.S. Department of Health, Education and Welfare, *Measure of Poverty: A Report to Congress as Mandated by the Education Amendments of 1974* (Washington, D.C.: U.S. Government Printing Office, 1976), p. 10, cited in Trudi Renwick, *Poverty and Single Parent Families: A Study of Minimal Subsistence Household Budgets*, (New York: Garland Publishing, Inc., 1998), p. 12.

14 Cited in Fisher, "The Development of the Orshansky Poverty Thresholds and Their Subsequent History as the Official U.S. Poverty Measure." See note 169. Orshansky also articulated this view in a March 23, 1971 Congressional hearing.

15 See, for example, Constance F. Citro and Robert T. Michael, eds., *Measuring Poverty: A New Approach*, (Washington, D.C.: National Academy Press, 1995), pp. 1-15, 25-31; Patricia Ruggles, *Drawing the Line: Alternative Poverty Measures and their Implications for Public Policy* (Washington, D.C.: Urban Institute Press, 1990); Renwick, *Poverty and Single Parent Families*, pp. 9-51; John E. Schwarz and Thomas J. Volgy, *The Forgotten Americans: Thirty Million Working Poor in the Land of Opportunity* (New York: W.W. Norton, 1992); General Accounting Office, *Poverty Measurement: Issues in Revising and Updating the Official Definition*, April 1997.

16 The Consumer Price Index for all urban consumers (CPI-U) measures "the average change over time in the prices paid by urban consumers for a market basket of consumer goods and services. The CPI-U represents about 87 percent of the total U.S. population. It is based on the expenditures of almost all residents of urban or metropolitan areas, including professionals, the self-employed, the poor, the unemployed and retired persons as well as urban wage earners and clerical workers. Not included in the CPI are the spending patterns of persons living in rural non-metropolitan areas, farm families, persons in the Armed Forces, and those in institutions, such as prisons and mental hospitals." http://stats.bls.gov/cpifaq.htm#Question 1.

17 From U.S. Bureau of Labor Statistics, *Consumer Expenditure Survey 1998*, Table 45: Quintiles of income before taxes: Shares of average annual expenditures and sources of income. http://stats.bls.gov/csx/1998/share/quintile.pdf.

18 M.P. Taylor, "Budget blues," *Dallas Morning News*, March 9, 1993.

19 Citro and Michael, *Measuring Poverty*, p.1.

20 Ibid., pp. 4-5.

21 Unstandardized rates from U.S. Census Bureau, "Standardized and Unstandardized Experimental Poverty Rates: 1990-1999." Standardized poverty rates are less useful in comparing NAS-related rates with the official rate in a given year because they are calculated by adjusting the experimental poverty thresholds to produce the same rate as the official rate for 1997. For more information on the derivation of experimental poverty measures, see Kathleen Short, Thesia Garner, David Johnson and Patricia Doyle, *Experimental Poverty Measures, 1990-1997*, U.S. Census Bureau, June 1999. See also Thesia I. Garner, Kathleen Short, Stephanie Shipp, Charles Nelson and Geoffrey Paulin, "Experimental Poverty Measurement for the 1990s," *Monthly Labor Review*, March 1998.

22 Patricia Ruggles, *Drawing the Line: Alternative Poverty Measures and their Implications for Public Policy* (Washington, D.C.: Urban Institute Press, 1990); Daniel H. Weinberg and Enrique J. Lamas, "Some experimental results on alternative poverty measures," *Proceedings of the American Statistical Association, Social Statistics Section*, 1993, pp. 549-555.

23 David S. Johnson, John M. Rogers and Lucilla Tan, "A century of family budgets in the United States," *Monthly Labor Review*, May 2001, p. 28.

24 Citro and Michael, *Measuring Poverty*, pp. 120-122. Also see Johnson, et al., "A century of family budgets," p.28.

25 Renwick, *Poverty and Single Parent Families*, p. 32.

26 Department of Labor Employment and Training Administration, "Lower Living Standard Income Level (for a family of four persons) by Region," 2001, http://wdsc.doleta.gov/llsil/2001table1.htm.

27 Trudi J. Renwick and Barbara R. Bergmann, "A Budget-Based Definition of Poverty: With an Application to Single-Parent Families," *Journal of Human Resources*, Vol. XXVIII, No. 1, (1993); Renwick, *Poverty and Single Parent Families*; Bergmann, "Deciding Who's Poor," *Dollars and Sense*, March-April 2000; Jared Bernstein, Chauna Brocht, and Maggie Spade-Aguilar, *How Much Is Enough? Basic Needs Budgets for Working Families* (Washington, D.C.: Economic Policy Institute, 2000), pp. 18 and 73; Citro and Michael, *Measuring Poverty*, pp. 116-118. Also see John E. Schwarz and Thomas J. Volgy, *The Forgotten Americans: Thirty Million Working Poor in the Land of Opportunity* (New York: W.W. Norton, 1992), for their detailed "economy budget" and case studies of working Americans who can't make ends meet.

28 Jared Bernstein, Chauna Brocht, and Maggie Spade-Aguilar, *How Much Is Enough? Basic Needs Budgets for Working Families* (Washington, D.C.: Economic Policy Institute, 2000).

29 Heather Boushey, Chauna Brocht, Bethney Gundersen and Jared Bernstein, Economic Policy Institute, *Hardships In America: The Real Story of Working Families*, July 2001. Sections of the report and the budgets for every MSA and one combined rural budget per state are available through the online Issue Guide "Poverty and Family Budgets," www.epinet.org.

30 Diana Pearce with Jennifer Brooks, *The Self-Sufficiency Standard for the City of New York*, prepared for the Women's Center for Education and Career Advancement, September 2000, p. 1.

31 See, for example, Rose Gutfeld, "The Real Cost of Living: 'Self-Sufficiency' may be the next frontier for U.S. welfare reform," *Ford Foundation Report*, Winter 2001.

32 *Boston Globe* editorial, May 8, 2001.

33 United Nations Children's Fund, Innocenti Research Centre, *A League Table of Child Poverty in Rich Nations*, pp. 6-9.

34 Denton R. Vaughan, "Exploring the Use of the Public's Views to Set Income Poverty Thresholds and Adjust Them Over Time," *Social Security Bulletin* 56 (2) (Summer 1993); Lee Rainwater, *What Money Buys: Inequality and the Social Meanings of Income* (New York: Basic Books, 1974). For a critique see, for example, Renwick, *Poverty and Single Parent Families*, pp. 26-27.

35 NPR/Kaiser/Kennedy School poll, "Poverty in America," NPR Online, 2001. Also see, for example, Citro and Michael, *Measuring Poverty*, pp. 134-140.

36 Lake Snell Perry & Associates, "A National Survey of American Attitudes Towards Low-Wage Workers and Welfare Reform," Jobs for the Future (www.jff.org), Boston, 2000.

37 Richard Berman, "Minimum wage needs some flexibility," *Providence Journal*, March 29, 2001.

38 See, for example: Theda Skocpol, *States and Social Revolutions* (Cambridge: Cambridge University Press, 1979); Theda Skocpol, "Bringing the State Back In: Strategies of Analysis in Current Research," in P. Evans, D. Rueschmeyer and T. Skocpol, eds., *Bringing the State Back In*, (Cambridge: Cambridge University Press, 1985); Edwin Amenta and Yvonne Zylan, "It happened here: political opportunity, the new institutionalism and the Townsend movement," *American Sociological Review*, Vol. 56, April: 260-265 (1991); Jill Quandango, *The Transformation of Old Age Security: Class and Politics in the American Welfare State*, (Chicago: University of Chicago Press, 1988); Robert W. Fogel, *The Fourth Great Awakening and the Future of Egalitarianism* (Chicago: University of Chicago Press, 2000).

39 Sar A. Levitan, Garth L. Mangum and Ray Marshall, *Human Resources and Labor Markets: Labor and Manpower in the American Economy* (New York: Harper and Row, 1972).

40 U.S. Department of Labor, *Report on the Youth Labor Force*, revised, November 2000, p. 3.

41 Sar Levitan and Frank Gallo, "Work and family: the impact of legislation (The American Family During the 20th Century)," *Monthly Labor Review*, March, 1990, pp. 34-37.

42 It was only in the 1940s, following two federal actions, that private pensions were given the support or protection needed to encourage their growth: First, in 1942, the Federal government excluded from taxation contributions that private employers invest in pension funds. Second, in 1949, the Supreme Court concluded that private sector pensions can be included in union agreements. This profoundly encouraged the growth of such funds. Levitan and Gallo, "Work and family: the impact of legislation."

CHAPTER 2

1 Alison Gregor, "Living wage crusade pays off," *San Antonio Express-News*, November 27, 2000.

2 See, for example, Bernstein, Brocht and Spade-Aguilar, *How Much Is Enough?* for a comprehensive review of needs budget methodologies.

3 U.S. Census Bureau, *America's Families and Living Arrangements*, June 2001.

4 For accessing state Self-Sufficiency Standards and other tools from WOW's Family Economic Self-Sufficiency Project, visit www.sixstrategies.org. The Economic Policy Institute (www.epinet.org) publishes an online guide, "Poverty and Family Budgets," which provides an interactive tool for figuring family budgets; provides family budgets for every Metropolitan Statistical Area and one combined rural budget per state; and includes a section on "Basic family budgets by state," with hyperlinks to state studies by other organizations.

5 U.S. Department of Housing and Urban Development, 24 CFR Part 888 [Docket No. FR-4496-02], *Fair Market Rents for the Section 8 Housing Assistance Payments Program—Fiscal Year 2000*, October 1, 1999.

6 U.S. Census Bureau, *Health Insurance Coverage 1999*, September 2000.

7 Economic Policy Institute, *The State of Working America 2000/2001*,Table 2.15, p. 140.

8 Jon Gabel, Larry Levitt, Jeremy Pickreign, Heidi Whitmore, Erin Holve, Samantha Hawkins and Nick Miller, "Job-Based Health Insurance In 2000: Premiums Rise Sharply While Coverage Grows," *Health Affairs* (September/October 2000), pp. 144-151. Despite the increase over the last decade, workers' monthly contribution toward job-based health insurance premiums remained stable in the last few years (1999-2000) and have even decreased slightly (for single coverage) since 1996.

9 Citro and Michael, *Measuring Poverty*, pp. 27-28.

10 Jeffrey Capizzano, Gina Adams and Freya Sonenstein, "Child Care Arrangements for Children Under Five: Variation Across States," Urban Institute, Series B, No. B-7, March 2000; Jeffrey Capizzano and Gina Adams, "The Number of Child Care Arrangements Used by Children Under Five: Variation Across States," Urban Institute, Series B, No. B-12, March 2000. A recent U.S. Census Bureau report based on data from the Survey of Income and Program Participation (SIPP) found similar differences in child care arrangements. According to this report, preschool children in poverty were more likely to be cared for by relatives (67.9 percent v. 61.0 percent) than by non-relatives (52.5 percent v. 62.1 percent) in 1995. Note that the percentages do not sum to 100 percent because many families use multiple care arrangements. Kristin Smith, *Who's Minding the Kids? Child Care Arrangements Fall 1995*, U.S. Census Bureau, October 2000.

11 Note that the percentages do not sum to 100 percent because many families use multiple care arrangements. Smith, *Who's Minding the Kids? Child Care Arrangements, Fall 1995*, U.S. Census Bureau, October 2000.

12 Elaine Murakami and Jennifer Young, "Daily Travel by Persons with Low Income," presented at the NPTS Symposium, Bethesda, MD, October 1997, Figure 1.

13 Patricia S. Hu and Jennifer R. Young, *A Summary of Travel Trends: 1995 National Personal Transportation Survey*, January 8, 1999 (Draft), prepared for U.S. Department of Transportation, Federal Highway Administration, Table 18; Murakami and Young, "Daily Travel by Persons with Low Income," Figure 1.

14 Steven Rafael and Michael Stoll, "Can Boosting Minority Car-Ownership Rates Narrow Inter-Racial Employment Gaps?" June 2000.

15 Ed Lazere, Shawn Fremstad and Heidi Goldberg, *States and Counties Are Taking Steps to Help Low-Income Working Families Make Ends Meet and Move Up the Economic Ladder*, (Washington, D.C.: Center on Budget and Policy Priorities), November 27, 2000.

16 Murakami and Young, "Daily Travel by Persons with Low Income," Table 6.

17 See, for example, Congressional Budget Office, *Estimates of Federal Tax Liabilities for Individuals and Families by Income Category and Family Type for 1995 and 1999*, May 1998, http://www.cbo.gov; Nicholas Johnson, Robert Zahradnik and Elizabeth C. McNichol, *State Income Tax Burdens on Low-Income Families in 1999*, Center on Budget and Policy Priorities, March 2000.

18 Chris McComb, "Few say it's ideal for both parents to work full time outside of home," Gallup News Service, May 4, 2001, Gallup poll conducted April 20-22, 2001.

19 These estimates are based on data from the March 2000 Current Population Survey Annual Demographic Supplement. The six household compositions for which a minimum needs budget was estimated account for 82 percent of households and 78.4 percent of working households. We use "household" to define individuals living alone and all families in the March 2000 CPS. Our working household estimates are based on individuals and families (households) with some wage or salary income. They include households with only self-employment income. Note also that the self-employed are included in calculations that reflect "all families" independent of employment status.

CHAPTER 3

1 Andrew C. Revkin, "Welfare Policies Alter the Face of Food Lines," *New York Times*, February 26, 1999.

2 Jonathan Grossman, "Fair Labor Standards Act of 1938: Maximum Struggle for a Minimum Wage," U.S. Department of Labor, www.dol.gov/dol/esa/public/minwage/history.htm.

3 Franklin D. Roosevelt, *Public Papers*, VI (May 24, 1937), pp. 209-214, cited in Grossman, "Fair Labor Standards Act of 1938."

4 Jared Bernstein and John Schmitt, Economic Policy Institute, *The Impact of the Minimum Wage: Policy lifts wages, maintains floor for low-wage labor market*, June 2000, p. 10. Also see Oren M. Levin-Waldman, *The Rhetorical Evolution of the Minimum Wage*, Working Paper No. 280, The Jerome Levy Economics Institute, September 1999.

5 Historical data for congressional pay can be found on the Dirksen Congressional Center website at http://www.congresslink.org/sources/salaries.html.

6 We calculated the real value of the minimum wage in 2003 (2000 dollars) using inflation projections from Congressional Budget Office, *Budget and Economic Outlook, Fiscal Years 2002-2011* (January 2001).

7 Wendy W. Simmons and Frank Newport, "Issue Referendum reveals mix of liberal and conservative views in America today," Gallup News Service, November 1, 2000.

8 Pew Research Center for the People and the Press, "Credit crunch and energy costs shadow financial outlook: Economic inequality seen as rising, boom bypasses poor," June 21, 2001.

9 Adjusted using inflation projections from Congressional Budget Office, *Budget and Economic Outlook, Fiscal Years 2002-2011* (January 2001).

10 U.S. Department of Labor, "Minimum Wage Laws in the States," http://www.dol.gov/dol/esa/public/minwage/america.htm; IOMA (Institute of Management and Administration), "Report on Hourly Compensation," August 2001.

11 Edith Rasell, Jared Bernstein and Heather Boushey, Economic Policy Institute, *Step Up, Not Out: The Case for Raising the Federal Minimum Wage for Workers in Every State*, February 7, 2001, pp. 5-6.

12 Grossman, "Fair Labor Standards Act of 1938."

13 Department of Labor, *Minimum Wage and Overtime Hours Under the Fair Labor Standards Act*, January 2001, pp. 17, 19.

14 *Economic Report of the President 2001*. As the Department of Labor notes in *Minimum Wage and Overtime Hours Under the Fair Labor Standards Act*, p. 17, data is not available to isolate out the productivity of minimum wage workers.

15 *Statistical Abstract of the United States 2000*, Table 647, and *Statistical Abstract of the United States 1991*, Table 634.

16 Amy Dean, "Fighting for working families in a Bush era," speech to the Next Agenda Conference, Washington, D.C., February 28, 200l, transcript available at www.ourfuture.org.

17 Barbara Ehrenreich, Cambridge Public Library, June 25, 2001.

18 Economic Policy Institute, "Measuring prosperity: When better isn't good enough," *EPI Journal*, Fall 2000.

19 Department of Labor, *Minimum Wage and Overtime Hours Under the Fair Labor Standards Act*, January 2001, p. 19.

20 Franklin Roosevelt, *Public Papers and Addresses*, Vol. VII (New York: Random House, 1937), p. 392, cited in Grossman, "Fair Labor Standards Act of 1938."

21 Eric Schlosser, *Fast Food Nation* (New York: Houghton Mifflin, 2001), p. 73.

22 Joann S. Lublin, "Pay for no performance," *Wall Street Journal*, April 9, 1998.

23 *Fortune*, "Inside the great CEO pay heist: a special report," June 25, 2001.

24 Matthew Miller, "Market forces buffet the little people—CEO salary is in a different class," *Sacramento Bee*, April 20, 2001. Also see, Scott Klinger, *The Bigger They Come, The Harder They Fall: High CEO pay and the effect on long-term stock prices*, United for a Fair Economy, April 6, 2001 (www.ufenet.org).

25 See, for example, Matt Bloom, "The performance effects of pay dispersion on individuals and organizations," *Academy of Management Journal*, February 1, 1999.

26 Department of Labor, *Minimum Wage and Overtime Hours Under the Fair Labor Standards Act*, 2001, p. 3; U.S. Bureau of Labor Statistics, *Employment and Earnings*, Table 44, January 2001.

27 Schlosser, *Fast Food Nation*, pp. 72-73.

28 John Schmitt, "Minimum Wage Careers," *The American Prospect*, March 27-April 10, 2000.

29 William J. Carrington and Bruce C. Fallick, "Do some workers have minimum wage careers?" *Monthly Labor Review*, May 2001, pp. 18, 25.

30 *Statistical Abstract of the United States 2000*, Table 295. The figures of those enrolled in college were 45.1 percent in 1960, 51.8 percent in 1970, 49.3 percent in 1980, 59.9 percent in 1990, and 65.6 percent in 1998.

31 Schlosser, *Fast Food Nation*, pp. 82-84.

32 Ibid., pp. 84-85.

33 Ibid., pp. 72-73.

CHAPTER 4

1 Small Business Survival Committee, Legislative Issues, "An Opportunity to Set a Pro-Entrepreneur Tone for a New Century," 2001, www.sbsc.org.

2 A Report by the National Economic Council with the Assistance of the Council of Economic Advisers and the Office of the Chief Economist, U.S. Department of Labor, *The Minimum Wage: Increasing the Reward for Work*, March 2000.

3 Jennifer L. Martel and David S. Langdon, "The job market in 2000: slowing down as the year ended," *Monthly Labor Review*, February 2001, pp. 18-19, 24, 26.

4 National Economic Council, *The Minimum Wage: Increasing the Reward for Work*, p. 3. Also see these Economic Policy Institute reports: Bernstein and Schmitt, *The Impact of the Minimum Wage*; Rasell, Bernstein and Boushey, *Step Up, Not Out: The Case for Raising the Federal Minimum Wage for Workers in Every State*; Chauna Brocht, *The Next Step: The New Minimum Wage Proposals and the Old Opposition*, Revised March 8, 2000; Jared Bernstein and John Schmitt, *Making Work Pay: The Impact of the 1996-97 Minimum Wage Increase*, 1998.

5 John T. Addison and McKinley Blackburn, "Minimum Wages and Poverty," *Industrial and Labor Relations Review*, April 1999.

6 David Card and Alan Krueger, *Myth and Measurement: The New Economics of the Minimum Wage*, (Princeton, NJ: Princeton University Press, 1995).

7 Jeff Thompson and Anna Braun, "The Effects of the Minimum Wage on the Restaurant Industry," Oregon Center for Public Policy, March 23, 1999. Oregon's minimum wage was increased as the result of a 1996 voter initiative. The increase took place in three stages: the minimum wage increased from $4.75 to $5.50, effective January 1, 1997; to $6.00, effective January 1, 1998; and to $6.50, effective January 1, 1999. The report cited here examines the impact of the 1997 and 1998 increase on the restaurant and retail trade industries in Oregon.

8 Bernstein and Schmitt, *The Impact of the Minimum Wage*, p. 16.

9 Martel and Langdon, "The job market in 2000," p. 18.

10 Robert D. Hershey, Jr., "The Cost of Not Living On A $5.15 Minimum; Little Impact Seen In Raising Wage Now," *New York Times*, September 19, 2000; "You Can Go Home Again—With A Raise: Businesses Are Going To Unusual Lengths To Fill Jobs," *Business Week*, July 19, 1999; Louis Uchitelle, "The Floor Under Wages: How Low Can It Fall?" *New York Times*, December 24, 2000.

Upward movement in the wage distribution is evident in our own analysis of the Current Population Survey Outgoing Rotation Group Files from October 1998 through September 1999 and from July 1999 through June 2000. In the earlier period, 13.3 percent of the workforce earned less than $6.15 per hour and 26.1 percent earned less than $8 per hour. In the later period, 10.6 percent of the workforce earned less than $6.15 per hour while 23.1 percent earned less than $8. In all industries except forestry and fisheries, the percentage of the workforce earning less than $8 per hour declined. We used the Current Population Survey Outgoing Rotation Group files since this dataset provides the most current data source from which workers' hourly wages can be readily calculated since respondents are asked questions about earnings and hours worked in the prior week. In contrast, for the March supplement to the Current Population Survey (another data set frequently used in wage and earnings analyses), respondents are asked for information on earnings and income the prior year. Individuals and households sampled for the Current Population Survey answer a set of questions for four consecutive months, are "off" for eight months and participate for four more consecutive months. The Outgoing Rotation Group files are used because the questions pertaining to wages and hours worked are only asked of respondents in their fourth and eighth months of the survey.

11 See, for example, Robert E. Scott and Christian Weller, Economic Policy Institute, *Fed Up: The Federal Reserve must lower interest rates now to avoid a recession, rising unemployment*, January 29, 2001; Jeff Faux, Economic Policy Institute, *The Fed's Unnecessary Assault on Wages*, March 2, 2000; Willem Thorbecke, *A Dual Mandate for the Federal Reserve: The Pursuit of Price Stability and Full Employment*, Jerome Levy Economics Institute, Public Policy Brief 60, 2000.

12 Rick Wartzman, "Falling Behind," *Wall Street Journal*, July 19, 2001.

13 Rasell, Bernstein and Boushey, *Step Up, Not Out*, p. 6.

14 Scott and Weller, *Fed Up*.

15 Rochelle Sharpe, "What exactly is a living wage?" *Business Week*, May 28, 2001.

16 Jane Steinfels Hussain, "Not a minimum wage but a living wage," *The Tennessean*, March 28, 2001.

17 Ana M. Cabrera, "Jobs For Justice: Pay the people a living wage demand local community groups," *The Providence American*, March 23, 2000.

18 Bobbi Murray, "Living Wage Comes of Age," *The Nation*, July 23/30, 2001.

19 On federal contractors, see Chauna Brocht, Economic Policy Institute, *The Forgotten Workforce: More Than One in 10 Federal Contract Workers Earn Less than a Living Wage*, November 2000.

20 In addition to those cited in the text, see, for example, Robert Pollin and Stephanie Luce, *The Living Wage: Building a Fair Economy* (New York: The New Press, 1998); Economic Policy Institute, *Issue Guide on the Living Wage* at www.epinet.org; Robert Pollin, Stephanie Luce and Mark Brenner, *An Economic Analysis of the New Orleans Minimum Wage Proposal*, Political Economy Research Institute (July 1999); Bruce Nissen, "The Impact of a Living Wage Ordinance on Miami-Dade County," Center for Labor Research and Studies, Florida International University (October 23, 1998); Michael Reich, Peter Hall and Fiona Hsu, "Living Wages and the San Francisco Economy: The Benefits and The Costs" (June 1999). For the opposition case, see Employment Policies Institute, *Living Wage Policy: The Basics* (2000).

21 Mark Weisbrot and Michelle Sforza-Roderick, *Baltimore's Living Wage Law: An Analysis of the Fiscal and Economic Costs of Baltimore City Ordinance 442* (Washington, D.C.: Preamble Center, October 1996).

22 Jared Bernstein, Economic Policy Institute, *Higher Wages Lead to More Efficient Service Provision: The Impact of Living Wage Ordinances on the Public Service Contracting Process*, August 2000.

23 Steven V. Brull, "What's So Bad About a Living Wage? Paying above the minimum seems to do more good than harm," *Business Week*, September 4, 2000.

24 Sharpe, "What exactly is a living wage?"

25 A recent study examining businesses started in 1992 found that 53 percent ceased operations prior to 1996. The same study found that 55.2 percent of eating and drinking places (a sector considered to have high turnover) opened in 1992 ceased operations prior to 1996. Dr. Richard J. Boden, Jr., "Analyses of Business Dissolution by Demographic Category of Business Ownership," Final Report Prepared for the Office of Advocacy of the U.S. Small Business Administration (December 2000), http://www.sba.gov/advo/research/rs204tot.pdf.

26 U.S. Small Business Administration, Office of Advocacy, *The State of Small Business, 1999*, http://www.sba.gov/advo/stats/facts99.pdf. Also see U.S. Small Business Administration, Office Of Advocacy, "Small Business Economic Indicators, 1998" (March 2000), http://www.sba.gov/advo/stats/sbei98.pdf.

27 The authors of the study grouped 65 discrete types of answers from the debtors into eight broad categories. Outside business conditions included factors such as new competition, increases in rent, insurance or other costs of doing business, declining real estate values, etc.; financing included high debt service, loss of financing or the inability to get financing; inside business conditions included factors such as mismanagement, a decline in production, a bad location, the loss of major clients and the inability to collect accounts receivable, and tax obligations included problems with the IRS, state or local tax authority. Teresa A. Sullivan, Elizabeth Warren and Jay Westbrook, "Financial Difficulties of Small Firms and Reasons for Their Failure" (Austin, TX: Business Bankruptcy Project, 1998), http://www.sba.gov/advo/research/rs188tot.pdf.

28 *Statistical Abstract of the United States 2000*, Tables 875 and 877.

29 Correspondence, November 2, 2000, from Brian Headd, economist, U.S. Small Business Administration, Office of Advocacy; U.S. Small Business Administration, Office of Advocacy, *Small Business Indicators, 1998* (2000), http://www.sba.gov.advo/stats/sbei98.pdf.

30 "Inflation and Deflation," *Microsoft Encarta Encyclopedia 2000*.

31 Robert Pollin, Stephanie Luce and Mark Brenner, "Economic Analysis of the New Orleans Minimum Wage Proposal," Political Economy Research Institute, July 1999.

32 Gene Koretz, "Minimum Wage: A Hike Won't Hurt, Weighing the inflationary impact," *Business Week*, October 9, 2000.

33 Christopher Niedt, Greg Ruiters, Dana Wise and Erica Schoenberger, Economic Policy Institute, *The Effects of the Living Wage in Baltimore* (1999), p. 6.

34 Michael LeBlanc, *Poverty, Policy and the Macroeconomy*, USDA Economic Research Service, Technical Bulletin No. 1889, p.23.

35 Schlosser, *Fast Food Nation*, p. 73.

36 Ibid., pp. 9, 195, 263.

37 Karen Kraut, Scott Klinger and Chuck Collins, *Choosing the High Road: Businesses That Pay A Living Wage and Prosper*, (Boston: Responsible Wealth, 2000), available at www.responsiblewealth.org; Steven V. Brull, "What's So Bad About a Living Wage?"; Bernstein, *Higher Wages Lead to More Efficient Service Provision*; Department of Labor, *Minimum Wage and Overtime Hours Under the Fair Labor Standards Act*, June 1998.

38 Kraut, et al., *Choosing the High Road*, p. 6.

39 Bernstein, *Higher Wages Lead to More Efficient Service Provision*.

40 Watson Wyatt Worldwide, "Employers That Focus On People Strategy Provide Greater Returns to Shareholders," December 1, 1999. Also see "Companies with Superior Human Capital Practices Provided 70 Percent Return to Shareholders in 1999," March 2, 2000, www.watsonwyatt.com.

41 We have not estimated the multiplier effect of the increased income to low wage workers generated from a mandated wage increase. A study of the San Francisco Living Wage Ordinance estimates a net benefit of $20.8 million to the San Francisco economy as a result of the multiplier effect. Michael Reich, Peter Hall and Fiona Hsu, "Living Wages and the San Francisco Economy: The Benefits and The Costs," Bay Area Living Wage Research Group, Center on Pay and Inequality, Institute of Industrial Relations, University of California (Berkeley), June 1999.

42 U.S. Small Business Administration, "State Winner! Mo's Enterprises, Inc.," and SBA News Release, "Alabama Entrepreneur is National Small Business Person of the Year: Oregon, Pennsylvania and Florida Winners are Runners-Up," May 8, 2001, www.sba.gov.

43 Teresa Carp, "Mo's Success Recipe," *Oregon Business,* February 1992; "President of Mo's to receive SBA honor," *The Oregonian,* April 20, 2001.

44 "The 2001 ICIC-Inc Magazine *Inner City 100* Fast Facts," www.innercity100.org. Also see Initiative for a Competitive Inner City, press release, "Leaders of the New Economy: 2nd Annual ICIC-Inc. Magazine Inner City 100," 2000, www.icic.org.

45 2001 Inner City 100 company summary.

46 Jill Priluck, "Vision Quest," *City Limits,* September/October 2000.

47 Dudley Street Neighborhood Initiative Economic Development Committee, "Economics With People In Mind: A Summary of DSNI's Approach to Economic Development," 1993, cited in Peter Medoff and Holly Sklar, *Streets of Hope: The Fall and Rise of an Urban Neighborhood* (Boston: South End Press, 1994), p. 189.

48 Conversation with authors, March 20, 2001.

49 Richard D. Bingham and Zhongcai Zhang, "Poverty and Economic Morphology of Ohio Central-City Neighborhoods," *Urban Affairs Review,* July 1997.

50 The Boston Consulting Group in partnership with the Initiative for a Competitive Inner City, *The Business Case for Pursuing Retail Opportunities in the Inner City,* Boston, June 1998, www.icic.org.

51 Initiative for a Competitive Inner City with PricewaterhouseCoopers, *Inner-City Shoppers Make Cents (and Dollars),* Boston, October 2000.

CHAPTER 5

1 Department of Labor, *Minimum Wage and Overtime Hours Under the Fair Labor Standards Act,* p. ix.

2 The ripple effect occurs as employers increase the wages of workers earning more than the new minimum wage in order to maintain the wage structure within the firm. Although there is uncertainty in the empirical literature concerning the extent of the ripple effect, there is general consensus among economists that the ripple effect occurs. See, for example, Card and Krueger, *Myth and Measurement*; and Pollin and Luce, *The Living Wage,* pp.104-106.

3 Low-wage workers are disproportionately represented in a sector if the proportion of low-wage workers employed in that sector to all low-wage workers exceeds the proportion of workers employed in that sector to total employment.

4 Retail trade includes lumber and building material retail stores, hardware stores, retail nurseries and garden, mobile home dealers, department stores, variety stores, miscellaneous general merchandise stores, grocery stores, dairy products stores, retail bakeries, food stores not elsewhere classified, motor vehicle dealers, auto and home supply stores, gasoline service stations, miscellaneous vehicle dealers, apparel and accessory stores, shoe stores, furniture and home furnishings, household appliance stores, radio, TV and computer stores, music stores, eating and drinking places, drug stores, liquor stores, sporting goods, bicycles, and hobby stores, book and stationery stores, jewelry stores, gift, novelty and souvenir shops, sewing, needlework and piece goods stores, catalog and mail order houses, vending machine operators, direct selling establishments, fuel dealers, retail florists, miscellaneous retail stores and not specified retail trade.

5 Center for the Child Care Workforce, *Current Data on Child Care Salaries and Benefits in the United States,* March 2001, p. 4.

6 U.S. Bureau of Labor Statistics, News Release, "Occupational Employment and Wages in 1999 Based on the New Standard Occupational Classification System," December 20, 2000.

7 U.S. Census Bureau, *Income in the United States 1999* (September 2000), p. xiii.

8 Ibid., Table 7.

9 "Fact Sheet: 2000 Catalyst Census of Women Corporate Officers and Top Earners of the Fortune 500" and Press Release, "Number of Women Chief Executives in Fortune 500 Doubles in 2001," [From 2 CEOs to 4], April 18, 2001, www.catalystwomen.org.

10 Anne B. Fisher, "When Will Women Get To The Top?" *Fortune*, September 21, 1992.

11 CBS News Poll, December 13-16, 1999, www.pollingreport.com.

12 Karin Stallard, Barbara Ehrenreich and Holly Sklar, *Poverty in the American Dream: Women and Children First* (Boston: South End Press, 1983), p. 9, citing, Patricia C. Sexton, *Women and Work*, R. and D. Monograph No. 46, U.S. Department of Labor, Employment and Training Administration (1977).

13 AFL-CIO and Institute for Women's Policy Research, *Equal Pay for Working Families: National and State Data on the Pay Gap and Its Costs*, 1999. Also see Jared Bernstein, Heidi Hartmann and John Schmitt, Economic Policy Institute and the Institute for Women's Policy Research, *The Minimum Wage Increase: A Working Woman's Issue*, September 16, 1999.

14 See wage methodology appendix for further explanation and sources.

15 Internal Revenue Service, *1996 Corporation Returns, Explanation of Terms*, p. 169.

16 Total industry receipts and payroll data are from the U.S. Census Bureau Company Statistics data (1997 data adjusted to 1999 dollars using CPI-U). Benefits data are computed from BLS Employer Costs for Employee Compensation data (March 1999).

17 Exemptions to the current federal minimum wage and hour legislation include: executive, administrative and professional employees and outside salesmen; employees of amusement or recreational establishment organized camps or religious or nonprofit educational conference centers not operating for more than seven months in any calendar year if its receipts in any six months were not more than one-third of its receipts in the other six months of a calendar year, except for employees of such organizations providing services or facilities in a national park or national forest, or on land in the National Wildlife Refuge System, under a contract with the federal government; employees engaged in catching or harvesting of aquatic animal and vegetable life, including fish, shellfish, sponges and seaweed, or in the processing or packing of such products at sea; employees employed in agriculture if the employer did not use more than 500 man-days of agricultural labor, if the employee is an immediate family member of the employer, if the employee is paid on a piece rate basis in an operation which is customarily recognized as having been paid on a piece rate basis, commutes daily from his or her permanent home and has been employed in agriculture less than 13 weeks in the previous calendar year; if the employee is 16 years of age as a hand harvest laborer, if the employee is paid on a piece rate basis in an operation which is customarily recognized as having been paid on a piece rate basis, is employed on the same farm as his/her parent or guardian and is paid at the same rate as employees over 16 years of age; or if the employee is engaged in the range production of livestock; employees exempt under special certificate, for example, students, messengers, and handicapped workers; employees employed in connection with the publication of a newspaper with a circulation of less than 4,000; switchboard operators employed by independently owned telephone companies with less than 750 stations; employees on maritime vessels other than American maritime vessels; employees providing domestic services, including babysitting or companionship services for disabled individuals, on a casual basis; criminal investigators paid availability pay; computer systems analysts, computer programmers, software engineers or other similarly skilled workers paid at least $27.63 per hour. Employees of enterprises with annual sales less than $500,000 may be exempt from the minimum wage provisions of the FLSA if they are not engaged in interstate commerce in the course of their employment.

The 1996 legislation also allows employers to maintain a "youth minimum" wage of $4.25 per hour for employees under 20 years of age during their first 90 consecutive days on the job. Some employees receiving tips as part of their earnings are also exempt from the $5.15 per hour current minimum wage. The FLSA does not define a tipped employee under the act on the basis of industry or occupation. Rather, tipped employees are defined as "those who customarily and regularly receive more than $30 a month in tips." Tips actually received by tipped employees may be counted as wages as long as the employer pays at least $2.13 an hour in direct wages. Any difference between the sum of the employee's base wage and any tips earned and the current minimum wage must be paid by the employer. U.S. Department of Labor, Employment Standards Administration, Wage and Hour Division, *Minimum Wage and Overtime Hours Under the Fair Labor Standards Act*, January 2001.

18 While for most industries the impact is less than 1 or 2 percent of net receipts and the cost of goods sold, the impact is higher in a few sectors. In *The Living Wage*, for example, Pollin and Luce found that the proposed living wage ordinance in Los Angeles County would cost less than 2 percent of covered firms' total production costs. Pollin and Luce consider firms for which living wage increases would raise production costs by 2.4 percent as "low-impact" firms, i.e. firms that would be able to readily absorb these costs.

Data on total payroll, net receipts and cost of goods sold were not available for the private household and public administration industries. Payroll and net receipts data were available only for agricultural services industries, but not agricultural product industries. Thus we were not able to determine the complete relative impact of a minimum wage increase on these sectors. However, both the agricultural and private household sectors are sectors that employ an extraordinarily high proportion of low-wage workers. We therefore expect that the relative impact of a minimum wage increase on these sectors will be larger.

19 The social services sector includes: individual and family services, job training and related services, child day care services, residential care and social services, not elsewhere classified. The educational services sector includes: elementary and secondary schools, colleges and universities, libraries, vocational schools, and schools and educational services, not elsewhere classified. The personal services industry includes: laundry, cleaning and garment services, photographic studios, beauty shops, barber shops, shoe repair shops and shoeshine parlors, funeral services and crematories, tax return preparation services and miscellaneous personal services, not elsewhere classified.

20 Cited in Joan Fitzgerald, "Better-Paid Caregivers, Better Care," *American Prospect*, May 21, 2001.

21 Fitzgerald, "Better-Paid Caregivers, Better Care."

22 "Results of a Follow-Up Survey to States on Wage Supplements for Medicaid and Other Public Funding to Address Aide Recruitment and Retention in Long-Term Care Settings," North Carolina Division of Facility Services (November 4, 2000), http://facility-services.state.nc.us/survy.pdf; "Comparing State Efforts to Address the Recruitment and Retention of Nurse Aide and Other Paraprofessional Aide Workers," North Carolina Division of Facility Services (September 1999).

23 Fitzgerald, "Better-Paid Caregivers, Better Care."

24 Jack L. Runyan, *Profile of Hired Farmworkers, 1998*, USDA Economic Research Service, November 2000, pp. 29, 32. Also see Chinkook Lee, Gerald Schluter and Brian O'Roark, "How Much Would Increasing the Minimum Wage Affect Food Prices?" *Current Issues in Economics of Food Markets*, U.S. Department of Agriculture, Economic Research Service, Agriculture Information Bulletin No. 747-03 (May 2000).

25 Mitchell Morehart, James Ryan and Robert Green, *Farm Income and Finance: The Importance of Government Payments*, USDA Economic Research Service, February 22, 2001.

26 Timothy Egan, "Failing Farmers Learn To Profit From Federal Aid" *New York Times*, December 24, 2000. Also see Dan Morgan, "Farming's chronic woes confront new USDA chief," *Washington Post*, January 26, 2001.

27 Morehart, Ryan and Green, *Farm Income and Finance*. Also see Robert A. Hoppe, editor, *Structural and Financial Characteristics of U.S. Farms: 2001 Family Farm Report*, USDA Economic Research Service, May 2001.

28 Craig Gundersen, et al., *A Safety Net for Farm Households*, USDA Economic Research Service, October 2000.

29 Runyan, *Profile of Hired Farmworkers*, p. 4.

30 Katti Gray, "A Clean Start," *Newsday*, September 21, 1999; authors' conversation with Workplace Project, July 18, 2001.

31 These estimates were derived using the U.S. Census Bureau Current Population Survey Annual Demographic Supplement March 2000.

32 LeBlanc, *Poverty, Policy and the Macroeconomy*, pp. 6, 23.

33 Nicole Fortin and Thomas Lemieux, "Institutional Changes and Rising Wage Inequality: Is There a Linkage?" *Journal of Economic Perspectives*, 11(2), 1997, pp. 75-96.

CHAPTER 6

1 In seven western nations, public polices reduce the poverty rate by 63 to 89 percent; U.S. government policy reduces poverty by only 37 percent. Timothy M. Smeeding and K. Ross Phillips, "Social Protection for the Poor in the Developed World," in N. Lustig, ed., *Shielding the Poor: Social Protection in the Developing World* (Washington, D.C.: Brookings Press, 2001), pp. 267-304; Timothy Smeeding, Lee Rainwater and Gary Burtless, "United States Poverty in a Cross-National Context," prepared for the IRP Conference Volume, *Understanding Poverty in America: Progress and Problems* (May 2001), http://www-cpr.maxwell.syr.edu/faculty/smeeding/papers/irpconf.pdf.

   To measure poverty internationally, UNICEF defines the poverty line as half the median income after taxes and transfer income. (Social Security and TANF payments are an example of transfers in the United States.). With government action, the UK's child poverty rate drops from 36.1 percent to 19.8 percent and Sweden's plummets from 23.4 percent to 2.6 percent (1995 data). The U.S. reduced child poverty from 26.7 percent to 22.4 percent (1997 data). The UK and Sweden both have higher proportions of children in single parent families than the United States. UNICEF, *Child Poverty in Rich Nations*, pp. 10, 15-16.

2 The earliest a person can start receiving partial Social Security retirement benefits is age 62; persons born in 1937 or earlier receive full retirement benefits at age 65, but the eligibility age gradually increases in 2-month increments for persons born after 1937. Persons born during 1943-1954 receive full benefits at age 66; persons born in 1960 and later are not scheduled to receive full benefits until age 67. Social Security Administration, "Social Security Full Retirement and Reductions by Age," http://www.ssa.gov/retirechartred.htm.

3 See *A Citizen's Guide to the Federal Budget, Budget of the United States Government Fiscal Year 2001*, Chart 2-6: The Federal Government Dollar—Where it Goes, http://w3.access.gpo.gov/usbudget/fy2001/guide02.html.

4 Center on Budget and Policy Priorities, *The Earned Income Credit Campaign 2001 Outreach Kit*, opening letter and p. 23. Also see Robert Greenstein and Isaac Shapiro, Center on Budget and Policy Priorities, *New Research Findings on the Effects of the Earned Income Tax Credit*, March 11, 1998; Timothy M. Smeeding, Hatherin E. Ross, Michael O'Connor and Michael Simon, *The Economic Impact of the Earned Income Tax Credit (EITC)*, Joint Center for Poverty Research, 1999.

5 Robert Greenstein, Center on Budget and Policy Priorities, *The Changes the New Tax Law Makes in Refundable Tax Credits for Low-Income Working Families*, Revised June 18, 2001.

6 Center on Budget and Policy Priorities, *The Earned Income Credit Campaign 2001 Outreach Kit*, p. 6.

7 From Statement of Lynda D. Willis, Director, Tax Policy and Administration Issues, U.S. General Accounting Office, http://www.house.gov/ways_means/full-comm/105cong/5-8-97/5-8will.htm.

8 "Second Class," *Consumer Reports* investigative report, September 2000, p. 50.

9 Melissa B. Jacoby, Teresa A. Sullivan and Elizabeth Warren, "Medical Problems and Bankruptcy Filings," *Norton Bankruptcy Law Adviser*, May 2000.

10 Employee Benefit Research Institute, "The Working Uninsured: Who They Are, How They Have Changed, and the Consequences of Being Uninsured," *EBRI Issue Brief*, August 2000.

11 Kaiser Family Foundation and Health Research and Educational Trust, *Employer Health Benefits: 2000 Summary of Findings*, www.kff.org. Also see Peter T. Kilborn, "Uninsured in U.S. Span Many Groups," *New York Times*, February 26, 1999.

12 *Statistical Abstract of the United States 2000*, Table 180; U.S. Bureau of Labor Statistics, "Employee Benefits in Medium and Large Private Establishments, 1997," USDL-99-02; U.S. Bureau of Labor Statistics, "Employee Benefits in Small Private Industry Establishments, 1996," USDL-98-240; Center for Studying Health System Change, "Who Declines Employer-Sponsored Health Insurance and Is Uninsured?" Issue Brief Number 22 (October 1999), citing results from the 1997 Robert Wood Johnson Employer Health Insurance Survey. This survey found that employees in firms paying wages averaging less than $7 per hour were required to contribute $7 more per month for single coverage and $24.00 more per month for family coverage than the average employee contribution for single and family coverage for all firms.

13 Employee Benefit Research Institute, *EBRI Issue Brief*, "Small Employers and Health Benefits: Findings from the 2000 Small Employer Health Benefits Survey," October 2000.

14 *Statistical Abstract of the United States 2000*, Table 539.

15 Matthew Broaddus and Leighton Ku, Center on Budget and Policy Priorities, *Nearly 95 Percent of Low-Income Uninsured Children Now are Eligible for Medicaid or SCHIP*, December 6, 2000.

16 Center on Budget and Policy Priorities, *Congress Has a $28 Billion Opportunity to Expand Coverage for Low-Income Families with Children*, July 18, 2001. Also see Families USA, *Go Directly To Work, Do Not Collect Health Insurance: Low-Income Parents Lose Medicaid*, Washington, D.C., June 2000.

17 Bowen Garrett and John Holahan, *Welfare Leavers, Medicaid Coverage, and Private Health Insurance*, (Washington, D.C.: Urban Institute), March 2000. See also Jocelyn Guyer and Cindy Mann, Center on Budget and Policy Priorities, *Taking the Next Step: States Can Now Take Advantage of Federal Medicaid Matching Funds to Expand Health Care Coverage to Low-income Working Adults*, August 20, 1998, citing Abt Associates, *The Indiana Welfare Reform Evaluation: Who Is On and Who Is Off? Comparing Characteristics and Outcomes for Current and Former TANF Recipients* (September 1997) and South Carolina Department of Social Services, *Survey of Former Family Independence Program Clients: Cases Closed During April Through June 1997* (South Carolina: June 1998).

18 Jocelyn Guyer, Center on Budget and Policy Priorities, *Uninsured Rate of Poor Children Declines, But Remains Above Pre-Welfare Reform Levels: Nearly One in Two Working Poor Adults Remain Uninsured*, September 29, 2000.

19 World Health Organization, *World Health Report 2000*. www.who.int/whr/2000/en/report.htm.

20 Physicians for a National Health Program, *Proposal of the Physicians' Working Group for Single-Payer National Health Insurance*, May 2001, www.pnhp.org.

21 "Executive Summary," *No Health Insurance? It's Enough to Make You Sick*, Decision 2000 Campaign, www.acponline.org.

22 Press Release, "Uninsured Americans Not Receiving Necessary Care According to Newly Released JAMA Study," October 24, 2000.

23 Physicians for a National Health Program, *Proposal of the Physicians' Working Group for Single-Payer National Health Insurance*.

24 Jonathan Oberlander and Theodore R. Marmor, "The Path to Universal Care," in Robert L. Borosage and Roger Hickey, eds., Campaign for America's Future, *The Next Agenda: Blueprint for a New Progressive Movement* (Boulder, CO: Westview Press, 2001) and Phineas Baxandall, "Spending #1, Performance #37: How U.S. Health Care Stacks Up Internationally," *Dollars and Sense*, May-June 2001.

25 Economic Policy Institute, "Medicare at the crossroads: Vouchers take us in the wrong direction," *Paycheck Economics*, January 2001.

26 Physicians for a National Health Program, *Proposal of the Physicians' Working Group for Single-Payer National Health Insurance*.

27 Jody Heymann, *The Widening Gap: Why America's Working Families Are in Jeopardy—and What Can Be Done About It* (New York: Basic Books, 2000), p. 3.

28 Janet C. Gornick and Marcia K. Meyers, "Support for Working Families: What the United States Can Learn from Europe," *The American Prospect*, January 1-15, 2001; *Statistical Abstract of the United States 2000*, Tables 644, 652, 653; Census Bureau, *Employment Characteristics of Families in 2000*, April 19, 2001.

29 Holly Sklar, *Chaos or Community? Seeking Solutions, Not Scapegoats for Bad Economics* (Boston: South End Press, 1995), citing Susan Faludi, *Backlash: The Undeclared War Against American Women* (New York: Crown, 1991), pp. 51-52.

30 Nancy Duff Campbell, Judith Appelbaum, Karin Martinson and Emily Martin, *Be All That We can Be: Lessons from the Military for Improving our Nation's Child Care System*, National Women's Law Center, April 2000, pp. 1-2.

31 Ibid., pp. 15-16.

32 Barbara Bergmann, *Saving Our Children from Poverty: What the United States Can Learn from France*, Russell Sage Foundation, New York, 1996, p. 142.

33 Ann Crittenden, *The Price of Motherhood: Why the Most Important Job in the World is Still the Least Valued*, (New York: Henry Holt and Company, 2001), p. 2.

34 Gornick and Meyers, "Support for Working Families," p. 6.

35 National Partnership for Women and Families, "Leave Policies for New Parents Worldwide"; Gornick and Meyers, "Support for Working Families," pp. 4, 6; UNICEF, *Child Poverty in Rich Nations*, p.8.

36 Institute for Women's Policy Research, *Essential Support for Working Men and Women: Paid Family and Medical Leave*, November 2000; National Partnership for Working Families: Family Leave Benefits Campaign, "Family Leave Benefits Campaign Measures Progress in State Legislatures in 2001," Bulletin, Issue 5, July 17, 2001.

37 "Facts About Pregnancy Discrimination," The U.S. Equal Employment Opportunity Commission, http://www.eeoc.gov/facts/fs-preg.html.

38 Gornick and Meyers, "Support for Working Families, p. 6.

39 National Partnership for Working Families, "Campaign for Family Leave Benefits."

40 Robert Greenstein, *The Changes the New Tax Law Makes in Refundable Tax Credits for Low-Income Working Families*, Center on Budget and Policy Priorities, revised June 18, 2001. See also Deepak Bhargava, *Victory!*, National Campaign for Jobs and Income Support, May 31, 2001, http://www.nationalcampaign.org/victory.asp. CBPP estimates 15 million children benefiting while the National Campaign estimates 17 million. We are using the more conservative figure.

41 "Leave No Child Behind?" Briefing Paper, *National Campaign for Jobs and Income Support*, February 6, 2001.

42 *Caregivers Tax Credit Campaign*, www.caregivercredit.org.

43 Children's Defense Fund, "Increase Investments in After-School Care." See also, DeeAnn W. Brimhall, Lizaberth M. Reaney and Jerry West, "Participation of Kindergarteners Through Third Graders in Before- and After- School Care," *Education Statistics Quarterly*, Fall 1999.

44 *U.S. News & World Report*, April 30, 2001.

45 National Women's Law Center, *New Tax Bill Contains Some Important Benefits for Low-Income Families*, June 2001.

46 National Women's Law Center, "Tax Relief for Employed Families: Improving the Dependent Care Tax Credit," July 2000; U.S. Internal Revenue Services, *Statistics Of Income*, Individual Tax Returns, 1997, Table 2.

47 Center on Budget and Policy Priorities, *Earned Income Credit Outreach Kit 2001*, p. 29.

48 U.S. Department of Health and Human Services, Administration for Children and Families, Child Care Bureau, "Child Care and Development Fund," http://www.acf.dhhs.gov/programs/ccb/geninfo/ccdfdesc.html.

49 U.S. Department of Health and Human Services, Administration for Children and Families, Child Care Bureau, "Access to Child Care for Low-Income Working Families," http://www.acf.dhhs.gov/programs/ccb/reports/ccreport.htm.

50 Mark H. Greenberg, "Child Care Policy Two Years Later" (Washington, D.C.: Center for Law and Social Policy, June 1998); Mark Greenberg, "A Summary of Key Child Care Provisions of H.R. 3734," Center for Law and Social Policy, August, 1996; Rachel Schumacher and Mark Greenberg, "Child Care After Leaving Welfare: Early Evidence from State Studies," Center for Law and Social Policy, October 1999; Institute for Women's Policy Research, "Child Care and Welfare Reform" IWPR *Welfare Reform Network News*, May 30, 1997.

51 Barbara Bergmann, "Decent Child Care at Decent Wages," *The American Prospect:*, January 1-15, 2001, p. 8.

52 Ibid., p.9.

53 Gornick and Meyers, "Support for Working Families," p. 5.

54 Helen Blank, Karen Schulman and Danielle Ewen, *State Prekindergarden Initiatives 1998-1999*, Children's Defense Fund, September 1999, executive summary, p. 32.

55 Gladys M. Martinez and Andrea E. Curry, U.S. Census Bureau, *School Enrollment— Social and Economic Characteristics of Students: October 1998*, September 1999.

56 Children's Defense Fund, "Fact Sheet: Increase Investments in Head Start;" U.S. House Democratic Policy Committee, Special Report, *The Bush Budget and Children: Leaving Too Many Behind*, April 26, 2001.

57 Edward F. Zigler and Matia Finn-Stevenson, "Funding Child Care and Public Education," *The Future of Children*, Financing Child Care, Vol. 6, No. 2.

58 Blank, et al, "State Prekindergarden Initiatives 1998-1999," p. 37.

59 Children's Defense Fund, "Fact Sheet: Increase Investments in After-School Care." See also, Brimhall, Reaney and West, "Participation of Kindergarteners Through Third Graders in Before- and After- School Care."

60 U.S. Department of Health and Human Services, Administration for Children and Families, Child Care Bureau, "Child Care and Development Fund," http://www.acf.dhhs.gov/programs/ccb/policy1/current/im0103/alloce02.html.

61 Center for the Child Care Workforce, "Model Work Standards."

62 Bergmann, "Decent Child Care at Decent Wages," p. 9.

63 Author conversation with Shannah Kurland, then executive director of Direct Action for Rights and Equality (DARE), December 1998. DARE organized family child care providers in Rhode Island who were providing state-subsidized child care. After a five-year campaign, the providers won health insurance through the state's Medicaid program.

64 Michael Bodaken, "We Must Preserve the Nation's Supply of Affordable Housing," National Housing Institute Research and Reports.

65 Cushing N. Dolbeare, "Housing Budget Trends," National Low Income Housing Coalition/LIHIS, *2000 Advocate's Guide to Housing and Community Development Policy*; Lynn A. Curtis and Vesta Kimble, *Investing in Children and Youth, Reconstructing Our Cities* (Washington, D.C.: The Milton S. Eisenhower Foundation, 1993), p. 14.

66 "Weekly Housing Update: Memo to Members," Vol. 6, No. 28, July 13, 2001, National Low Income Housing Coalition, www.nlihc.org.

67 Jennifer Daskal, *In Search of Shelter: The Growing Shortage of Affordable Rental Housing*, Center on Budget and Policy Priorities, June 15, 1998.

68 HUD, *A Report on Worst Case Housing Needs in 1999*, January 2001, pp. 2, 5.

69 Daskal, *In Search of Shelter*.

70 U.S. Conference of Mayors, *A Status Report on Hunger and Homelessness in America's Cities 2000* (December 2000), p. iii.

71 National Low Income Housing Coalition/LIHIS, *2000 Advocate's Guide to Housing and Community Development Policy*.

72 See, for example, HUD, *The State of the Cities 2000* (June 2000); David Stout, "Odds Worsen in Hunt for Low-Income Rentals," *The New York Times*, September 24, 1999.

73 HUD, *A Report on Worst Case Housing Needs in 1999*, p. 9.

74 Martha Burt and Laudan Aron, America's Homeless II: Populations and Services, Urban Institute, February 2000; National Low Income Housing Coalition/LIHIS, "Homelessness," *2000 Advocate's Guide to Housing and Community Development Policy*; National Alliance to End Homelessness, "Facts about Homelessness;" National Coalition for the Homeless, "How Many People Experience Homelessness," NCH Fact Sheet #2, February 1999 and "Who is Homeless?" NCH Fact Sheet #3, February 1999; National Law Center on Homelessness and Poverty.

75 U.S. Conference of Mayors, *A Status Report on Hunger and Homelessness in America's Cities 2000*, p. ii

76 David Cay Johnston, "Mortgage Tax Break: Who Gets What," *New York Times*, January 10, 1999.

77 Dolbeare, "Housing Budget Trends."

78 *Statistical Abstract of the United States 2000*, Tables 537-39. Also see Appendix A.

79 HUD, *A Report on Worst Case Housing Needs in 1999*, p. 11.

80 The payment standard can be set by the local Public Housing Authority (PHA) anywhere between 90 percent and 110 percent of the fair market rent set by HUD. PHAs must request HUD permission to use exception rents to set payment standards outside this basic range. Brian Maney and Sheila Crowley, Ph.D., "Scarcity and Success: Perspectives on Assisted Housing," Part I: Tenant-Based Housing Assistance, http://www/nlihc.org/bookshelf/scarcity/chap1.htm.

81 Michael Bodaken, "We Must Preserve the Nation's Supply of Affordable Housing."

82 National Housing Institute, *A Progressive Housing Plan for America*. Also see Barbara Sard and Jeff Lubell, Center on Budget and Policy Priorities, *The Value of Housing Subsidies to Welfare Reform Efforts* (February 24, 2000) and National Low Income Housing Coalition/LIHIS, *Scarcity and Success: Perspectives on Assisted Housing*.

83 Statement of HUD Secretary Andrew Cuomo, September 20, 2000, upon release of the National Low Income Housing Coalition/LIHIS report, *Out of Reach: The Growing Gap Between Housing Costs and Income of Poor People in the United States* (Washington D.C.: September 2000).

84 National Housing Trust Fund Campaign, Policy Recommendations, March 7, 2001, website recommendations and correspondence with authors about homeownership assistance, www.nlihc.org.

85 The Federal Housing Administration (FHA) was established under the National Housing Act of 1934 to "improve housing standards and conditions...[and] plays a critical role in funding low-income housing, by providing insurance to lenders otherwise fearful of selling mortgages to borrowers who present a higher risk than average." Administered by the HUD, FHA insures single family mortgages and allows first-time home buyers and minority home buyers to obtain mortgages with very low down payments. FHA also has multifamily insurance programs that insure lenders against loss on mortgages that are used to finance the construction or rehabilitation of housing for moderate-income families, the elderly and disabled. "Federal Housing Administration," National Low Income Housing Coalition, *2000 Advocates Guide to Housing and Community Development Policy*.
  Ginnie Mae, the Government National Mortgage Association, is a government corporation within HUD that guarantees mortgage-backed securities sold to investors. These mortgages are insured by FHA, the Veterans Administration (VA), and the Rural Housing Service (RHS). It provides a continual supply of capital to lenders, who in turn provide mortgages to borrowers who qualify for FHA, VA and RHS insured loans. It generates $400-600 million per year in revenue for the government. National Low Income Housing Coalition, "Don't Sell Ginnie Mae: Call to Action," September 29, 1999.

86 See, for example, Peter Medoff and Holly Sklar, *Streets of Hope: The Fall and Rise of an Urban Neighborhood* (Boston: South End Press, 1994) and the Dudley Street Neighborhood Initiative website, www.dsni.org; Institute for Community Economics, www.iceclt.org; Pratt Institute Center for Community and Environmental Development, www.picced.org; Urban Homesteading Assistance Board, www.uhab.org; Planners Network, www.plannersnetwork.org; The McAuley Institute, www.bhconline.org/mcauley/index.html; the Enterprise Foundation, www.enterprisefoundation.org.

87 Arloc Sherman, *Rescuing the American Dream: Halting the Economic Freefall of Today's Young Families with Children* (Washington, D.C.: Children's Defense Fund, 1997), p.35.

88 U.S. Census Bureau, Table 15, "Homeownership Rates for the United States, by Age of Householder and by Family Status: 1982 to 2000, (February 22, 2001) in "Housing Vacancies and Homeownership Annual Statistics: 2000"; HUD, Office of Policy Development and Research, *Issue Brief: Homeownership: Progress and Work Remaining*," December 2000.

89 U.S. Census Bureau, Table 20: "Homeownership Rates by Race and Ethnicity of Householder: 1994 to 2000," in "Housing Vacancies and Homeownership Annual Statistics: 2000.

90 Chuck Collins, Betsy Leondar-Wright and Holly Sklar, *Shifting Fortunes: The Perils of the Growing American Wealth Gap* (Boston: United for a Fair Economy, 1999), pp. 55-56. Also see Sklar, *Chaos or Community?*, pp. 79-84.

91 Medoff and Sklar, *Streets of Hope*, p. 14.

92 Dennis R. Judd, "Segregation Forever?" The Nation, December 9, 1991, cited in Medoff and Sklar, *Streets of Hope*, p. 15.

93 Medoff and Sklar, *Streets of Hope*, pp. 15-16.

94 Ted Sickinger, "When the door is blocked to buying a home," *Kansas City Star*, February 28, 1999. Also see Sickinger, "Hard-to-prove cases can be put to test," "Sides often keep bias settlements confidential," "Critics say regulators and laws too lenient," all February 28, and Chris Lester, "Minorities, mortgages and denial," *Kansas City Star*, March 2, 1999.

95 HUD Press Release, April 12, 2000, on the release of *Unequal Burden: Income and Racial Disparities in Subprime Lending in America.* Also see HUD, *Curbing Predatory Home Lending* (2000).

96 See, for example, "Poverty Inc.," *Consumer Reports,* July 1998; Ted Sickinger, "'Fringe banks' eye low-income areas" and "Laws provide consumers little protection from unscrupulous lenders, critics say," *Kansas City Star,* March 1, 1999; Medoff and Sklar, *Streets of Hope,* pp. 27-30; Michael Hudson, ed., *Merchants of Misery: How Corporate America Profits From Poverty* (Monroe, ME: Common Courage Press, 1996); David Dante Troutt, *The Thin Red Line: How the Poor Still Pay More* (San Francisco: West Coast Regional Office of Consumers Union, 1993).

97 BLS, *Employment and Earnings,* January 2001, Table 41.

98 "Why America Needs Unions But Not The Kind It Has Now," *Business Week,* May 23, 1994, pp. 70-71.

99 Ibid., p. 78, citing illegal firing figures by University of Chicago professors Robert LaLonde and Bernard Metlzer.

100 "Why America Needs Unions But Not The Kind It Has Now," *Business Week,* pp. 70-71.

101 *Statistical Abstract of the United States 2000,* Table 712; U.S. Bureau of Labor Statistics, *Employment and Earnings 2000,* Table 40.

102 Human Rights Watch, *Unfair Advantage: Worker's Freedom of Association in the United States under International Human Rights Standards,* August 2000, p. 9. This book provides detailed case studies that reflect violations and obstacles when workers attempt to exercise their right to join trade unions, to bargain collectively, and to strike.

103 Kate Bronfenbrenner, Cornell University, Commission on the Future of Worker-Management Relations, cited on the AFL-CIO web page *The Threat to Workers' Freedom to Choose a Union;* Human Rights Watch, pp. 2, 9-10.

104 Bronfenbrenner, AFL-CIO; Human Rights Watch, *Unfair Advantage,* pp. 19, 23.

105 Bronfenbrenner, AFL-CIO; Human Rights Watch, *Unfair Advantage,* p. 28.

106 Human Rights Watch, *Unfair Advantage,* p. 33-35.

107 Los Angeles Alliance for a New Economy, *The Other Los Angeles,* p. 50.

108 The National Alliance for Fair Employment, *Contingent Workers: Fight for Fairness,* Boston, pp. 2, 12, 24.

109 Occupational Safety & Health Administration (OSHA), U.S. Department of Labor, *The New OSHA: Reinventing Worker Safety and Health.*

110 Steven Greenhouse, "Rules' Repeal Heightens Workplace Safety Battle," *New York Times,* March 12, 2001; AFL-CIO, *Ergonomics.*

111 *Leaving Women and Children Behind: The First 100 Days of the Bush Administration,* 2001, www.wisnotforwomen.org.

112 Greenhouse, "Rules' Repeal Heightens Workplace Safety Battle."

113 *Statistical Abstract of the United States 2000,* Table 618; Department of Labor, *Unemployment Insurance Chartbook,* May 2001; Making Wages Work website, http://www.makingwageswork.org/unemployment.htm.

114 General Accounting Office, *Unemployment Insurance: Role as Safety Net for Low-Wage Workers is Limited,* December 2000.

115 Ibid.

116 See, for example, Annisah Um'rani and Vicky Lovell, *Unemployment Insurance and Welfare Reform: Fair Access to Economic Supports for Low-Income Working Women,* Institute for Women's Policy Research, December 2000.

117 National Committee on Pay Equity, *Questions and Answers on Pay Equity,* http://www.feminist.com/fairpay/f_qape.html.

118 AFL-CIO, *The Case for Equal Pay: Responding to Common Arguments Against Equal Pay.*

119 Ibid.

120 National Committee on Pay Equity, *Questions and Answers on Pay Equity.*

121 Jonathan Kozol, *Savage Inequalities: Children in America's Schools* (New York: Crown Publishers, 1991), pp. 54-55.

122 U.S. Census Bureau, *Money Income in the United States: 1999*, Table 7.

123 "Inequality: How the Gap Between Rich and Poor Hurts the Economy," *Business Week*, August 15, 1994, p. 79.

124 Joshua Wolf Shenk, "In Debt All the Way up to Their Nose Rings," *US News & World Report*, June 9, 1997, p. 38.

125 Nellie Mae, "Life After Debt: Results of the National Student Loan Survey," 1998. The sample surveyed was composed of 65 percent undergraduates and 35 percent graduate students, all Nellie Mae borrowers, from across the United States. The survey was done in 1997.

126 Thomas Karier, "Welfare Graduates: College and Financial Independence," *Policy Notes*, The Jerome Levy Economics Institute, Bard College. 1998, www.levy.org; and M. Gittell, M. Schehl, C. Facri, "From Welfare to Independence: The College Option." Ford Foundation, March 1990.

127 Julie Strawn, "Workforce Development for the Unemployed and Low Wage Workers: the Role of Postsecondary Education," working draft, Center for Law and Social Policy, February 2000, and "Senate Amendment to Welfare Law Allows States to Train Hardest-to-Employ Adults, Help Others find Better Jobs," Center for Law and Social Policy, August 27, 1998; Thomas Karier, "Welfare College Students: Measuring the Impact of Welfare Reform," *Policy Notes*, The Jerome Levy Economics Institute, 2000.

128 Dillona C. Lewis, "School's Out for Welfare Recipients: College Students Forced to Abandon Studies by Welfare Reform," National Association of Social Workers, New York City Chapter, New York, NY, September 1999, http://www.naswnyc.org/w11.html.

129 Ibid.

130 Steven Greenhouse, "Many Participants in Workfare Take the Place of City Workers," April 13, 1998 and "Union to Sue Giuliani Administration Over Use Of Welfare Recipients in Jobs," February 4, 1999, *New York Times*.

131 Rima Shore, *Our Basic Dream: Keeping Faith with America's Working Families and their Children*, Foundation for Child Development, New York, October 2000; Paul Osterman, "Reforming employment and training policies," *USA Today Magazine*, January 1998.

132 See www.work4women.org, a site sponsored by Wider Opportunities for Women in conjunction with Workplace Solutions.

133 See www.womenwork.org.

134 Collins, Leondar-Wright and Sklar, *Shifting Fortunes*, p. 62.

135 Corporation for Enterprise Development, www.cfed.org.

136 If, after May 6, 1997, your home was owned by you and used as your main home for at least two out of the five years prior to sale (or exchange) you do not have to pay income tax on capital gains—the difference between the price you paid for your home, plus allowable capital improvements, and the price you sold your home for. See IRS tax topic 701, http://www.irs.gov/prod/tax_edu/teletax/tc701.html.

CHAPTER 7

1 Eleanor Roosevelt, "Social Responsibility for Individual Welfare," in James Earl Russell, ed.,, *National Policies for Education Health and Social Services*, Columbia University Bicentennial Conference Series (New York: Doubleday, 1955).

2 See, for example, Lake Snell Perry & Associates, *A National Survey of American Attitudes Towards Low-Wage Workers and Welfare Reform*, Jobs for the Future (www.jff.org), Boston, 2000; National Public Radio/Henry J. Kaiser Family Foundation/Harvard University Kennedy School of Government, July 28, 2000, http://www.npr.org/programs/specials/poll/govt/summary.html; Martin Gilens, *Why Americans Hate Welfare: Race, Media, and the Politics of Antipoverty Policy* (Chicago: University of Chicago Press, 1999); the Pew Research Center for the People and the Press, *Deconstructing Distrust: How Americans View Government* (Washington, D.C., 1998); Alan Wolfe, *One Nation, After All: What Middle-Class Americans Really Think About: God, Country, Family, Racism, Welfare, Immigration, Homosexuality, Work, The Right, The Left, And Each Other* (New York: Viking Penguin, 1998); various surveys by the National Opinion Research Center and Gallup Poll.

On many of these issues, women's support is even stronger than men's. See *Women's Voices 2000: The Most Comprehensive Polling and Research Project on Women's Values and Policy Priorities for the Economy*, Center for Policy Alternatives and Lifetime Television.

3 Center on Budget and Policy Priorities, *Is a Large Tax Cut Needed to Forestall an Explosion in Spending?* February 27, 2001.

4 Stephanie Coontz, *The Way We Never Were: American Families and the Nostalgia Trap* (New York: Basic Books, 1992), p. 69.

5 Citizens for Tax Justice, "Final Version of Bush Tax Plan Keeps High-End Tax Cuts, Adds to Long-Term Cost," May 26, 2001.

6 Isaac Shapiro, Robert Greenstein and Wendell Primus, *Pathbreaking CBO Study Shows Dramatic Increases in Income Disparities in 1980s and 1990s*, Center on Budget and Policy Priorities. revised May 31, 2001. Also see Isaac Shapiro, *The Latest IRS Data on After-Tax Income Trends*, Center on Budget and Policy Priorities, February 26, 2001, and Isaac Shapiro and Joel Friedman, *Income Tax Rates and High-Income Taxpayers*, March 2001.

7 Citizens for Tax Justice, "51 Million Taxpayers Won't Get Full Rebates from 2001 Tax Bill," June 1, 2001.

8 *USA Today*, July 25, 2001.

9 William Greider, "The Education of David Stockman," *Atlantic Monthly*, December 1981; William Greider, *The Education of David Stockman and Other Americans* (Dutton, 1982).

10 William Greider, "Stockman Returneth," *The Nation*, April 2, 2001.

11 Citizens for Tax Justice, "Post-2001 Tax Cuts Offer Little to Most Americans," June 18, 2001.

12 Children's Defense Fund, *The State of America's Children Yearbook 2001*, pp. xiii, xxiii.

APPENDIX B

1 U.S. Department of Housing and Urban Development, 24 CFR Part 888 [Docket No. FR-4496-02], *Fair Market Rents for the Section 8 Housing Assistance Payments Program—Fiscal Year 2000*, October 1, 1999. With the exception of Renwick and Bergmann's Basic Needs Budget, all of the other studies reviewed use HUD Fair Market Rents to assess housing costs.

2 Gail Shearer, *Hidden from View: The Growing Burden of Health Care Costs*, Consumers Union, January 22, 1998.

3 Agency for Health Care Policy and Research, Center for Cost and Financing Studies, *1996 Medical Expenditure Panel Survey Insurance Component*, Tables 2R, 2S, 2U and 2V. The premium costs used represent costs for private employers. Because these employers are eligible for group rates, premium costs may likely be lower relative to the cost of privately purchased insurance.

4 To access the monthly average cost of food for the Official USDA Food Plans, see http://www.usda.gov/cnpp.

5 Bernstein, Brocht and Spade-Aguilar, *How Much Is Enough?*

6 From U.S. Bureau of Labor Statistics, Table 1: Quintiles of income before taxes: Average annual expenditures and characteristics, Consumer Expenditure Survey 1998.

7 Household composition data for this calculation was taken from U.S. Census Bureau, *Household and Family Characteristics, March 1998* (Update), Summary Tables, Table A: Households by Type and Selected Characteristics: 1998 (single adults) and Table 11: Family Groups with Own Children Under 19 Years, By Marital Status, Sex, Race and Hispanic Origin of Parent: March 1998.

8 Gina Adams and Karen Schulman, *Child Care Challenges*, Children's Defense Fund, May 1998.

9 Jeffrey Capizzano, Gina Adams, and Freya Sonenstein, "Child Care Arrangements for Children Under Five: Variation Across States," Urban Institute, Series B, No. B-7, March 2000.

10 Cost data derived from the 1995 National Household Education Survey and reported in DeeAnn W. Brimhall, Lizabeth M. Reaney and Jerry West, "Participation of Kindergartners through Third-Graders in Before- and After-School Care," National Center for Education Statistics, August 1999.

11 Ibid.

12 1998 Consumer Expenditure Survey, Tables 1, 5 and 6; "Expenditures on Public Transportation," Bureau of Labor Statistics Summary 99-9; Hu and Young, *A Summary of Travel Trends*, Table 4.

13 Murakami and Young, "Daily Travel by Persons with Low Income," Table 9.

14 U.S. Bureau of Labor Statistics, Consumer Expenditure Survey 1998, Tables 5 and 6.

15 Ibid., Table 1.

16 Household composition data for this calculation was taken from U.S. Census Bureau, *Household and Family Characteristics, March 1998* (Update), Summary Tables, Table A: Households by Type and Selected Characteristics: 1998.

17 U.S. Bureau of Labor Statistics, Consumer Expenditure Survey 1998, Table 1.

18 Phil Cheilik, "Reference Book of Rates, Price Indices and Expenditures for Telephone Service," Industry Analysis Division, Common Carrier Bureau, Federal Communications Commission (June 1999), Table 3.1.

APPENDIX C

1 Diana Pearce with Jennifer Brooks, *The Self-Sufficiency Standard for the City of New York*, Women's Center for Education and Career Advancement, September 2000, p.17; Wider Opportunities for Women, "The Self-Sufficiency Standard Hourly Wages, Selected Family Types, Selected Jurisdictions in 14 States and Metropolitan Areas," table provided to authors, January 2001.

2 Boushey, Brocht, Gundersen and Bernstein, *Hardships In America*; "New EPI Report Determines Basic Family Budgets for Every Community Nationwide," tables on ten highest- and ten lowest-cost communities, press release, July 24, 2001.

3 HUD Fair Market Rents were used to estimate housing costs. U.S. Bureau of Labor Statistics, Consumer Expenditure Survey, 1997-1998, Tables 21 (New York City), 22 (Kansas City) and 24 (Los Angeles); U.S. Bureau of Labor Statistics, Consumer Expenditure Survey, 1998, Table 8 (using Midwest for Des Moines and South for Gadsden; also used for national average expenditures).

4 Bernstein, Brocht and Spade-Aguilar, *How Much Is Enough?*, pp. 32-33.

5 Pearce with Brooks, *The Self-Sufficiency Standard for the City of New York*, pp.5-6; tables.

6 For example, the recent study conducted by WOW for New York City assumes that school-age children receive part-time care in before- and after-school programs and estimated the annual cost of such care at $5,976. Pearce with Brooks, *The Self-Sufficiency Standard for the City of New York*, p. 5.

7 Agency for Health Care Policy and Research, Center for Cost and Financing Studies, 1996 Medical Expenditure Panel Survey Insurance Component, Tables 2R, 2S, 2U and 2V. The premium costs used represent costs for private employers. Because these employers are eligible for group rates, premium costs may likely be lower relative to the cost of privately purchased insurance.

8 In addition to the standard deduction and exemptions for each household configuration, some families in New York City with incomes sufficient to meet their minimum needs would be eligible for the New York State and New York City Household Credit, Child and Dependent Care Credit and School Tax Credit; some families in Los Angeles with incomes sufficient to meet their minimum needs would be eligible for a Renter's Credit; some families in Des Moines with incomes sufficient to meet their minimum needs would be eligible for an Earned Income Credit, a Child and Dependent Care Credit and (for those purchasing their own health coverage) a health insurance deduction; and families in Kansas City with incomes sufficient to meet their minimum needs would not be eligible for additional credits.

APPENDIX E

1 For workers who held more than one job, we assumed that their hourly wage rate was the same in each job. We also adjusted for overtime earnings if the worker indicated that they had earnings from overtime, tips or commission and if they worked more than 40 hours.

2 The FLSA does not define a tipped employee under the act on the basis of indus-

try or occupation. Rather, tipped employees are defined as "those who customarily and regularly receive more than $30 a month in tips." Tips actually received by tipped employees may be counted as wages as long as the employer pays at least $2.13 an hour in direct wages. Any difference between the sum of the employee's base wage and any tips earned and the current minimum wage must be paid by the employer.

The IRS has entered into tip reporting agreements with the food and beverage, cosmetology and barber and gaming industries and has developed agreements for other industries in which tipping is customary. The IRS estimates that the number of employees receiving cash and charged tips in industries other than the food and beverage industry or cosmetology and barber industry is relatively small.

We assumed that workers in the following occupations earn tips which supplement their wages: Bartenders, Waiters and Waitresses, Food counter, fountain and related occupations, Waiters' and Waitresses' Assistants, Barbers, Hairdressers and Cosmetologists, Baggage Porters and Bellhops, Taxicab Drivers and Chauffeurs and Parking Lot Attendants.

3 For example, see Robert Pollin and Stephanie Luce, *The Living Wage: Building a Fair Economy* (New York: The New Press, 1998); Also, Robert Pollin, Stephanie Luce and Mark Brenner, *An Economic Analysis of the New Orleans Minimum Wage Proposal*, Political Economy Research Institute (July 1999); Bruce Nissen, "The Impact of a Living Wage Ordinance on Miami-Dade County," Center for Labor Research and Studies, Florida International University (October 23, 1998); Michael Reich, Peter Hall and Fiona Hsu, "Living Wages and the San Francisco Economy: The Benefits and The Costs" (June 1999).

4 Estimates of the number of workers earning below a given wage, the average hourly wage earned by workers earning below a given wage, and the average hours worked per week by workers earning below a given wage were derived from the U.S. Census Bureau's Current Population Survey Outgoing Rotation Group Files for July 1999 through June 2000. Estimates of the average weeks worked by workers earning below a given wage were derived from the U.S. Census Bureau's Current Population Survey March 2000 Annual Demographic Supplement.

5 The ripple effect occurs as employers increase the wages of workers earning more than the new minimum wage in order to maintain the wage structure within the firm. Although there is not agreement in the empirical literature concerning the extent of the ripple effect, there is general consensus among economists that the ripple effect occurs as wages increase. See, for example, David Card and Alan B. Krueger, *Myth and Measurement: The New Economics of the Minimum Wage* (Princeton, NJ: Princeton University Press, 1995); See also, Robert Pollin and Stephanie Luce, *The Living Wage: Building a Fair Economy* (New York: The New Press, 1998), pp.104-106.

6 U.S. Bureau of Labor Statistics, *Employer Costs for Employee Compensation–March 1999*, (June 24, 1999), Tables 2, 10 and 16.

7 IRS Statistics of Income, *1996 Corporation Returns, Explanation of Terms.*

RAISE THE FLOOR
PARTNER ORGANIZATIONS

■ ■ ■ ■ ■

Ms. Foundation for Women
120 Wall Street, 33rd Floor
New York, NY 10005
p (212) 742-2300
f (212) 742-1653
info@ms.foundation.org
www.ms.foundation.org

MediaVision
PO Box 1045
Boston, MA 02130
p (617) 522-2923
f (617) 522-1872
hsklar@aol.com

Solutions for Progress
1800 JFK Boulevard, 5th Floor
Philadelphia, PA 19103
p (215) 972-5558
f (215) 972-8109
lmykyta@solfopro.com
www.solfopro.com

Social Research Corporation
813 Pardee Lane
Wyncote, PA 19095
p (215) 576-8221
f (215) 576-8346
rkoppel@sas.upenn.edu

**9to5, National Association
of Working Women**
231 W. Wisconsin Avenue, Suite 900
Milwaukee, WI 53203
p (414) 274-0925
f (414) 272-2870
naww9to5@execpc.com
www.9to5.org

Campaign on Contingent Work
33 Harrison Avenue, 4th floor
Boston, MA 02111
p (617) 338-9966
f (617) 426-7684
ccw@igc.org
www.fairjobs.org

**Center for the Child
Care Workforce**
733 15th Street, NW, Suite 1037
Washington, DC 20005
p (202) 737-7700
f (202) 737-0370
ccw@ccw.org
www.ccw.org

**Center for Third World
Organizing**
1218 East 21 Street
Oakland, CA 94606
p (510) 533-7583
f (510) 533-0923
ctwo@ctwo.org
www.ctwo.org

**Chinese Staff and
Workers Association**
5411 Seventh Avenue
Brooklyn, NY 11220
p (718) 633-9752
f (718) 437-6991
info@cswa.org
www.cswa.org

**Direct Action for Rights
and Equality**
340 Lockwood Street
Providence, RI 02907
p (401) 351-6960
f (401) 351-6977
DARE@ids.net
www.providence.edu/polisci/
projects/dare/welcome.htm

Just Economics
1600 Shattuck Ave., Suite 124
Berkeley, CA 94709
p (510) 548-4760
f (510) 548-4762
justecon@igc.org

...ignity and
...men
...uite 260
... Utah 84111
...4-8562
...1) 323-9452
jedi@networld.com
www.jedi4women.org

**Los Angeles Alliance
for a New Economy**
548 Spring Street, Suite 630
Los Angeles, CA 90013
p (213) 486-9880
f (213) 486-9886
info@laane.org
www.laane.org

**Southeast Regional Economic
Justice Network**
PO Box 240
Durham, NC 27702
p (919) 683-4310
f (919) 683-3428
serejn@rejn.org
www.rejn.org

**Wider Opportunities
for Women**
815 15th Street, NW, Suite 916
Washington, DC 20005
p (202) 638-3143
f (202) 638-4885
info@wowonline.org
www.wowonline.org

**Women's Association for
Women's Alternatives**
225 South Chester Road, Suite 6
Swarthmore, PA 19081
p (610) 543 5022
f (610) 543-6483
www.womensassoc.org

**Women's Institute for
Leadership Development**
33 Harrison Avenue, 4th floor
Boston, MA 02111
p (617) 426-0520
f (617) 426-6519
wildlabor@aol.com

The Workplace Project
91 N. Franklin Street, Suite 207
Hempstead, NY 11550-3003
p (516) 565-5377
f (516) 565-5470
workplace@igc.org
www.peggybrowningfund.org/
wpp.html

Working Partnerships USA
2102 Almaden Road, Suite 100
San Jose, CA 95125
p (408) 269-7872
f (408) 266-2653
wpusa@atwork.org
www.atwork.org

ABOUT THE AUTHORS

■ ■ ■ ■ ■

HOLLY SKLAR

Holly Sklar's standout commentaries on economic and political affairs have appeared in hundreds of newspapers nationwide. She is the coauthor of *Shifting Fortunes: The Perils of the Growing American Wealth Gap* and author of *Chaos or Community? Seeking Solutions, Not Scapegoats for Bad Economics.* Sklar's other books include *Streets of Hope: The Fall and Rise of an Urban Neighborhood* (coauthored), the remarkable story of how the Dudley Street Neighborhood Initiative is rebuilding a long impoverished Boston community as a dynamic urban village. Sklar is the director of MediaVision, a strategic research, analysis and communications firm based in Boston.
Email: hsklar@aol.com.

LARYSSA MYKYTA

Laryssa Mykyta is a senior policy analyst at Solutions for Progress. While her primary interest lies in labor market policy and effective anti-poverty policy, she has also applied her research and database management skills to projects on health care and education policy. Mykyta's past research addressed the effects of inequality on labor market outcomes for female and minority workers and examined the impact of racial divisions on society. Mykyta also teaches at Temple University where her courses include "Women and the Economy."
Email: lmykyta@solfopro.com.

SUSAN WEFALD

Susan Wefald is director of institutional planning at the Ms. Foundation for Women and coordinator of the Raise the Floor campaign. Wefald previously ran a community development consulting business, where she conducted training in the U.S. and Russia. As former staff director of the Naugatuck Valley Project, Wefald coordinated the organizing and economic development work of a coalition of unions, churches and community organizations in Western Connecticut. She is the former assistant director of the Urban Homesteading Assistance Board and taught "Community Organizing and Community Economic Development" at New Hampshire College.
Email: swefald@ms.foundation.org.

With research by

...TIONS FOR PROGRESS, INC.

...for Progress (Philadelphia, PA), founded by Robert Brand, ...ivate consulting firm whose mission is to work to solve complex and seemingly intractable social and economic problems. Solutions for Progress works with governmental and nongovernmental clients in the areas of economic analysis and modeling, economic development, job creation, sustainable economics, environmental policy, health care, public education, strategic planning and government accountability.
Email: rbrand@solfopro.com. www.solfopro.com.

SOCIAL RESEARCH CORPORATION

Ross Koppel is president of the Social Research Corporation (Wyncote, PA) and teaches sociology and research methods at the University of Pennsylvania. His work, and the work of the Social Research Corporation, focus largely on the impact of technology on jobs and skills, health costs and health policy, evaluation, ethics of social research, discrimination at work and in schools, nutrition and deregulation. Koppel received the 1998 William Foote Whyte Award for Distinguished Career in the Practice of Sociology given by the American Sociological Association.
Email: rkoppel@sas.upenn.edu.

About the

MS. FOUNDATION FOR WOMEN

The Ms. Foundation for Women has been creating opportunities for women, girls and families for almost thirty years. We conduct advocacy and public education campaigns, and direct resources of all kinds to cutting-edge projects across the country that nurture girls' leadership, protect the health and safety of women and girls, and provide low-income women with the tools to lift themselves and their families out of poverty. Creator of the award-winning Take Our Daughters To Work® Day program, the Ms. Foundation is also a recipient of a Presidential Award for Excellence in Microenterprise Development.